The *Art* of Coaching

JB JOSSEY-BASS™
A Wiley Brand

The *Art* of Coaching

Effective Strategies for School Transformation

ELENA AGUILAR

WILEY

Cover design by Michael Cook
Cover photo by @ Jelena Veskovic/iStockphoto

Published by Jossey-Bass
A Wiley Imprint
One Montgomery Street, Suite 1200, San Francisco, CA 94104-4594-www.josseybass.com

Jossey-Bass books and products are available through most bookstores. To contact Jossey-Bass directly call our Customer Care Department within the U.S. at 800-956-7739, outside the U.S. at 317-572-3986, or fax 317-572-4002.

Wiley also publishes its books in a variety of electronic formats and by print-on-demand. Some material included with standard print versions of this book may not be included in e-books or in print-on-demand. If the version of this book that you purchased references media such as CD or DVD that was not included in your purchase, you may download this material at http://booksupport.wiley.com. For more information about Wiley products, visit www.wiley.com.

Library of Congress Cataloging-in-Publication Data has been applied for.
ISBN 978-1-118-20653-9 (pbk.);
ISBN 978-1-118-41943-4 (ePDF);
ISBN 978-1-118-42102-4 (ePub);
ISBN 978-1-118-54014-5 (eMobi)

Printed in the United States of America

FIRST EDITION

PB Printing   V10010421_052119

CONTENTS

PART TWO: ESTABLISHING COACHING WITH A CLIENT   73

PART THREE: THE COACHING DANCE   145

PART FOUR: PROFESSIONAL DEVELOPMENT FOR COACHES   265

FOR MY MOTHER, LINDA,
MY FIRST AND FINEST COACH

"Another world is not only possible, she is on her way.
On a quiet day, I can hear her breathing."
— Arundhati Roy (2003)

INTRODUCTION

Some years ago, during a very difficult time in my coaching career, I was coached by Leslie Plettner, who was then with the Bay Area Coalition for Equitable Schools, a nonprofit organization supporting school transformation. It was hard to describe what happened when we met for our sessions at a café, but I always left renewed and empowered, bursting with new understandings about myself and my work. Sometimes Leslie asked provocative questions, other times she guided me in looking at situations from a perspective I'd never considered, and often she pushed me to try something different in my work—I usually felt stretched, but supported; my coaching improved quickly. After a while, I realized that I could express my fears and expose my worst flaws, and Leslie would still believe in me and work with me. Leslie communicated an unconditional acceptance that I had never encountered in schools.

During the time I worked with her, I found it hard to identify what Leslie "did" as a coach. I couldn't identify the specific "coaching moves" she made, I couldn't figure out how she was thinking or how she made decisions about what to ask me. She was an amazing coach, and I wanted to be just like her.

In the following years, as my coaching practice developed, I explored the complicated processes that result in effective coaching and learned how to see the elements that made up Leslie's coaching. This book is an attempt to make what goes on in an effective coach's mind visible—to make a coach's thoughts, beliefs, knowledge, core values, and feelings explicit so that they can be replicated by others. Coaching is an art, and just as the process of producing a piece of art can be broken down, so can coaching.

Art is a useful metaphor to help us understand coaching. Consider, for example, just a sliver of what a visual artist must know in order to produce a painting: how the chemical elements in the mediums he's working with interact with each other, how they are affected by humidity, and the order in which they need to be applied. A musician plans a piece of music, then carefully crafts and rehearses it many times before it is performed. Although art may seem magical, sometimes effortless, and perhaps impossible to replicate, it requires scientific knowledge and skills and an ability to precisely use a range of available tools and materials. The end product may be a delightful surprise, different perhaps from the artist's original vision, but a great deal of intention, planning, thought, and knowledge lie deeply embedded within the outcome.

Coaching can be perceived as a mysterious process, but in fact it requires intention, a plan, and a lot of practice; it requires a knowledge of adult learning theory and an understanding of systems and communication. An effective coach must possess certain analytical capacities and an ability to think sequentially. Coaching, like creating art, requires intuitive capacities, an ability to see something that is not yet—but could be—in existence, and the willingness to surrender to the process and trust that a worthwhile product will emerge. Like any visual or performing art, coaching requires attention to detail as well as an appreciation for the whole, and an understanding that the artistry is in the process as well as the product.

Although a coach plans and applies a body of knowledge and skills, an artful coach also engages in the work creatively. Our education system is a heavy and serious place these days. The need to improve our schools is urgent. But when a coach taps into and harnesses creative energy, when the process is enjoyable, even fun, the end result is more likely to be transformational.

COACHING FOR TRANSFORMATION

I coach for transformation—transformation of the adults with whom I work, the institutions in which they work, the lives of the children and communities they serve, and our society as a whole. I coach to help teachers, principals, central office administrators, and all educators transform their behaviors, beliefs, and being. The model of coaching that I propose holds transformation as the end goal; it also assumes that to meet this goal, the process must be transformational. Transformation describes both the destination and the journey.

Transformation is a term that is at risk of being overused and drained of meaning, so a definition is necessary here. The prefix *trans-* means across, on the other side of, beyond—where we are going is unknown and yet to be defined. A transformation is an end result almost unrecognizable from its previous form, a change so massive and complete, so thorough and comprehensive that until we are there, it is unimaginable. For example, mist transforms when it solidifies into an iceberg; a caterpillar transforms when it becomes a butterfly. How can we create something we can barely imagine? Working toward something unclear and ambiguous can be uncomfortable. This process of creation will require us to suspend our beliefs about whether or not it can be done and to forge onward, creating and transforming in spite of our own preconceptions. Transformation, of course, can be positive or negative. The assumption in my definition is that the destination is a tremendous, positive improvement over the current state.

Coaching that is practiced as an art is coaching that has the power to transform—to completely change the substance, appearance, and even essence of one thing into another. This can be a challenging craft, at first, for those who are goal oriented, driven by strategic plans, seeking benchmarks, and secure working in a sequential, linear progression. Goals and plans will be crucial for this journey, as long as they are guides and not dictators. However, transforming individuals, institutions, student experience, and our society will require a new set of tools and some new ways of being.

WHAT MIGHT A TRANSFORMED EDUCATION SYSTEM BE LIKE?

I envision an education system that is equitable for all children. Because so many definitions are used for the term *equity*, I would like to share mine here.

In its most simplistic definition, *equity* means that every child gets what he or she needs in our schools—*every child*, regardless of where she comes from, what she looks like, who her parents are, what her temperament is, or what she shows up knowing or not knowing. Every child gets what she needs every day in order to have all the skills and tools that she needs to pursue whatever she wants after leaving our schools, and to lead a fulfilling life. Equity is about outcomes and experiences—for every child, every day.

An equitable education system, therefore, is one in which student achievement and learning are not predictable by race, class, language, gender, sexual orientation, or other such social factors. An equitable school system will be one in which

African American and Latino males do not constitute the largest groups of students who do not graduate from high school. Nor will English language learners with learning disabilities have the lowest passing scores on a high school exit exam, as they do currently in California. Equitable classrooms will be those in which boys are not routinely the students found in time-out chairs. According to a range of measurements including, but not limited to, standardized test scores and high school graduation rates, we will not be able to predict who will perform well in school. All students, regardless of family income levels, home zip codes, primary language, skin tone and gender, will have access to experiences, conditions, and support so that they can graduate from high school ready for college and careers.

This definition of equity is no small task. It describes a transformation that might be hard to imagine. It is this mind-set—that transformation is unimaginable, unattainable—that we must transform. The natural world abounds with transformation: life on Earth emerged from star dust! Human societies have undergone equally massive transformations. Consider the women's suffrage movement in the United States, Mahatma Gandhi's nonviolent resistance to British colonialism, and the end of apartheid in South Africa. We can transform our schools. It is possible.

In order to meet the needs of all students, we must also transform the experience for the adults who work in schools. Until we address the social, emotional, and learning needs of educators, we won't be able to transform the experience for students. We can start by identifying the needs that teachers and administrators have, finding ways to meet those needs, and bringing groups of educators together in different ways. In this way, together and in healthy relationships with each other, we can explore solutions to current challenges and improve outcomes and experiences for kids. This is where coaching comes in. It is a holistic approach to working with people that incorporates an understanding of how institutions and systems impact experience and learning and that fosters transformation at multiple levels.

Coaching alone, however, will not result in the kind of transformation that I envision. First of all, coaching for transformation is not possible in a vacuum—certain conditions must be established in an educational context in order for coaching to be effective. Second, coaching alone will do nothing to address the loss of funding for American schools, an issue that results in fundamentally inequitable schools. Until the current funding structure is changed, we will continue to have difficulty developing equitable schools. Finally, some educational policy and national "reform" efforts have actually made the creation of equitable schools more difficult: as long as the evaluation of a teacher's quality is reduced to a number, we will not have equitable classrooms. A single number can never encapsulate the experience and outcomes for all students.

It will take time to transform our education system. I find consolation in the Dalai Lama's advice: "Do not despair," he counseled a group of activists. "Your work will bear fruit in 700 years or so" (Wheatley, 2009, p. 83). I also recognize that I have no choice but to engage in this process of transformation. The sages who wrote the Talmud declared, "It is not up to you to finish the work, but neither are you free not to take it up."

While the whole system may take generations to transform, the coaching you do today can impact students immediately. The effort is well worth it for them. We cause transformation all along the road to greater transformation.

ONE PURPOSE AND TWO PROMISES

My intent in this book is to propose a model of coaching that can foster transformation in schools and beyond. This model emerges from several theoretical frameworks, proposes dozens of specific activities, and suggests belief stances and habits of mind that coaches can adopt. Coaching in schools is an emerging field. I hope to contribute to our knowledge and understanding of what coaching is and what it can do.

I make two commitments to you. First, I promise that this book will be full of immediately applicable and useful ideas and resources. I write for an audience who may not have much time to read and who may read this book in short chunks, consulting it when looking for information that might provide guidance at a specific moment. With this awareness, I promise that this book will be useful and that you won't need to read more than a few pages without getting ideas for something you can do today. At the same time, I don't want to give the impression that coaching is merely a checklist of strategies. It is much more than a set of tools, and a coach must cultivate a particular way of being—I will define this "way of being" and suggest how it can be developed.

Second, I promise to tell a lot of stories. Our brains are wired to learn through stories, we remember what we hear in a narrative, and we enjoy stories. I will use stories to illustrate theories, to provide concrete examples of the ideas I'm presenting, and to share how these coaching practices actually play out.

WHERE I'M COMING FROM AND WHO THIS BOOK IS FOR

After one year teaching high school in rural Salinas, California, I moved to Oakland (in the San Francisco Bay Area), where I have taught and coached in our public schools for seventeen years. For most of the time I've worked here, the demographics in our schools have been roughly 40 percent Latino, 40 percent African American, and the remainder divided between Asian Americans, whites, Native Americans, and Pacific Islanders. About 25 percent of our students are English language learners, and over 70 percent are eligible for free and reduced-cost lunches. My stories and experiences emerge from this complicated and dynamic urban context.

I transitioned into coaching after over a decade of teaching. First, I coached teachers new to the school where I taught. Working with adults was a shift—sometimes rewarding and other times frustrating, but something about it hooked me. After a few years in the hybrid teaching-coaching role, I left the classroom for a full-time instructional coaching position in a large middle school. I knew I was in for a challenge, but assumed I'd find resources to help me.

I learn best by watching others—and as a teacher I was lucky to work with a fantastic coach, but I also learn from books. When I turned to the usual places for resources in print, I found barely a handful of books written on coaching. I read everything I could, but some of it was too specific, or not basic enough, or not grounded in an education context.

I've always heard that you should write the book you want to read. This is the book I wanted to read as a new, struggling coach, and it's still the book I want to read. I am not yet fully the artful coach I aspire to be—I have many years of practice to go to approach mastery. Writing this book is a way for me to reflect on and develop my coaching.

One note: this book focuses on coaches working with individuals. Many of the approaches are applicable to facilitating groups of educators, but the art of coaching teams is worthy of an entire volume itself.

Beyond myself, I write for three audiences:

1. **Coaches working in schools**. I hope that regardless of which area a coach works in—whether beginning teacher support, math, literacy, classroom management, leadership, or school improvement—you will find relevant resources, tools, and ideas. I also hope that regardless of whether you are a brand new coach or an experienced coach, you will find something here to augment your practice.

2. **Principals and other administrators working toward school transformation**. Coaching strategies can be used by anyone. Site-based leaders, central office administrators, school counselors, deans, and other educators engaged in school change will find resources for refining skills such as listening and asking questions, building trusting relationships, understanding adult learners, and more.

   In order to highlight sections that might be useful to those who are not coaches but who want to use coaching strategies—primarily principals and other site-based administrators—specific sections throughout this book have been flagged as tips for principals. Look for the circular arrow icon.

3. **The coaching community outside of education**. I frequently read literature from the broader field of coaching. Regardless of where they work, the goals for many coaches are similar—the growth and development of an individual and the authentic integration of skills and passion for a greater good. I hope to share some of what has been learned in the education context with coaches who work in other fields; we have much to learn from each other.

SUMMARY OF THE CONTENTS AND HOW TO USE THIS BOOK

Even if you could read this book cover to cover in one sitting, I'm not sure I'd recommend you do so. Coaching is effective in part because it is experienced over time: you keep coming back to your coach, exploring a different aspect of your work, and then venturing out to try new approaches. In the same way, I hope this book will act as a coach—that you'll get some ideas, go try them, and then come back to reflect and learn more.

Part One, "Foundations of Coaching," will be very useful to those new to the field. It's what I wish I could have read during my first year. This is also the information I review with principals when they're considering hiring a coach. I recommend that you read this section first.

Part Two, "Establishing Coaching with a Client" explores how to build trust, get to know a client, and determine a coaching focus. The information in this section will help a coach set up the coaching agreements and relationship.

Part Three, "The Coaching Dance" describes the listening, questioning, conversational approaches, and activities that a coach typically engages a client in. At the end of the chapters in Parts Two and Three are sections on Common Challenges that coaches experience, followed by suggested solutions.

Part Four, "Professional Development for Coaches," is geared for coaches and those who supervise them. It proposes some structures and activities that coaches can engage in either independently or in teams to refine their practice. (See the following table of Essential Frameworks for Transformational Coaching.)

Essential Frameworks for Transformational Coaching

I offer three frameworks that I suggest are essential in transformational coaching.

	Framework	Description
1	The Ladder of Inference (See Chapter Three)	A framework to help us understand what's underneath behaviors that we observe and to help us deconstruct beliefs. This is based on the work of Peter Senge.
2	The Coach's Optical Refractor (See Chapter Four)	A set of analytical tools that can help us see a situation in many different ways. There are six lenses which help us look at evidence from different perspectives. These are based on the work of the National Equity Project and Daniel Goleman.
3	Coaching Stances (See Chapters Nine–Twelve)	An analytical framework for coaching conversations and activities. These can help us plan coaching conversations, make decisions during the conversation, and guide the next steps we take. These are based on the work of John Heron.

The Appendixes offer a glossary of commonly used terms and recommended resources on topics raised in each chapter. On my website, www.elenaaguilar.com, you'll find a bank of additional tools and tips.

A COUPLE NOTES

On Terminology

As someone very interested in the power of words, I am unsatisfied with any of the terms that are currently used to describe the person who receives coaching: the "coachee" or the "client." *Coachee* sounds too cute, informal, and like a derivative of "coach." *Client* references the business world, but our work in schools is about transformation, which lies too close to the heart and soul to be associated with financial transactions. As much as I dislike these two terms, there are no other alternatives currently in use, and rather than attempting to be innovative, I'm going to grudgingly settle for using these two interchangeably.

On Anonymity and Pseudonyms

To protect the privacy of every teacher and administrator I have ever coached, as well as the schools where they worked, I have changed names and most identity markers so that the people about whom I write will be unrecognizable even to themselves.

The *Art* of Coaching

PART ONE

Foundations of Coaching

CHAPTER 1

How Can Coaching Transform Schools?

Read this when:

- You are a coach, supervisor of coaches, or principal who wants to articulate what coaching is and can be
- You are an administrator considering developing a coaching program in your school

A STORY ABOUT WHAT COACHING CAN DO

The best way to describe how coaching can transform schools—through improving teacher practices, addressing systemic issues, and improving outcomes for children—is by offering an example.

Karen, a young white woman, was in her third year teaching English in an urban middle school. Before I started working with her, I had been warned that she was "not good with Mexican kids." One principal had already moved her out of his school, and her new principal, whose student population was 80 percent Latino, was very concerned. I found Karen to be well intentioned, able to create engaging lessons, and capable of building good rapport with students. She was also eager to receive coaching.

A significant percentage of Karen's eighth graders were several years below grade level in reading. Karen agreed to explore her students' skill gaps and selected Angel, a Mexican-American boy, as a focal student. She hoped that digging deep into what was going on with one student would reveal insights and practices that could be applied to other struggling students. Angel was bright, well liked, and had a stable home life; his parents had both graduated from high school in California. He was also goofy and frequently off task in class. Karen had no idea why Angel read at a second-grade level.

As a first step, I coached Karen in using a set of reading diagnostics. She discovered that while Angel had a tremendous mastery of a set of sight words, and therefore could read some text, he could not decode multisyllabic words. Karen dug deeper, finding that Angel struggled with the sounds of certain phonemes. Karen identified the precise skill gaps that made reading difficult for Angel. Now it was just a matter of filling those gaps. Angel leapt at the offer of extra help and extra homework, regularly skipping recess and coming in after school; Karen was enthusiastic about supporting him. In the course of six months, Angel's reading advanced three grade levels.

In an end-of-year reflection with me, Karen revealed that initially she had thought that Angel was "just lazy." She looked at the boy's photo, which decorated the outside of his file. "I really thought he was just a lazy boy," she admitted. She was embarrassed by her previous beliefs and that she'd fallen into believing stereotypes about Mexican immigrants. In our coaching, I carefully and intentionally pushed Karen to explore her belief system; I challenged it and helped her shatter an assumption that she held about some of her students.

I also coached the English department to which Karen belonged. That year, I facilitated an inquiry process to help teachers identify students' key missing skills and provide small-group and individual instruction to close those gaps. By the end of the year, these teachers concluded that it was an imperative to know, from day one, what their incoming students' exact gap areas were. They devised a process in which information could be gathered on students in certain achievement groups as part of the registration process. With these data, teachers could get a head start on planning to close these gaps.

As a result, my coaching led to a systems change—a change in how much teachers at one school know about their students, when and how they get certain information, and what they do with the information they gather. This change was initiated by teachers, welcomed by them, and resulted in a sense of empowerment about changing the outcomes for children. As evidenced by multiple measures, student achievement increased dramatically at this school for the next two years. This is what coaching can offer.

WHAT WILL IT TAKE TO TRANSFORM OUR SCHOOLS?

Speaking in the early 1980s, poet and activist Audre Lorde warned that true change could only be realized when those engaged in enacting it operate from an entirely different set of thoughts, beliefs, and values and take radically different actions from those taken in the past. Without a

The master's tools will never dismantle the master's house.

AUDRE LORDE (1984)

new set of tools, Lorde warned that we risk reproducing structures of oppression. Coaching offers a new set of tools that have the potential to radically transform our schools.

In the United States, our public school system is in crisis. On this point there is little disagreement. Something must be done. Beyond that, there is a raging debate on what to do and how to do it. Those who ride the chariot of No Child Left Behind (NCLB) deliver one message, which perhaps crudely summarized comes down to this—teachers, principals: improve your test scores or you will be penalized or even fired. Perhaps their intentions are positive, but over ten years have passed since NCLB went into effect, and this method has not worked. The "achievement gap" remains, and there have been many devastating side effects from NCLB, such as the narrowing of curriculum, the time and focus dedicated to test preparation, and the increase in rote learning. Coaching must be contextualized within a broader conversation to "reform," save, or transform public education. As such, coaching—as a method and theory—is a political stance. Coaching rests on a few basic assumptions that place its supporters in a unique location in this discussion of school transformation.

First, a coaching stance views teachers, principals, and all the adults who work in schools *as capable of changing practices*—coaches fundamentally believe that people can learn and change. Second, in order to understand the current reality and challenges in schools, coaches analyze larger systems at play as well as the historical context. We consider the impact of complex organizations, the macro socioeconomic system, and the roles of all individuals; we do not blame one group of people or seek any quick fixes.

It is essential that we explore the nature of the so-called "achievement gap"—why it exists, who benefits from it, and why current federal legislation can't eliminate it. But it is more important and absolutely critical that we are thoughtful about the way we are going about doing things—the "how": how we reflect on and analyze the past, how we confront the present, how we change our schools and create the future. If we are not mindful, the change process will end up replicating the structures of oppression that produced our current system.

This is where coaching comes in: when we explore the "how." An understanding of this historical context is essential when we work in schools. Teachers have been blamed for poverty and told they are lazy, untrustworthy, and unintelligent. I believe that the most effective coaches were once teachers, and that they carry this awareness with them. Our communication with teachers and principals must be imbued with this empathy and contextual understanding or we risk (perhaps unconsciously) falling into the dominant discourse around what's wrong with schools.

Former superintendent of San Diego's schools, Carl Cohn, cautions that "school reform is a slow, steady labor-intensive process" contingent on "harnessing the talent of individuals . . . " (quoted in Ravitch, 2010, p. 66). Herein lies the essential question for us to grapple with: How do we harness the talent of individuals? How do we develop conditions for adults to learn and develop their talents?

A NEW TOOL KIT BASED ON ANCIENT KNOWLEDGE

Coaching is a form of professional development that brings out the best in people, uncovers strengths and skills, builds effective teams, cultivates compassion, and builds emotionally resilient educators. Coaching at its essence is the way that human beings, and individuals, have always learned best.

The apprenticeship is an ancient form of coaching. An experienced practitioner welcomes a learner who improves her practice by watching, listening, asking questions, and trying things out under the supportive gaze of the mentor. While there are critical distinguishing factors between a mentor and a coach, the sensibility and outcome are the same: the learner is met and accepted wherever she is in her learning trajectory, she is encouraged and supported, she may be pushed, and in the end, she's a competent practitioner.

Coaching is also, essentially, what any parent does with a child. When my son learned to walk, I supported him in his first steps, standing close by and offering a hand when necessary. I let him stumble and fall, looking for that fine line between his need for reassurance and his need to remain upright. I'd crouch a few feet away, with my hands outstretched, rambling, "Come on, sweetie, I know you can do it! Come on—take a step, you can do it." Gradually, I'd scoot backward on the floor, allowing my toddler to take more steps as he was ready, until eventually he was running across the living room.

With our children, we use a gradual release of responsibility model, providing just enough help for them to do it, but not so much that they don't develop the skills by themselves. When they're nine months old, we don't scream, "I can't carry you any longer. You need to walk now or I'm leaving you here!" Threats and coercion don't work.

In order to transform our education system, we need to pay attention to the people who make up this system and all of their needs. This requires everyone to develop tremendous patience, compassion, humility, attentiveness, and a willingness to listen deeply. We need to meet people wherever they are and then together devise a "how," and, most likely, we'll have to try a few "hows" before we see the results we want. There's just no other way.

WHAT CAN COACHING DO FOR A SCHOOL? WHAT DOES THE RESEARCH SAY?

 Administrators: this next section will be very useful if you are considering hiring a coach or setting up a coaching program.

There's generally an agreement that educators need more knowledge, skills, practice, and support after they enter the profession. Malcolm Gladwell, the author of *Outliers: The Story of Success* (2008), calculates that it takes ten thousand hours of deliberate practice—practice that promotes continuous improvement—to master a complex skill. This translates into about seven years for those working in schools. The majority of teachers and principals want professional development; they want to improve their craft, be more effective, implement new skills, and see students learn more.

Opinions diverge as to what professional development (PD) should look like. Traditionally, PD has taken the form of a three-day training, say in August before school starts, and then perhaps a couple of follow-up sessions throughout the year. This kind of PD by itself, which just about every teacher has experienced, rarely results in a significant change in teacher practice and rarely results in increased learning for children. According to a 2009 study on professional development, teachers need close to fifty hours of PD in a given area to improve their skills and their students' learning (Darling-Hammond and others, 2009). While the research on the ineffectiveness of "one-shot" PD continues to pile up, a search is under way for PD that might work. Learning Forward (the international association of educators formerly known as the National Staff Development Council) has developed an invaluable set of Standards for Professional Learning that identifies the characteristics of professional learning that lead to effective teaching practices, supportive leadership, and improved student results. It is very useful to all engaged in designing or leading PD. You can find these standards online here: www.learningforward.org/standards.

Coaching is an essential component of an effective professional development program. Coaching can build will, skill, knowledge, and capacity because it can go where no other professional development has gone before: into the intellect, behaviors, practices, beliefs, values, and feelings of an educator. Coaching creates a relationship in which a client feels cared for and is therefore able to access and implement new knowledge. A coach can foster conditions in which deep reflection and learning can take place, where a teacher can take risks to change her practice, where powerful conversations can take place and where growth is recognized and celebrated. Finally, a coach holds a space where healing can take place and where resilient, joyful communities can be built.

When considering hiring a coach, principals often ask the following kinds of questions about the impact of coaching: What does the research say about how coaching can transform a school? Is there a model that is most effective? Is there evidence that coaching will result in increased student achievement?

As coaches, it is our responsibility to know what can be expected. We can't go into schools purporting to raise test scores by 50 percent in the first year. We need to articulate what we might be able to accomplish. Fortunately, there is a growing body of research indicating that coaching can help create the conditions necessary for instructional practices to change and student outcomes to improve. These are valuable data points for coaches to be aware of as they help direct the work we do; our work is not simply about working individually with teachers to improve their practice—it must extend farther.

To date, the most thorough and comprehensive study on coaching was done in 2004 by the Annenberg Foundation for Education Reform. It reports a number of findings that offer powerful validation for coaching. First, the report concludes that effective coaching encourages collaborative, reflective practice. Coaching allows teachers to apply their learning more deeply, frequently, and consistently than teachers working alone. Coaching supports teachers to improve their capacity to reflect and apply their learning to their work with students and also in their work with each other.

A second finding from the Annenberg report is that effective embedded professional learning promotes positive cultural change. The conditions, behaviors, and practices required by an effective coaching program can affect the culture of a school or system, thus embedding instructional change within broader efforts to improve school-based culture and conditions.

Coaching was also linked to teachers' increase in using data to inform practice. Effective coaching programs respond to particular needs suggested by data, allowing improvement efforts to target issues such as closing achievement gaps and advocating for equity. The Annenberg report found that coaching programs guided by data helped create coherence within a school by focusing on strategic areas of need that were suggested by evidence, rather than by individual and sometimes conflicting opinions.

Another key finding was that coaching promotes the implementation of learning and reciprocal accountability. Coaching is an embedded support that attempts to respond to student and teacher needs in ongoing, consistent, dedicated ways. The likelihood of using new learning and sharing responsibility rises when colleagues, guided by a coach, work together and hold each other accountable for improved teaching and learning.

Finally, the Annenberg report determined that coaching supports collective leadership across a school system. An essential feature of coaching is that it uses the relationships between coaches, principals, and teachers to create the conversation that leads to behavioral, pedagogical, and content knowledge change. Effective coaching distributes leadership and keeps the focus on teaching and learning. This focus promotes the development of leadership skills, professional learning, and support for teachers that target ways to improve student outcomes.

Additional research studies indicate that effective coaching structures promote a collaborative culture where school staffs feel ownership and responsibility for leading improvement efforts in teaching and learning. Coaching attends to the "social infrastructure" issues of schools and systems that often impede the deep and lasting change that school reform requires. These issues include school climate, teacher isolation, insufficient support, and limited instructional and leadership capacity. In 2010, the *Elementary School Journal* published eight studies on the impact of coaching on teacher practice and student achievement. This included a three-year study on literacy coaches working in grades K–2 in seventeen schools. In these schools, they found that student literacy learning increased by 16 percent in its first year, 28 percent in its second year, and 32 percent in the third (Biancarosa, Bryk, and Dexter, 2010).

Another study investigated the effect of coaching on new teachers in a high-turnover school. It found that schools with coaching programs saw significant improvement in measures of teacher practices and student outcomes compared to schools without coaching programs. The findings suggest that new teachers benefit from teaching in schools with strong coaching programs in place, and that coaching programs could have an added benefit in high-turnover urban schools (Matsumura and others, 2010). Reflecting on the eight different studies, the *Elementary School Journal* editors write: "Many in the field have trusted that intuitive feeling that putting a knowledgeable coach in a classroom to work with a teacher will result in improved teacher practices and increased student learning. The jury of these researchers and the peer reviewers of their work have delivered its verdict: while coaching may be new, it is no longer unproven" (Sailors and Shanklin, 2010).

As the field of coaching in schools develops, it is critical that we identify and gather sets of qualitative and quantitative data that can reveal the impact of our work on student learning. We need to track the changes we see in teacher and leader practice and gather evidence that our work is resulting in improved student learning. This can be an exciting and validating effort—it is these data that help us feel effective and that let us know objectively that we're doing good work. In order to do this, we need to make sure that the scope of our work is defined and narrow, that we're gathering data on how our clients make progress, and that we're articulating these findings. A highly effective, comprehensive coaching program in a school or district supports coaches to systematically gather a range of evidence to illustrate the impact of coaching on teachers, administrators, and students.

THE NECESSARY CONDITIONS

The potential for coaching within the education system has yet to be reached for several reasons. First, in most schools and districts, there is no formal pathway or training for entering a coaching role. The majority of coaches were strong teachers who demonstrated mastery of content and pedagogy and who were encouraged, or self-selected, to pursue coaching. While content and pedagogy are foundational knowledge for a school coach, there are many more skills and capacities required for working with adults. Furthermore, once in the position, most coaches receive little professional development. Therefore, given the inconsistency with which coaches are trained and supported, there is bound to be a discrepancy between what coaching can offer and the reality.

In addition, the potential of coaching cannot be realized if certain conditions are not in place. Daniel Coyle, author of *The Talent Code* (2009), describes coaches as farmers who cultivate talent in others. As someone who has long admired the patience, attentiveness, and groundedness of farmers, I love this analogy. It is also apt when considering what needs to be in place for coaching to be effective: the land must be fertile, invasive weeds need to have been removed, and the seeds can't be old and moldy. A farmer must be aware of local climate—you can't plant pineapples in Alaska and expect them to thrive.

Coaches, similarly, need to be able to analyze systems and identify situations primed for coaching. It is partly our responsibility as coaches to accept positions in schools where the foundation is laid for us to do our best work. Principals, or supervisors of coaches, are also responsible for assessing how "ready" a coach is to undertake the work.

Let's consider these conditions that need to be in place in order for coaching to work. It is critical that these be delineated, because when the status of these conditions is murky, it is hard to assess the impact of coaching or draw conclusions about its impact. For example, if a principal invests scarce resources to bring coaches into his school and sees little change in test scores after two years, he might conclude that "coaching doesn't work." While this appears to be an obvious conclusion, is it correct? If taken at face value, it could result in a school culture that does not value or utilize coaching.

There are two sets of variables to assess for readiness: the readiness of the coach and of the site.

The Coach's Readiness

A coach working with teachers or principals must have been an effective teacher for at least five years; there is just no other way to have developed the kind of empathy and foundational knowledge and understanding that teachers or principals need in a coach. A dynamic teacher or principal may not necessarily segue into being an effective coach without additional training. Fortunately, many of the technical skills and knowledge about coaching can be learned, but a prospective coach must at a minimum have strong communication skills, particularly listening skills, and high emotional intelligence.

Principals interviewing coaches might also explore how the coach became a coach—did she participate in any training? Has she ever been coached? What draws her to the domain of adult learning? Without a deep interest in—and perhaps passion for—adult learners, a coach will struggle. The following list offers questions that principals might ask applicants for a coaching position.

Interview Questions for a Principal or Hiring Manager to Ask a Coach-Applicant

1. Tell us a little about yourself and your background in education.

2. Why do you want to be a coach? Why do you want to be a coach here?

3. What has your experience been with coaching? If you were coached in the past, what worked for you? What didn't work?

4. Which coaching skills do you feel you're strong in?

5. Which coaching skills would you like to develop?

6. What conditions do you think need to be present at a site in order for you to have an impact as a coach?

7. What does a really good classroom look like to you?

8. When you go into a classroom as an observer, what are you looking for? Or looking at? What catches your attention?

9. What would you do if you were coaching a new teacher who couldn't manage a class?

10. What would you do to get to know a site that you were assigned to coach at?

11. How would you work with a teacher or administrator who didn't seem to want coaching?

12. What experience have you had working in teams?

13. What are your thoughts about how teams develop? What do you anticipate doing as a coach to support team development?

14. What are your thoughts and beliefs about how systems change? As a coach, how do you see yourself affecting system change at a site?

15. How would you measure or evaluate the impact you have as a coach on your client?

16. Tell us about a time when you experienced big change that may have been outside of your sphere of control. How did you manage it?

17. Most teachers and administrators experience significant stress. How have you managed stress and emotional turmoil at work? What ideas do you have for supporting clients in this area?

18. How do you learn best? How do you see yourself developing as a coach?

The Site's Readiness

There are definitely conditions in which an experienced, trained, highly skilled coach can fail to produce any kind of change in teacher practice or student outcome. In this case, we want to be careful not to come to the easy or obvious conclusion that the coach was ineffective without also looking at the conditions at the site.

An abundance of research describes the determining impact that a leader has on a school. In order for a site to be ripe for a coach, the principal must demonstrate some degree of effective leadership. The main areas to assess for are in the domains of how a leader fosters vision or mission, determines instructional foci, creates and sustains a collaborative culture, organizes professional development, and makes decisions. A site that is under a time-bound threat of sanctions for not meeting external goals (such as not making NCLB's adequate yearly progress, or AYP) is one where the range of a coach's impact will be limited—at least for the immediate future. A coach *can* help a site improve markers such as AYP, but it takes years. In a school with ineffective leadership, coaching won't result in whole-school change. While it is very likely that some of these conditions may be in place in any school that seeks to bring in a coach, prospective coaches would be wise to consider for themselves how many conditions need to be in place in order to allow them to be effective, or which ones are nonnegotiable. The following list offers questions for coaches to consider when applying for a coaching position.

> *Most transformation programs satisfy themselves with shifting the same old furniture about in the same old room. But real transformation requires that we redesign the room itself. Perhaps even blow up the old room. It requires that we change the thinking behind our thinking.*
>
> DANAH ZOHAR (1997, P. 243)

Questions for a Coach to Ask at an Interview

1. What are your school's overarching goals? Who has set these goals? What was that process like?

2. What is your school's vision and mission? When were they created? When and where are the vision and mission revisited? What percentage of your staff, students, and parents would you guess know the vision and mission well?

3. What do you see as your teachers' areas of strengths? Areas for growth? How have you gathered these data?

4. What does professional development look like at your site? When and where does professional development occur? What role do you play in professional development? What impact does professional development have on your teachers' practice? How do you know?

5. Have you had coaches working in this school before? What was that experience like?

6. What is your vision of how you'd like to partner with a coach?

7. How do teachers feel about getting a coach? How do you know what they feel?

SPEAKING OF RACE

In June 2011, in the Oakland Unified School District where I work, fewer than 50 percent of the African American and Latino boys who had enrolled in high school four years earlier graduated; almost 75 percent of Asian American and white males graduated. One in three African American boys in Oakland middle schools is suspended in a given year; this exceeds the suspension rate of white males by six times. In our schools that are 100 percent students of color, it's not uncommon to find that the majority of teachers are young white women from middle-class backgrounds. Oakland is not unique among urban districts in facing these issues. Rural and suburban schools grapple with some of the same challenges on a different scale, and with other issues that reflect their contexts. It's hard to work in schools these days without recognizing the patterns in outcomes that correlate to socioeconomic factors and reflect broader patterns of achievement and power.

In order to talk about transformational coaching that works toward equitable schools, we're going to have to talk about race and class and gender and all those other issues that have divided people. There's no way around it. And yet we don't live in a society where these topics are discussed, we may have little experience engaging in this dialogue, and we may not know how. So what can coaches do?

Let's start with three truths about this work, offered with the hope of bringing relief:

1. *This isn't going to be easy.* Whether we're talking to people who share our particular cultural group or skin tones, or we're in mixed company, speaking about race, classism, patriarchy, homophobia, and the like is going to be uncomfortable.

2. *There is no "right way" to have these conversations.* We're going to struggle to find the right words and get them out; we're going to blunder and stumble.

3. *We have to do it anyway.* We need to gather skills, manage our own discomfort, and engage in conversations about race, class, privilege, and power because children need us to.

This book will offer some ways to speak about race, but you'll also want to read other authors, attend workshops, and engage in other forms of learning. You'll find suggestions for these in the recommended resources in Appendix E.

THE VALUE OF COACHING

The fact that coaching has been taken up in so many personal and professional realms in the last couple of decades is another data set to consider as we make the case for coaching in our schools. Athletic coaches have long been recognized as those who play the determining role in a team's success—their disproportionately high salaries may reflect this appreciation (a value that is not reflected in the salaries of coaches working in schools). The business world has engaged coaches at all levels, and various companies attribute their successes to coaching. Life coaches have proliferated in recent years; clients who once went to therapy are now trying coaching as a self-help approach. Spiritual coaches are emerging from many traditions. Finally, experienced surgeons are discovering that coaching can improve their practice and they are recommending it to their ranks (Gawande, 2011).

Coaching has proliferated because it is responsive to what we know about what adults need in order to be able to learn. Coaching is at its essence a nurturing structure, but it is also one where there is always a subtle push for change. It grants space for emotions, but doesn't linger in feelings; our intention is to address them, process them, and then move on. Coaches encourage us to explore our core values, behaviors, beliefs, and ways of being and compel us to venture into new behaviors, beliefs, and ways of being. It is this essential combination of safety, support, encouragement, and forward movement that makes coaching feel so satisfying, that allows us to make changes in what we do, and even to transform who we are.

Coaching, however, is not a panacea for our education system. As Diane Ravitch cautions, "In education, there are no shortcuts, no utopias, and no silver bullets" (Ravitch, 2010, p. 3). But coaching is one piece—an essential piece—of the multilayered approach that will be necessary to transform schools. Teachers and leaders need high-quality professional development that takes many shapes and forms, and that development includes coaching, but they also need living wages, improved working conditions, and a whole lot more respect. Our schools need a tremendous influx of cash: decrepit, antiquated buildings need to be repaired, basic supplies dwindle every year, class sizes keep increasing, support staff is slashed out of the budget, and so on. Curriculum must be improved in order to meet the needs of all our students. Our schools cannot continue to exist or be treated as isolated entities in a community—those of us working with and in schools must support them to become more tightly connected to, in service of, and responsive to the communities in which they are located. And on the policy front, the necessary changes are too many to list. The transformation of our education system will need to happen on many levels from the macro to the micro, from policy changes and taxation reform to the interpersonal relationships between people in a school.

But we must devote more time, money, and attention to improving the practice of the adults who work in schools. Coaching offers a model for professional development that can support teachers and principals in making immediate and long-term changes and becoming artful masters in our profession; these changes can lead to the transformation of our education system and the experiences and outcomes of the children it is meant to serve.

CHAPTER 2

What Is Coaching?

Read this when:

- You're beginning a new coaching assignment; a clear definition will help you articulate your role and responsibilities, which in turn helps build trusting relationships
- You're a principal considering hiring a coach or establishing a coaching program
- You're looking for a coaching job and you want to find the best fit

A STORY ABOUT A COACH WHO DIDN'T KNOW WHAT SHE WAS

"What does she do?" they whispered behind my back during my first months as an English language arts coach.

"Are you here to help us with *Holt*?" Ms. X asked me in the hallway. When I said no, that I wasn't there to enforce usage of the mandated curriculum, and that in fact I didn't like textbooks (a statement that I hoped would earn me points—who likes curriculum police?), she threw up her hands and turned away, shaking her head.

The requests came: "Can you make some copies for me, put up a bulletin board, order books?" "Can you cover my class while I go to the bathroom?" "Can you find out why Dominique's mom won't return my calls?" "Can you get the principal to do something about these kids?"

I met some of these requests. And then I tried to observe a few English teachers, model lessons, compile student data, and facilitate the English department's meetings. I designed and delivered some professional development (PD) sessions. But most of my efforts were met with resistance. I struggled to build trusting relationships, I didn't see changes in teacher practice, and I felt ineffective and frustrated most of the time.

At first I wanted to blame the principal; he hadn't positioned me well, he hadn't defined my role, and he had thrown me into the most toxic department in a dysfunctional school. But it wasn't his fault—he was a new leader in a very difficult situation. And the school needed way more than a coach to solve its problems. It wasn't my fault that I was ineffective, either—I had good intentions and I knew a few things about instruction—but I had no training as a coach. I didn't know what to do or how to do it.

Unfortunately, I know that my experience at this school was not unique. The majority of coaches I have met say that they feel that their job description is not clear. A coach's need to have a sense of the field of coaching and then define her own work is an essential starting place. This chapter puts forth some definitions of coaching and the model described in this book—transformational coaching. After becoming familiar with coaching models, I suggest that coaches construct a vision for themselves as a coach.

WHY WE NEED A DEFINITION

 Administrators: this next section will be useful when you are deciding how to make the best use of coaching.

The title *coach* has been loosely and widely applied in the field of education. New teachers are sometimes appointed a coach who might be a mentor and confidant, or simply someone who stops in every other week to fill out paperwork. Many mandated curricula initiatives deploy "coaches" to enforce implementation. Some schools have "data coaches" who gather and analyze data, prepare reports, meet with teachers to discuss the results, and suggest actions to take. Some districts assign coaches to underperforming veteran teachers as a step in the complicated process of firing a teacher. Central office administrators have also appointed "school improvement coaches" to schools that have failed to improve test scores. Finally, some teachers have experienced a coach who coplans lessons, observes instruction and offers feedback, models instructional strategies, gathers resources, and offers support with new curricula. There have been enough coaches passing through schools in recent decades that most educators have some idea about what a coach does. Coaches have a responsibility to understand this context and to provide a definition for what their work entails.

A definition of coaching is also necessary to help us come to agreement about what coaching *is not*. Let me suggest a few things that coaching must never be used for:

1. *Coaching is not a way to enforce a program.* Coaches should never be used as enforcers, reporters, or evaluators. This approach has many negative implications and demeans the field of coaching.

2. *Coaching is not a tool for fixing people.* It is not something you should do with or to ineffective teachers. It is not a box to be checked so that a district can move toward disciplinary measures. Coaching should not be mandated, and teachers or principals should be able to opt out of coaching. Coaching (as a form of professional development) won't be effective if the client doesn't want to engage in it. We can't force people to learn.

3. *Coaching is not therapy.* A coach does not pursue in-depth explorations of someone's psyche, childhood, or emotional issues. While these areas may arise in coaching—and, in fact, they frequently do—the role of a coach is not to dwell here. Sometimes a coach needs to delineate the lines between what she knows and can do and what a mental health expert knows and can do for a client. A coach needs to be very clear about the boundaries between coaching and therapy, and to remember that the focus of coaching is on learning and developing new skills and capacities.

4. *Coaching is not consulting.* A coach is not necessarily an expert who trains others in a way of doing something; a coach helps build the capacity of others by facilitating their learning.

Because coaching has been linked to enforcement of a program or disciplinary measures, and as such has disempowered educators, those of us who intend to practice it as a vehicle for transformation must be responsible for presenting a clear definition of what it is, who we are, what we do, and why we do it. We need to interrupt any stories that are not in alignment with what we're doing. Entering into a school or a coaching relationship with a clear definition that you can communicate will enable you to build much stronger relationships from the beginning.

Because there are so many different ideas circulating about what a coach is, when you start working with a new client it's important to ask him about his past experiences with coaching (even if your own definition of the role is clear). You need to know what he thinks the role entails, how he defines coaching, and what he wants and expects from coaching. See Chapter Five for more questions to ask in an initial meeting with a new client.

WHAT ARE THE DIFFERENT COACHING MODELS?

New coaches tend to focus on the actions, behaviors, and outward indicators of coaching, such as questioning techniques, observations, and giving feedback—the *doing* of coaching. Below the surface of what we *do* is what we *think* and *believe* about what we're doing. Finally, below that layer of beliefs and thinking is a layer of *being*—who we're being when we're coaching. The art of coaching is doing, thinking, and being: doing a set of actions, holding a set of beliefs, and being in a way that results in those actions leading to change. These are the three things that can make coaching transformational.

Let's first consider coaching models through two lenses: those that support only teachers and leaders in changing their *behaviors*, and those that support teachers and leaders in also considering changing their *beliefs* and ways of *being*. Directive coaching, which is also sometimes called instructive coaching, generally focuses on changing behaviors. When a coach suggests that a teacher circulate around the classroom while students are responding to a discussion prompt, her coaching is directive. Facilitative coaching can build on changes in behavior to support someone in developing ways of being or it can explore beliefs in order to change behaviors. When a coach asks a teacher to explain her decision making behind the delivery of a lesson, her coaching is facilitative. Finally, I'll describe transformational coaching, the model that I'm putting forth in this book and that I believe offers the greatest possibility for transforming our education system.

Coaches are much more effective when they can name the approach they're taking at a particular time. Having that awareness allows us to make decisions and take actions that are aligned to a specific model. We can also determine when shifting into a different approach might be more effective.

Directive (or Instructive) Coaching

An Example of Directive Coaching

Tania, a first-year teacher, collapsed into her chair when I entered her room. "I am completely overwhelmed," she said, her head dropping into her open palms. "I don't know if I can do this."

"What's going on?" I asked. We were three weeks into the school year.

Tania described a day that was typical, in many ways, for a novice teacher: struggles with classroom management and organization, lessons that were partially completed, a frustrated parent after school, and her own fatigue and insecurities. "I don't know what to do," she said, after relaying these challenges. "Just tell me. Tell me what to do!"

Although I am not inclined to be a directive coach, I recognized this as a moment in which I needed to do just that.

"OK, Tania," I said. "Let's start with a couple of high-leverage areas." I decided I would identify these areas based on what I know about teaching—I could have guided her through a process to think about what she already knows, and arrive at what would probably have been the same areas that I settled on, but because of her emotional and physical fatigue, I decided to name them.

"Let's deal with some organizational and classroom management strategies," I said. I made various suggestions and then encouraged Tania to make decisions about what she felt she could do. I did not tell her what to do or what I had done as a teacher, but I did name two or three strategies that "many teachers find effective."

Tania was relieved at the end of our ninety-minute meeting. She had a solid plan for the next day on how she'd address behavior and organize materials for her lesson. "I think I can do this," she said as we wrapped up. "I can implement this plan. I can get through tomorrow. And I can actually see how eventually I might just be able to do this teaching thing." This comment was the evidence I needed to validate my decision to be *instructive* in my coaching.

Directive (or instructive) coaching (the terms are used interchangeably in the literature) generally focuses on changing a client's behaviors. The coach shows up as an expert in a content or strategy and shares her expertise. She might provide resources, make suggestions, model lessons, and teach someone how to do something.

This kind of coaching is frequently practiced by those who coach in a particular content, discipline, or instructional framework. For example, a district may adopt a new curriculum and provide coaches who will help teachers master the material. Or a school may take on a behavior management program and hire coaches who can support implementation. As the United States transitions to the Common Core State Standards, I anticipate many schools will hire coaches to support teachers in putting these standards into practice. In this model, the coach is seen as an expert who is responsible for teaching a set of skills or sharing a body of knowledge.

Directive coaching strategies are relevant and necessary at times, as in the case Tania at the beginning of her first year of teaching. However, these strategies are also limited. Directive coaching alone is less likely to result in long-term changes of practice or internalization of learning. A coach may notice that she returns to visit a teacher she worked with, only to find that the teacher has given up using the strategies that she appeared to have adopted in coaching. "What happened?" the coach might bemoan.

Such a scenario is often seen when a coach limits her coaching tools to directive strategies; the coaching did not expand the teacher's internal capacity to reflect, make decisions, or explore her ways of being. What was accomplished was a change in practice, for a limited time. For coaching to have deep, long lasting impact, it is imperative that a coach uses additional coaching strategies that support educators to explore, develop, and/or change their beliefs and ways of being.

Facilitative Coaching

An Example of Facilitative Coaching

It was early March of Tania's first year teaching.

"Today's lesson went so well!" she said as I walked in. "I wish you'd seen the first part. They were in teams and were totally engaged in analyzing the document I gave them. They asked each other great questions and challenged each other."

"Tania, it's so great to hear that you're feeling able to design a learning sequence that challenged your students. I'm also hearing that you felt they worked well in their teams. Congratulations!"

"It really was satisfying. I'm just afraid it was a fluke and it won't happen again."

"Can you identify what you did to set up the lesson and group work to make it effective?" I asked.

"Well, I made my expectations very clear. The directions were projected on the wall. The documents were relevant and interesting to kids. And I scaffolded the packets they had to complete so that they could be successful."

"Tania, when I was in here last week I observed a lesson on group work and the different roles that students need to play in order for them to function well. Do you think that helped?"

"Yeah, of course. And another thing—yesterday one group modeled doing an assignment in a fishbowl. The whole class watched and commented. That was really helpful."

"That's great, Tania! So what could get in the way of this being repeated?"

"I guess I'm just afraid. Teaching is so hard! I feel like for every good lesson I teach, there are four duds."

"That's to be expected for new teachers. But because you can identify what you did to set up a successful lesson, there's a greater possibility that you'll have more days like today. Does that seem like a possibility to you?"

"Sure, it does. It's definitely a possibility."

Facilitative coaching supports clients to learn new ways of thinking and being through reflection, analysis, observation, and experimentation; this awareness influences their behaviors. The coach does not share expert knowledge; she works to build on the client's existing skills, knowledge, and beliefs and helps the client to construct new skills, knowledge, and beliefs that will form the basis for future actions.

An essential concept in many coaching models, including facilitative coaching, is the zone of proximal development (ZPD), which was developed by the Russian psychologist Lev Vygotsky. The ZPD is the difference between what a learner can do without help and what he can do with help. It is the range of abilities that one can perform with assistance, but cannot yet perform independently. When a learner is in the ZPD, if he is provided with appropriate assistance and tools — the scaffolding — then he can accomplish the skill. Eventually the scaffolding can be removed and the learner can complete the task independently. A learner's ZPD, therefore, is constantly shifting; the teacher or coach needs to have an acute understanding of it. Scaffolded instruction is also known as the gradual release of responsibility.

Coaching is the art of creating an environment, through conversation and a way of being, that facilitates the process by which a person can move toward desired goals in a fulfilling manner.

TIM GALLWEY (2000, P. 177)

A number of coaching models lie within the broad domain of facilitative coaching. Cognitive coaching is a foundation for facilitative coaching because it addresses our *ways of thinking* and aims to build metacognition. It focuses on exploring and changing the way we think, in order to change the way we behave. Cognitive coaches encourage reflective practices and guide clients to self-directed learning.

Ontological coaching has also deeply influenced facilitative coaching. It emerges from the philosophical study of being and focuses on how our way of being manifests in language, body, and emotions. Our perceptions and attitudes are seen as the

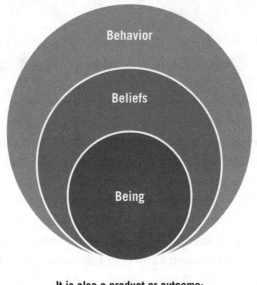

Transformational coaching is a process that explores the following:

Behavior

Beliefs

Being

It is also a product or outcome:

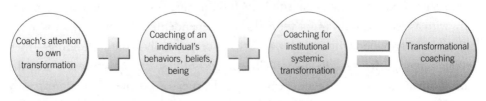

Coach's attention to own transformation + Coaching of an individual's behaviors, beliefs, being + Coaching for institutional systemic transformation = Transformational coaching

Figure 2.1. What Is Transformational Coaching?

underlying driver of behavior and communication, and coaching focuses on exploring these. Resources for learning more about these coaching models can be found in Appendix E.

Transformational Coaching

Transformational coaching, the model that I'm putting forth, has not been widely used in schools. It draws from ontology, the philosophical study of being, from Robert Hargrove, the author of *Masterful Coaching* and a pioneer in using transformational coaching in the business world, from the work of Peter Senge and the field of systems thinking, and from Margaret Wheatley's writing and teachings. Transformational coaching incorporates strategies from directive and facilitative coaching, as well as cognitive and ontological coaching; what makes it distinct is *the scope* that it attempts to affect and *the processes* used.

Transformational coaching is directed at three domains and intends to affect all three areas:

1. The individual client and his behaviors, beliefs, and being

2. The institutions and systems (departments, teams, and schools) in which the client works—and the people who work within those systems (students, teachers, and administrators)

3. The broader educational and social systems in which we live

A transformational coach works to surface the connections between these three domains, to leverage change between them, and to intentionally direct our efforts so that the impact we have on an individual will reverberate on other levels. Transformational coaching is deeply grounded in systems thinking. Systems thinking is a conceptual framework for seeing interrelationships and patterns of change rather than isolated events. Systems thinking helps us identify the structures that underlie complex situations and discern high- and low-leverage changes. By seeing wholes, we are much more effective in working toward transformation (Senge, 1990).

Coaching Behaviors, Beliefs, and Being

Changing behaviors is the goal in many forms of coaching. Exploring beliefs is also incorporated into some coaching approaches. But what does it mean to change your way of being? What does it mean to coach people on how they are "being"?

For a couple years, I coached a high school math teacher who played several leadership roles in her school. Her instructional practices were exceptional, and her beliefs about children contributed to equitable outcomes: she believed all kids could learn algebra—girls, boys, newly arrived immigrants, and so on—and they did. However, when she met with her colleagues for collaboration time or the school's leadership team, she often felt frustrated and impatient. She didn't feel she could communicate in the way she wanted to, she didn't feel understood, and she didn't get the results she wanted. Her verbal and nonverbal communication betrayed these feelings: her colleagues made comments such as, "What's up with Rachel today? She seemed really annoyed or something." Or "I'm nervous about saying what I really think because Rachel is so smart and sometimes I feel like she dismisses my ideas even before they're out of my mouth."

As Rachel began to recognize the effect she was having on her colleagues, and as she acknowledged that this would limit her effectiveness as a leader, she asked that my coaching address this. We worked on changing the specific behaviors that she was demonstrating, on exploring the underlying beliefs and thoughts, and we worked on who Rachel was "being" when she showed up at meetings in this way.

"Who do you want to be?" I prodded over and over.

"Someone who listens to others, who respects their perspectives," she said. "Empathetic and compassionate, but I also want to push people in their practice."

I helped Rachel develop a vision for herself as a teacher-leader, I helped her align behaviors and beliefs to this vision, and I gathered and shared data about how she showed up in different contexts. "Here's a transcript of what you said at your last math meeting," I shared. "Which statements reflect your core values and the leader you aspire to be?"

At the end of our coaching work together, Rachel commented: "I feel like your coaching changed me from the inside out. I feel different way down deep inside of me and I see the impact of coaching in other areas of my life."

Transformational coaching directly and intentionally attends to ways of being. We explore language, nonverbal communication, and emotions, and how these affect relationships, performance, and results. As transformational coaches in schools, we explore how our clients' ways of being shift depending on their contexts. Shifting is natural as we move into different settings, but sometimes we shift into ways of being that are not aligned to our vision for ourselves. For example, a principal may be able to "be" a certain way when he's leading teachers that come from his cultural background and demographic; however, when he works with teachers who are different, his way of being can shift. A transformational coach helps a client look at these shifts and explore the effects.

In order to transform our schools, we'll need to improve the craft of instruction and leadership and support educators to manage the physical, emotional, social, and intellectual demands of working in very diverse schools in a constantly changing environment.

Coaching for Institutional and Systems Change

A transformational coach thinks in terms of systems, helps a client see systems, and directs her efforts at the levels of an individual and the systems in which we are embedded. When we think in terms of systems, we are always looking for the links between the discrete problems that are presented and broader systems that exist now or that may need to be created: between the new teacher who is struggling with classroom management and the school and district's systems for on-boarding new teachers; between the principal who is frustrated by his staff's lack of compliance with e-mail protocols and the school's formal and informal communication systems. If we truly believe that everything is connected, in time and space, then without surfacing and addressing these connections the solutions that we come up with may not have the greatest impact. We explore systems in order to identify high-leverage entry points that could result in transformational changes for children.

What does this sound like in coaching? Here's a snippet of a conversation in which the coach is working from a systems-thinking perspective:

"I'm so frustrated," says the teacher. "I only have about 40 percent of students turning in homework. What should I do?"

"What do you think is going on?" asks the coach.

"They're lazy. I want to institute detention for those who don't do it."

"Let's hold off for a few minutes on a solution and consider why this is happening. OK?" The teacher nods. "So what might be the reasons they aren't doing homework?"

The reasons included these: students didn't understand the assignments, there were no consequences for not doing homework, they didn't remember what the homework was once they got home, many students didn't have quiet places in which to do homework in the evenings, many students worked after school or had responsibilities at home, students lost the assignments or didn't bring backpacks, and so on. The initial problem identified by the client was a symptom of much larger, complex problems.

As a systems thinker, the coach's first role is to carve out the time and psychological space for the client to explore root causes. We guide our clients toward an awareness of the systems that are interrelated to our problems, and then we seek high-leverage areas in which to take action. Let's consider what this might sound like in conversation with the teacher who is frustrated by the lack of homework submitted.

"We've surfaced a number of reasons that might contribute to students not doing homework," says the coach. "Which of these are immediately within your sphere of influence?"

The teacher identifies several obvious areas. "Can you think of some that might be within your school's sphere of influence and might be something you could take to the leadership team to discuss?"

"For years we've talked about starting an after-school homework club," says the teacher. "I'd like to push for that."

"That sounds like a schoolwide support structure that could be developed—a systemic response to this dilemma. What other reasons might indicate a system response?"

"I think kids not remembering their homework might be about communication—how we communicate homework. They have six classes per day, and each teacher has a different process for telling kids what their homework is. I can see how it would be confusing," says the teacher.

"That's a great observation. You could even take that to the next tenth-grade team meeting and discuss it."

When a transformational coach works from a systems-thinking approach, many conversations will begin at many levels of an organization. Some changes can be implemented immediately; others will take time. Some conversations stretch into socioeconomic and political issues that are beyond our control, but about which we need to be aware. For example, a student without a quiet place to do his homework may be living in a small apartment with many people; he may be the eldest responsible for watching his younger siblings while his mother works nights; he may live in an apartment complex on a busy thoroughfare that is a center for the informal economy. These macro issues are hard for a school to exert a direct influence on, but without an understanding of the larger systems at play, our responses to the immediate problems will be misguided, often tend to blame individuals, and are not likely to result in sustainable change. Furthermore, when we understand the larger systemic issues affecting our students and classroom experiences, we may be able to influence decisions made on the political and policy level; for example, we can use this knowledge when voting for school board candidates, we can support organizations that address socioeconomic issues, or we may be less inclined to blame a local district or principal for circumstances outside of their control.

The systems-thinking approach in coaching is integrated into many aspects of this book. It is addressed throughout every chapter, and more specifically in Chapters Six and Fourteen.

The Coach's Transformation

Transformational coaching is possible only when the coach is engaged in a process of transforming her own behaviors, beliefs, and being along with the client. Transformational coaching, therefore, is the synergistic outcome from two people engaged in transformation of their individual behaviors, beliefs, and being. Transformational coaching is not something we do *to* another; it is not a process that is engaged in only by the client. It is a complex dynamic engaged in by both client and coach. Without the coach's participation in her own transformation, the client cannot achieve his goals. Therefore, to take up this kind of coaching necessitates a commitment on the coach's part. This distinguishes transformational coaching from other forms. Chapter Fifteen goes in depth into this process for a coach.

A masterful coach is a leader who by nature is a vision builder and value shaper, not just a technician who manages people to reach their goals and plans through tips and techniques. To be able to do this requires that the coach discover his or her own humanness and humanity, while being a clearing for others to do the same.

HARGROVE (2003, P. 18)

A VISION FOR COACHING

As coaches learn about this field and explore what kind of coaching they practice, it can be helpful to develop a personal vision statement. Just as a vision statement focuses, empowers, and guides those who work at a school, coaches can also be guided by a vision. When I question why I'm doing what I'm doing, or when I feel unmoored by the challenges in my daily practice, I return to my vision. It helps me remember, it energizes me, and it grounds me.

My vision developed as I learned what coaching means to others in this field. I love collecting quotes about coaching, and you'll find many of these shared in this book. These poetic descriptions often illuminate aspects of coaching that I hadn't recognized before. They inform my vision for coaching.

I encourage all coaches to articulate a vision for coaching. Why do you do what you do? What's the big picture you're working toward? Your vision can be for your eyes alone, or you can share it with others. The process of creating a vision statement is powerful and surprising. You can find suggestions for how to create one online or on my website. Here's my vision:

> I coach to heal and transform the world. I coach teachers and leaders to discover ways of working and being that are joyful and rewarding, that bring communities together, and that result in positive outcomes for children. I coach people to find their own power and to empower others so that we can transform our education system, our society, and our world.

A COACH WHO KNOWS WHO SHE IS AND CAN TRAVEL BACK IN TIME

Here's what I wish I had done when I began working at the school I mentioned at the beginning of this chapter. Had I really articulated my role and personal vision as a transformational coach, I think I could have alleviated a lot of anxieties, had more support from the principal, and been far more effective.

First, I would have asked for time at a staff meeting in the very beginning of the year to present myself as a coach. I'd share my vision for coaching, my definition of coaching, and my hopes for what coaching might be able to do at this school. I'd let people know that in order to figure out what my role should be at that site, I'd need to conduct a deep investigation into the site's current situation. I'd let them know that I intended to interview teachers, students, parents, staff, and the administrators to hear about how they defined the school's strengths and areas for growth. I'd let them know that the purpose of doing this was to learn about the school and figure out how I could be most helpful.

At this meeting with the staff, even though I'd be really nervous, I'd also demonstrate a coaching session with a willing teacher so that they could get an immediate sense of how I work. I'd want them to see how I listen, ask questions, and offer support. This would make coaching less abstract and intimidating.

In the interviews, I would have asked teachers about their own learning needs and how they might feel most supported in their learning. Using this feedback, I would have co-constructed my role with the principal, identifying goals that I'd work toward during the year. Chapter Seven goes in depth into this process.

I'd also have a better understanding of what coaching was, what a coach did, what can be expected from coaching, and why a coach does what she does. I'd anticipate the pushback, resistance, and fear that are frequent among those new to coaching, and I would not take these things personally.

Hindsight, of course, is always 20/20. My reflection on how I went into this first coaching scenario helped me tremendously when I began my subsequent coaching job. I was much clearer and more articulate about what I was doing and why. Making mistakes and learning from them are unavoidable parts of being alive. In this book, I am committed to helping new coaches avoid as many mistakes as possible.

CHAPTER 3

Which Beliefs Help a Coach Be More Effective?

Read this when:

- You're a new coach reflecting on why you do what you do
- You feel stuck in your practice or you suspect that your actions don't align with your beliefs
- You are working with clients on developing and articulating their belief systems

THE DANGERS OF UNMONITORED BELIEFS

There was a period of time when, unbeknownst to me, my belief system was driving my actions and making me miserable. These beliefs ran rampant, like deadly viruses, until a pivotal moment in a workshop on coaching with Leslie Plettner, the masterful coach I mentioned in the Introduction. Leslie responded to a question and, while I don't remember the question, her response is etched into the forefront of my memory.

We do not really see through our eyes or hear through our ears, but through our beliefs.

LISA DELPIT (1995)

What she said was this: "No one can learn from you if you think that they suck."

I felt sick as this statement echoed in my mind. In a flash of painful awakening, I realized that I had indeed thought that some of the teachers and administrators I coached sucked. Semiconsciously, I thought they were incompetent people determined to oppress children.

As this awareness crystalized, I felt ashamed. Why would *anyone* want to work with a coach who thought that he was incompetent? No wonder they didn't want to meet with me! No wonder they were defensive and resistant! I *really did* think that they sucked!

I had a hard conversation with myself: "Either you quit this job right now—*today*—or you shift this belief," I told myself. "It is not serving you, it's not helping kids, and you are contributing to anger and pain in the world."

As I reflected on what I was feeling, I also realized that these beliefs did not align with my core values. And actually, I wanted to be a powerful coach who could change the education system far more than I wanted to cling to those beliefs. "Goodbye, my nasty little friends. Be gone," I ordered. Easier said than done, of course.

I printed Leslie's words in two-hundred-point font and posted them on the inside of my office door. I used them as a mantra, calling them forth when I noticed I was tumbling into this black hole of thinking. And little by little, I started deconstructing my beliefs and shifting into a new set from which I could be an effective coach. It took a while, and occasionally a sneaky little thought comes into my mind that harks back to this old belief system, but more often than not I operate from a different set of beliefs and I know that as a result I'm a much better coach.

THE BASICS ABOUT BELIEFS

 Administrators: the following sections are useful in guiding educators through exploring their beliefs.

Here's the thing about beliefs: we all have them and they drive our actions. We experience our beliefs as truths, and we can usually find evidence to support them. Subsequently, they create boundaries around what we think we can and can't do, what can and can't be done in the world. Some of our beliefs are tucked into our subconscious, where they operate without our awareness. Sometimes our beliefs contradict each other or our core values. Some of our beliefs make us strong, powerful people; some do not serve us.

The good news is that beliefs can be updated or changed. Think about your own beliefs about your life—perhaps about what you have believed you could do or not do. Which have served you? Which have you given up? Although we experience them as truths, they are just mental creations. We can select the ones that will lead us to fulfill the vision we have for our work, or a relationship, or the kind of life we want to live. We created them, so we can modify, strengthen, or release them.

Here's another thing about beliefs: they are simply strongly held opinions. They are not facts, although they can appear to be. We might have plenty of experiences that seem to prove that they are real, but we can just as easily believe in the opposite experience and make it real in our lives. For example, have you ever embarked on any kind of exercise program and thought something like, "I can't run a 10K, I've never been physically active and I can barely walk a mile!" And then did you see your body adapt and strengthen and see yourself meet a physical fitness goal? Did you notice that along the way your beliefs about your capacities changed? You shifted from believing you couldn't do something to holding new beliefs about your abilities. In other words, we have a lot of agency over our belief systems, which is great news!

An essential component of coaching is supporting others to become conscious of their belief systems—about children, learning, students of color, immigrants, and so on. But before we can engage in this work, as coaches we need to become aware of our own beliefs. Otherwise we run the risk of rogue beliefs taking over our internal operating system. Understanding our own belief systems—how they were formed, how we can become conscious of them, how we can change them—makes us much more skilled at helping others do this work.

> *We don't see things the way they are; we see things the way we are.*
>
> THE TALMUD

Essential Framework 1

Where Do Beliefs Come From?

Chris Argyris's Ladder of Inference provides an invaluable tool for helping us see how our beliefs are formed and why we do what we do. This model describes how we unconsciously climb up a mental pathway of increasing abstraction that often produces misguided beliefs (Senge, 1994, p. 243).

Let me explain this framework by providing an example. A high school principal asked me to observe a teacher who had been struggling with management. We entered the classroom and stood at the back. Ms. Smith was at the front directing a whole-class discussion of a text. She asked a question, and twelve students raised their hands. She called on a girl sitting in the front row. She asked another question. A boy shouted out the answer. The teacher ignored him. He shouted it out again. She called on a girl in the back. The teacher asked another question and called on another girl. One of the boys got frustrated and said, "How come you don't call on me? I keep raising my hand. Why do you always ignore me?" Ms. Smith quietly redirected his behavior. He groaned and put his head down on the table. The teacher asked another question and called on another girl. Several boys in the back mumbled to each other, "See, she always calls on girls." Under his breath, one of them called the teacher a bad name.

Figure 3.1. The Ladder of Inference

The principal and I left the room. "Wow," the principal said. "Those boys were so disrespectful. I can't believe she let them get away with behaving like that—she's so weak. She needs to get tough and institute detention. That kind of talking back can't be tolerated. She's going to lose control. They can't be allowed to run the room. I'm going to insist that she implement a tough behavior management program immediately." The principal intended to take actions to move the teacher into this management program that afternoon. But before he could send her an e-mail requesting an emergency meeting after school, I asked if we could debrief and explore how he'd arrived at that decision.

You might have arrived at a different conclusion based on what I described, or you might have some questions about what I shared. Let's use Argyris's Ladder of Inference, shown in Figure 3.1, to trace how the principal arrived at his decision.

Visualize a ladder. On the first rung of the ladder is *observable data and experiences*. What is captured on this level is what a camera would record—a massive amount of data. If you could see a video of the classroom we were in, you'd also see the student work posted on the walls, the piles of boxes in the back of the room, the sunlight streaming through the windows, the torn jeans of the kid in the front, the teacher's red earrings; you'd hear the questions the teacher asked, the articulate responses by the students, the chuckles from some boys, the train passing outside, and so on. Because our brains cannot make sense of so much data, we need to sort. This is where things get interesting; this is where the principal started climbing up the ladder to his conclusion.

On the second rung of the ladder, the principal *selected data* from what he observed. Because of what he already believes, because he's seen some of these actions before in this class or elsewhere, he filters out most of what's going on and selects certain data points. In this class, the principal noticed that the boys were shouting out, criticizing the teacher, and calling her names. He's just ascended one rung.

On the third rung of the ladder, he *added meaning* to what he observed. Meaning often arises from our own cultural backgrounds and experiences, and/or the culture of the structure or organization in which we are working. According to the principal's cultural background, students must respect their teachers. They must *never* talk back to them, they must always raise their hands, and so forth. When they demonstrate this behavior, it means they don't respect their teacher. By adding meaning, he's ascended another rung.

On the fourth rung of the ladder, he *made assumptions* based on the meanings he had added. He assumed that the boys had no boundaries in class and that their behavior was not kept in check.

On the fifth rung of the ladder, he *drew conclusions*. He concluded that the boys are out of control. Without realizing it, the principal moved farther up the ladder.

On the sixth rung of the ladder, he *adopted a belief* about the boys (that they are unruly, disrespectful, and don't take learning seriously) and about the teacher (that she is weak and losing control of her class).

And on the seventh rung, at the top of the ladder, he *took an action* and was just about to mandate that Ms. Smith institute a tough behavior management plan immediately.

What could happen next is actually what propels someone up the ladder again. The principal's belief that boys are not serious and are out of control will influence him the next time he's observing a class—his attention will be drawn to how boys behave. Unconsciously, he's going to focus on data points that affirm his belief system—this is just what our brains do. Most likely, he'll constantly see the same thing: unruly boys who need discipline. This translates into a generalized belief about boys, and his actions will emerge from this belief.

We can't live our lives without adding meaning and making assumptions. We simply have to do these things in order to make sense of our world. But as you can probably see, there's a great danger in constantly charging up the ladder and taking actions based on unexamined assumptions—we end up operating from a distorted picture of reality.

As I described the principal's thoughts while he was climbing up the ladder, did you have any questions about what he was thinking? Did you want to interject something like, "But maybe ..." Or "Perhaps the teacher was ..."? Did you want to challenge his thinking because you saw other meanings to add, other assumptions that could be drawn, or different conclusions to arrive at?

To make this scenario more complex (and also more realistic), what if I'd told you that all the boys who shouted out were African American? And that the assumption the principal came to was that African American boys don't respect their teacher or take learning seriously? And that this assumption affirmed his belief that African Americans don't value education? And that the action he suggested amounted to a tougher policy toward boys who don't value education—perhaps he ruminated that "they should not attend our school, because we are focused on academic success"?

Back in the principal's office, I pulled out the image of the Ladder of Inference that I always carry and asked if we could explore how he'd arrived at his conclusion. He agreed, somewhat reluctantly. He just wanted to take action regarding what he'd seen in Ms. Smith's class. Two hours later, after we'd painfully worked our way down the Ladder of Inference, he dropped is head into his palms and said, "I feel like you just took a sledgehammer to my brain. I don't know what I think or believe anymore, but as hard as this was, I think I'm glad my brain has been shattered." The actions that he took in the coming weeks were very different than what he'd planned on doing that day.

Coaches help people delineate the cognitive steps that led them to a belief system. We work with them to change their actions, but unless we explore the underlying belief systems that drive actions, we may not see the kind of transformational, sustained change that we need in our schools. The Ladder of Inference is a tool to help us delineate the cognitive steps that lead to our belief systems. When we guide clients down the ladder, they can explore other ladders to climb up. This is how we can dismantle racist belief systems, or belief systems about boys and education, or girls and math, and so on.

The reflection tools we use when coaching clients allow them to slow down their thinking processes and hone their awareness of how they form beliefs. It also allows clients to identify gaps between their actions and their core values. Often when they recognize those discrepancies, they are motivated to change their behaviors. When we work on the level of examining values and beliefs, lasting changes can happen; transformation is possible (Argyris, 1990; Senge and others, 1999).

COACHING BELIEFS AND CORE VALUES

 Administrators: exploring beliefs and core values can be a powerful activity for building teams.

At the beginning of this chapter, I described my epiphany when I realized I was operating from destructive beliefs about the teachers I was supposed to coach. What I realized was that this declaration was in sharp contrast to my deeply held values; I just hadn't noticed that they conflicted. This belief—that the teachers sucked—was a recently acquired belief. I had only recently left the classroom and had worked with many phenomenal teachers. Naming the belief allowed me to dislodge it; it felt like a scab that I quickly picked off.

In order to become an artful coach, I needed to do two things: deconstruct how I'd arrived at that conclusion so that I could take the assumption of "truth" out of it, for there was no truth in this declaration—only a limited data set. Second, I needed to articulate the set of beliefs from which I intended to work as a coach.

One stop on this reflective journey was at my core values. Core values are deeply held personal codes that reflect our ethics and what is most important to us. They come from our families, religious teachings, schools, people we admire, and from our culture (CampbellJones, Lindsey, and CampbellJones, 2010). Research on school leaders has found that core values play a key role in how educators build personal resilience. It is the process of "privately clarifying, publicly articulating, and consciously acting on" core values that resilient leaders identify as the greatest source of strength in helping them face adversity and emerge stronger than before (Patterson and Kelleher, 2005, p. 51).

Within the context of our workplaces, very few of us have had an opportunity to clarify or articulate our core values. Given that they are our moral compass, it follows that we are often misguided or floundering when we aren't being regularly guided by them. Before you articulate your belief system, I encourage you to identify your core values. On my website you can find an exercise to help you do this. It is also a fantastic exercise to do with anyone you coach—it is empowering to your client and it offers you a set of data that can anchor many conversations.

MY TRANSFORMATIONAL COACHING MANIFESTO

Many schools and organizations have sets of norms or community agreements that guide the behavior of their members. This manifesto works in the same way for me: it emerges from my core values and helps me stay aligned to my vision.

I offer this manifesto to coaches as an opportunity for reflection on the beliefs we hold in this work. While there are some core beliefs that we might need to agree on as coaches, I also recognize that some of those on my list may not resonate with all readers. It has helped me to articulate them and make them explicit so that they are not quietly lurking around—on the forefront of my consciousness, they are far more powerful.

1. *Everything is connected.* I start with this premise, what systems thinkers call the "primacy of the whole." Everything is connected in space and time; every action has a reaction and influences other pieces of the whole now and in the future. We are all bound to each other by invisible webs of interrelated actions. From within this belief, there is no single person to blame for what's not working; we're all connected, we all share responsibility.

2. *Meet people where they are.* If a systems-thinking perspective is like looking through a wide-angle lens, then from this second belief I look through a telephoto lens. Here, my compassion is activated as I seek to understand *why* a client is where she is. I don't make her wrong for being wherever she is—she's just there. We're all somewhere. And we don't have to stay there. But if my work is not infused with and coming from compassion, there is no possibility for me to positively affect the world. Meeting people where they are means exercising compassion, and it really is the only place to start when trying to make meaningful change.

3. *There is no coaching without trust.* A teacher or principal will not reveal the areas that she's struggling in, or share beliefs that might be holding her back, until she absolutely trusts you; trust defines a coaching relationship. It takes time to build, and once it has developed, it should not be taken for granted. This statement comes into

my mind as a reminder that I must always tend to this fragile state—we don't work in a very trustworthy world of education these days, and many school teachers and leaders feel under attack. Chapter Five is devoted to translating this belief into action, as it is so essential.

4. *"Words create worlds"* (Hartman, 1991). This belief instructs me to listen very carefully, to explore what is possible given the language that a client uses, and to find a high-leverage entry point. It also reminds me to be mindful of every word that comes out of my mouth. If I remember that words create worlds, I can make choices every second that allow me to fulfill my vision for coaching.

5. *Be here now.* In order for me to meet someone where she is, I need to listen very carefully. To do that, I need to be fully present. Clients sense the quality of a coach's attention, and in order for them to take risks, a coach must be fully present. This is challenging to do, but it is a practice that can be developed. Sometimes when I'm distracted during a coaching conversation, I remind myself to "be here now." I feel calmer and more grounded when I do so, and I know that my clients need that.

6. *Transformation takes time.* Sometimes I get frustrated that the teachers or leaders I'm working with aren't changing fast enough, and then I remind myself, again, that transformation takes time—an undefined amount of time—and that I must be patient. Working from a place of impatience and urgency won't result in a transformed system—it'll simply reproduce what we have now or provide a quick-fix bandage that will not be sustainable. When I remind myself of this, I am able to be in the present with a client, and I can more effectively respond to where he is now and assist him in identifying and taking the step that comes next for him.

7. *Justice, justice shalt thou pursue* (Deuteronomy 16:20). I experience this belief as a mandate. It demands that my work be driven by a pursuit of justice and pushes me to explore my notions about justice. What is justice? What would it look like in our schools? How do we get there? And do the ends ever justify the means? These questions are especially important because I often feel impatient with the rate of change. It also helps me make personal decisions in coaching—who to coach, how to coach, what boundaries I draw. And it keeps me focused on the end goal—justice, which helps me manage the desires of my own ego and the results and beliefs I am attached to.

8. *The journey is the destination.* This statement follows the last for a very important reason—so that I don't get trapped in the-end-justifies-the-means thinking. It

reminds me that every action on the journey of transformation needs to be imbued with kindness, fairness, and compassion. Sometimes putting this principle into action presents ethical challenges and pushes me to consider questions such as: Would I coach a principal who is intent on firing her whole staff because they are ineffective? What if I agree with her that her teachers are not serving children? Can justice be pursued by traveling down this road? This belief, however, reminds me that for every action there is a reaction, that we are making the future today, and that if I envision a just, fair future, I must behave justly and fairly today.

9. *Be unattached to outcome.* Given that justice is the outcome, this statement makes me very uncomfortable, but it does so in a way that I welcome. I am attached to the outcome of transformation, but I also don't know what that outcome is or what it might look like (beyond a few characteristics), so as we move forward on this journey, I need to avoid getting attached to the possible outcomes that arise.

For example, I remind myself of this belief when I've been coaching a principal to lead a big meeting with her staff. It could be a meeting that moves the school in a positive direction, if she can carry it off. In my mind, as I'm coaching her to prepare for this meeting, I begin thinking about how important it is that she does this well, that all hinges on her ability to reach certain outcomes on that day—I develop a story about what should happen. Tumbling into this train of thought not only takes me away from being fully present with the principal, but it also locks me into thinking that there is a single right outcome. Perhaps there's an even better outcome that I can't imagine? Maybe the meeting falls apart and the agenda is scrapped and a real, honest conversation ensues among the staff and a new, more powerful outcome is reached. I cannot know the future; I cannot determine the "right" outcome for this group of people.

When I get attached, there's usually a part of my own ego that's getting sucked in. This belief reminds me to be humble and open on this journey and that I don't know what is right—and that's a hard one to give up. But from this stance, I can see infinite numbers of possibilities for coaching actions to take.

10. *We can transform our education system.* I have made a choice to believe that transformation can be realized. I struggled with this idea, because for a while I didn't really think it could happen. I'd try, I thought, I'd give it my best shot—but I felt pretty hopeless and cynical most of the time. Then I decided to stand in a place of neutrality—I don't know if we can do this. Maybe. Maybe not. Regardless of whether or not we would prove able to transform our schools, I worked toward that end.

Maybe this was an example of being unattached to outcome, but operating from this stance felt a little dull and lifeless. It didn't help me.

Now I work from a place of believing that we can transform our schools and heal our world. I have more energy when I come from this belief, I feel more true to myself, and I believe I'm a more effective coach. I'm much more likely to convince others to become leaders on this journey if I come from this belief. In this place, I can access tremendous reserves of energy. I can inspire others. I can share the "data" that I gather that makes me believe that this is possible. I see evidence everywhere that we can do this. I see transformational moments all around us. I have seen individual schools transform and the people within them. We need to transform our schools, and I believe we can do this.

With our lives we make our answers all the time, to this ravenous, beautiful, mutilated, gorgeous world.

REVEREND VICTORIA SAFFORD
(LOEB, 2004, P. 9)

IDENTIFYING AND USING YOUR COACHING BELIEFS

Administrators: teachers and other educators working in schools will be empowered by articulating their belief systems.

I encourage all coaches to articulate the beliefs from which they want to work. Start by identifying your core values. Then consider how a core value translates into a belief statement and how those show up as actions. If one of your core values is appreciation, then a corresponding belief statement might be "Always acknowledge the positive," which could guide your actions in a coaching conversation.

After you formulate your set of beliefs, try them on—stand inside of them and speak from them in different coaching situations. See how they feel. See which ones give you the most energy, power, clarity, and groundedness. Notice which resonate. These questions might help you reflect on your belief statements:

- Does the belief bring you a sense of relief?
- Do you feel more empowered when you stand in the belief?

- Does it open more paths for action? Does it point to new directions?
- Does your belief align with your core values?
- Does it allow you to fulfill your vision for coaching?

I print my coaching manifesto on small pieces of card stock. I carry them in my bag, tuck them into my notebooks, and sometimes stick them in my pocket. They reside with my vision statement (see Chapter Two) and remind me where I want to come from.

Out beyond ideas of wrongdoing and rightdoing, there is a field. I'll meet you there.

RUMI, THIRTEENTH-CENTURY POET (BANKS, 1995, P. 35)

My list of beliefs has changed over the years. You can change yours, too. The point is to be mindful of the beliefs from which we're working and to notice the effect of working from those beliefs. Then we can make a conscious choice about the actions we take.

CHAPTER 4

What Must a Coach Know?

Read this chapter when:

- You're a new coach feeling overwhelmed by the complicated situations you're encountering and you want some analytical lenses to look through
- You're interested in the theoretical foundations of transformational coaching
- You're an experienced coach looking to deepen your practice and refine your analyses
- You're a principal looking for additional ways of tackling dilemmas at your site

INTRODUCING NEW COACHING TOOLS: COACHING LENSES

Transformational coaching draws from a number of theories, and while I don't want to drown you in them, I want you to gain a sense of which ones are most useful. When we're not working from a sound theoretical basis, we're just throwing strands of spaghetti on the wall to see if they stick.

In this chapter, I'll introduce a set of tools to help us think in different ways about the situations we encounter. These tools are based on theories about adult learning, emotional intelligence, systems thinking, change management, systemic (or structural) oppression, and inquiry thinking. I will introduce you to these theories and illustrate their application. These tools will be referenced throughout the book, so this chapter is meant to provide an overview and the background you'll need to make sense of them when they show up.

A STORY ABOUT A TEACHER WHO SEEMS TO STRUGGLE WITH CLASSROOM MANAGEMENT: PART 1

It was late October before Mr. Delgado, a new Spanish teacher at Turtlerock Middle School, accepted my offer of coaching support. The principal had been asking me to work with Mr. Delgado since the first week of school, when he had observed the teacher's class and left with major concerns about his classroom management skills. Since then, parent complaints were piling up, students were being sent to the office en masse, and Mr. Delgado looked miserable most of the time. However, the teacher missed our scheduled appointments and deflected my inquiries about how he was doing.

I knew that the principal had had concerns about hiring Mr. Delgado, an Afro-Cuban man in his sixties who spoke English with a British accent. He had taught Spanish for several years in a local public high school, but his former supervisor recommended him with reservations: nice guy, she said, but weak classroom management. However, unable to find another candidate, the principal had hired Mr. Delgado just two days before school started. "'Weak' was an understatement," the principal shared after observing Mr. Delgado when school started: "It's chaotic in there. He has no authority, no command. They're running all over him."

One Monday afternoon, Mr. Delgado showed up at my office door. "OK, I'll accept your offer of help," he said. "Could you start by coming to observe me? I think you should see what I'm dealing with. Fourth period would be good."

"Of course," I said, surprised by his openness. Many teachers are reluctant to have me observe so early in a coaching relationship. "I can come tomorrow."

The following day I settled into a chair on the side of Mr. Delgado's classroom a few minutes before class started. As students entered the class, Mr. Delgado welcomed his eighth graders and passed out a worksheet. "You have fifteen minutes to work on this assignment," Mr. Delgado said in a soft voice. "Try to work alone, but if you need help, you can work with a partner."

About eight minutes into the class, Davontae, a tall, African American boy walked in, slamming the door as he entered, muttering a string of curse words under his breath. He ignored Mr. Delgado when he was asked to sign the tardy book, he sat in a seat in the back of the class, again ignoring Mr. Delgado's reminder of his assigned seat, and he began to make loud disruptive comments: "What the fuck we doing today? This is boring-ass shit. I hate Spanish. I don't want to learn this stupid language," and so on.

Mr. Delgado seemed to ignore this behavior and attempted to help a girl sitting in the front row. Davontae turned his worksheet into an airplane and threw it across the room, hitting another student in the back of the head.

"Settle down," Mr. Delgado said in English, his voice barely audible above the rising din of the eighth graders. Several students began throwing paper airplanes. Mr. Delgado's voice rose a little and he called out again, "Settle down, please!" Davontae mimicked Mr. Delgado's accent, repeating his mandate in a mocking tone. Other students laughed and elaborated on the mimicry. Davontae rested his feet on the back of the chair in front of him and continued making snide remarks about the teacher. A girl in the front row shouted to her classmates: "Shut the fuck up, you idiots! I want to learn!" Davontae mocked her and she rose from her seat. "Sit down," Mr. Delgado said to her. "What you gonna do about him, then?" she said.

"Davontae, you're going to have to leave," Mr. Delgado said, his volume rising a little.

"I don't want to leave. Things are just getting fun," Davontae said.

"If you cannot behave and demonstrate an appropriate attitude, then you are going to have to leave," Mr. Delgado said. "Please take your things now and go."

A paper airplane hit Mr. Delgado in the back of the head. A loud "Ooooh" came from the students, who started shouting about who had done it. Mr. Delgado's frustration was becoming more and more visible: his hands were shaking, his brow was furrowed. "Go, now!" he shouted at Davontae.

"Don't scream at me!" Davontae yelled. "That's disrespectful," the student mocked.

Mr. Delgado grabbed Davontae's backpack and threw it toward the door. "Get out of my class!" He yelled at the student. "Get out now! You don't belong here!"

"Don't touch my stuff," Davontae shouted, rising up and standing taller than the teacher. "Don't you ever touch my stuff again, or I'll mess you up. You don't know who you're dealing with."

"If you don't leave now, I'm calling security," Mr. Delgado said as he walked toward the phone. Davontae stood still, staring at the teacher. Several students made provocative noises. Davontae slowly wandered toward the door as Mr. Delgado stood with his trembling hand on the phone. As Davontae opened the door, Mr. Delgado yelled, "And don't come back unless you want to learn Spanish."

After Davontae left, students settled down fairly quickly. Mr. Delgado delivered a lesson on the musical instruments of Cuba. He played music, tried to talk to the class about the origins of the music, and offered a couple dozen new vocabulary terms. He did not reach his stated objective, the sequence of the lesson seemed disjointed, and fewer than half the students completed the worksheet he gave them. Davontae was suspended.

I left Mr. Delgado's class feeling overwhelmed. I had no idea where I'd start my debrief with Mr. Delgado later that afternoon. Fortunately, I had reserved some time to process and plan in between my observation and our debrief. And fortunately, I have my massive set of tools—what I call the Coach's Optical Refractor—to help me think through what I'd observed and construct a plan for my conversation with Mr. Delgado.

I will now introduce you to the Coach's Optical Refractor and describe its six lenses. After I describe each lens, I'll apply it to Mr. Delgado's class. Finally, I'll share the questions that I created to ask Mr. Delgado, along with our debrief conversation.

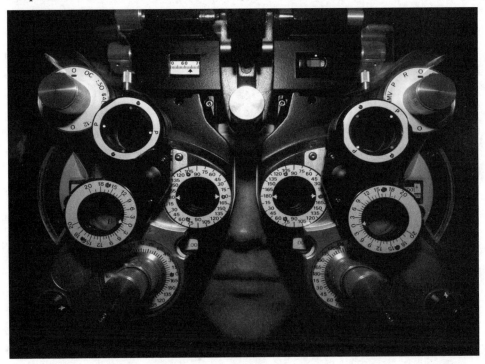

Essential Framework 2: The Coach's Optical Refractor

Optometrists use an instrument called an "optical refractor" in an eye examination to test vision. It's a massive device with six different lenses and multiple settings. Optometrists, concerned with visual systems, understand that a multitude of factors must be considered in order to understand how a person's vision is working. The final prescription will contain at least six numerical specifications, but an annual visit to the optometrist is necessary, as our vision changes and our prescription may change.

The refractor is an apt metaphor for the primary diagnostic instrument that coaches can use. Our work is about seeing a situation from different perspectives, in different ways. Our naked eyes alone are not powerful enough to see all that we need to see, to diagnose root causes or complex intertwining of issues. The first five lenses in the Coach's Optical Refractor are staples of the National Equity Project (NEP) coach's tool bag—the NEP authored the descriptors you'll soon read and I'm very grateful for their permission to share them here. The sixth lens, emotional intelligence, is one that I added based on the work of Daniel Goleman.

The six lenses in the Coach's Optical Refractor are

1. Inquiry
2. Change management
3. Systems thinking
4. Adult learning
5. Systemic oppression
6. Emotional intelligence

First five Coaching Lenses: © 2007 National Equity Project. All rights reserved. Used with permission. Credit Lines/Trademarks

But what is a lens? And how can we use one? The National Equity Project (2007) defines it this way:

> A "lens" is a metaphor to communicate the idea of looking at evidence from various perspectives. The meaning of the metaphor is that you can look at the same thing through different lenses and construct very different interpretations of the same reality. Each of us does this every day—it is how we individually and collectively make sense of the world around us. We know that we will define solutions based on the way that problems get defined. Similarly, we will define problems according to our interpretations or assessment of what we observe. For this reason, learning and applying these and other lenses is fundamental to coaching for equity.

The lenses are based on theories that attempt to explain human and organizational behavior. No one model alone is sufficient. Every situation requires that we look from multiple perspectives and examine relationships, individuals, institutions, and phenomena through multiple lenses. When we look at a situation through a particular lens, some things come into focus, while others are blocked out. The National Equity Project cautions: "This is the benefit of applying each lens as well as the inherent liability in using only one. At the same time, these lenses are interrelated and contain overlapping ideas. The purpose in using them is to think critically, particularly with regard to equity, and take informed action" (NEP, 2007, p. 1).

What follows in this chapter is an overview of each theory and some guiding questions to help you consider how the theory might be applied in a coaching setting. Then I'm going to use the lenses to think about Mr. Delgado's class and formulate some questions to ask him. At the end of the chapter, I'll describe the debrief conversation with Mr. Delgado and the coaching he engaged in that year.

In Appendix A, you will find all of the assumptions and questions for each lens laid out in a format that can be easily referenced and copied. These lenses are one of the few documents that I must always have tucked into my notebook.

The Six Lenses

 Administrators: these lenses are very useful to apply when you face dilemmas at a site.

The Lens of Inquiry

The lens of inquiry encourages questions, valuing them as much as the answers that we find. It purports that the way we define the problem dictates how we define the solution. Our field of possibility narrows depending on our definition, which is why we need to ask many questions from many perspectives. It also supposes that the way we pose the question determines the nature of the answer—if I ask a teacher, "Why did you shout at that student?" I may get a defensive answer.

The lens of inquiry suggests that evidence and multiple forms of data are critical to making informed decisions and judgments. It reminds us that there's usually more to the picture than what we initially see, and that we need to gather data from various stakeholders before we make decisions or determine a course of action. Finally, this lens reminds us that although we may ask good questions and gather a ton of data, we will never know everything we need to know and we will never have all the answers, but we must act anyway.

The lens of inquiry assumes the following:

- The way we pose the question determines the nature of the answer
- The way we define the problem dictates how we define the solution
- The questions we ask are as important as the answers we find
- People can create their own knowledge and solutions
- Seemingly intractable problems can be addressed
- It is easier to engage and enroll people to address inequities when we affirm that we don't yet know everything we need to know to create transformed systems, but we have a responsibility to do so, so we must ask questions together and move forward
- If you own the question, you will take responsibility for the answer
- Evidence and data are critical to making informed decisions and judgments
- Multiple forms of data—including authentic and qualitative measures produced by multiple constituencies—are necessary for effective decision making
- Knowledge is socially constructed
- We never know everything we need to know, but we need to act anyway

Questions that explore the lens of inquiry include the following:

- Who is defining the problem? Whose question is this?
- What data do we have on this problem? What problems do that data say we should address?
- Is this a question I really care about? Who does care about this question?
- From what perspective am I seeing this? What other perspectives would help me understand this?
- How is this connected to other things?

Applying the Lens of Inquiry in Mr. Delgado's Class

It was the principal who sent me to work with Mr. Delgado, saying that he had a "classroom management problem." When I walked into this classroom, I was primed to see this problem, with Mr. Delgado's deficiency as the cause. However, looking through the lens of inquiry, I began to wonder how Mr. Delgado would define the "problem?"

The principal has observed Mr. Delgado's class on several occasions; he has also gathered data on office referrals that indicate that Mr. Delgado struggles with classroom management. I would like to take a closer look at the referral data—are there specific groups of students with whom Mr. Delgado struggles? Are there times of the day, or certain periods, when he has more difficulty? I wonder what the students would identify as the cause of the classroom disruptions. Perhaps a student survey would yield useful data.

I know that the principal really cares about this question, but I wonder if Mr. Delgado does. I'm reminded that the teacher needs to "own the question," so that he'll take responsibility for the answer. I am seeing this problem from the principal's perspective at first. I clearly need to hear Mr. Delgado's perspective, and perhaps the perspective of students.

I went in to observe Mr. Delgado's classroom management, but I wondered about a number of other factors: the lesson plan, classroom routines and procedures, the assignment students were asked to complete, Davontae, and about Mr. Delgado himself. I wondered how he felt, what he thought about what was going on, what he envisioned for himself as a teacher.

I left Mr. Delgado's class not convinced that "the problem" was his management. I felt there were many dynamics going on that needed to be explored in order for solutions to be considered.

The Lens of Change Management

Now, let's shift the lenses on our optical refractor and see what is visible when we look through the lens of change management, which pushes us to consider how change might be made. First, this perspective reminds us that beneficial change *is* possible, which can be easy to forget when a situation looks particularly grim. Then it suggests an analysis of the conditions for change. This lens reminds us to look at the state of leadership within the problem area—certain leadership qualities need to be present in order for positive change to occur. We are also reminded to look for other conditions that need to be present in order for change to happen: incentives, resources, vision, and a clear action plan. Change cannot be made unless many, if not most, of these elements are in place.

The lens of change management also reminds us to consider a person's will, skill, knowledge, and capacity to change—and to understand where the gaps are in these four domains. Finally, we must look at the larger picture and the presence or absence of necessary conditions for change—and then we can determine how to go about supporting change.

The lens of change management assumes the following:

- Beneficial change is possible
- Conditions and strategies can be manipulated to get the system to produce different outcomes
- Change can be studied, understood, and influenced
- Analysis of conditions for change is necessary for effective implementation
- Certain elements need to be present for successful change to occur: leadership, vision, skills, incentives, resources, a clear plan of action
- People need to have the will, skill, knowledge, and capacity to change

Questions that explore the lens of change management include the following:

- What are the conditions for change here?
- What are the strengths that can be built on? What's working?
- Where are the opportunities for leveraging change? What threats to change are present?
- What is the vision people are working toward here?
- What skills are required of people to achieve the vision? What knowledge is necessary?
- Do people have the skills and knowledge necessary to implement change?
- Does the will for change exist here? Where?
- What incentives are in place for people to change? To improve their practice?
- What resources are available to support change?

Applying the Lens of Change Management in Mr. Delgado's Class

When I apply the lens of change management to Mr. Delgado's class, I am looking for opportunities for leveraging change. I wonder what Mr. Delgado's strengths are and what skills he feels competent in. I wonder which skills he might need to refine, and what knowledge might help him shift the dynamic in his classroom. I'm also curious about his will to change—I noticed his shaking hands, his frustration—I know he was unhappy, but how much does he want to change? Will, of course, is a tricky thing to assess and measure, and an even trickier thing to build up when reserves are low. I need to find out where his will for change is.

When I consider the conditions that are necessary for change, my musing shifts into the systems and structures in the whole school. Mr. Delgado's classroom does not exist as an isolated entity; applying this lens pushes me to think through the lens of systems thinking. Within the overlap between these two lenses, I am also wondering what resources exist to support Mr. Delgado in making change in his classroom. Once we identify the areas of skill and knowledge in which he'd like to expand his capacity, then I'll do some exploration into the resources that are available.

The Lens of Systems Thinking

The lens of systems thinking provides invaluable information and also builds an increasingly complicated picture. Schools are complex systems, and no single discrete element within a school exists in isolation from the others. Systems thinking helps us explore the ways that pieces are interwoven and affected by each other. It reflects the belief stance that everything is connected.

The lens of systems thinking presumes that what we observe, whatever is happening in the moment, is exactly what is supposed to happen in the system as it is—there is a logical, rational explanation for what we see. Although we may experience the system as chaotic or disorderly, this framework suggests there is an order. Everything we observe is the result of a complex set of interactions, and we must understand them if we want to intervene. This lens compels us to look at the pieces, the whole, and the interactions in order to understand how the system works and to change it.

The lens of systems thinking also makes some assumptions that can alleviate our anxiety when facing a seemingly disorderly system. It contends that change is a given, conflict and tension are necessary and natural, and that complexity and diversity are good, healthy things. Finally, it reminds us that all energy moves in cycles—the energy in a classroom, in a school, and in our education system is in some phase of a cycle. If we can identify that phase and understand conditions for change, we might be able to move it into a different phase of the cycle.

The lens of systems thinking assumes the following:

- What we observe, whatever is happening in this moment, is exactly what is supposed to happen in the system as it is
- Everything we observe is the result of a complex set of interactions
- We must seek to understand these interactions in order to intervene effectively to change them
- Process and product are part of the same whole
- Conflict and tension are necessary and natural
- Complexity and diversity are good, healthy things
- All energy moves in cycles

Questions that explore the lens of systems thinking include the following:

- How is the current system designed to produce these results?
- Why did that happen?
- What happens when this happens? What happens when that happens? What are the relationships between things here?
- Where is the energy here? Where are the stuck points?
- If I do this here, what will happen over here?

Applying the Lens of Systems Thinking in Mr. Delgado's class

When I apply the lens of systems thinking to Mr. Delgado's classroom, a long list of questions comes to mind about what I've observed. Leading from the principal's concern regarding Mr. Delgado's classroom management skills, I wonder about how the current system produced these results. I realize that I don't fully understand the schoolwide behavior management system and the process for bringing new teachers into an understanding of it. I'm curious about the relationships between these elements: the broader expectations for students, teachers, and staff and the process for communicating expectations.

I'm also curious about how class schedules are determined. I asked several students (who seemed very disengaged) about why they were taking Spanish and they told me that they didn't want to take it, that they'd been assigned to it. I realized that I didn't understand many pieces of the system that I was seeing. It also seemed like everyone in the system was stuck: the teacher, the students, the principal. Considering the different systems at play, and then jumping back to the lens of change management, I wasn't sure where the opportune points were for making change, because I didn't have a clear enough understanding of the systems that had produced this challenge. Using this lens, I realized I had a number of questions for the principal, the counselor who created student assignments, and Mr. Delgado. I also suspect that there may be a number of macro systems affecting what is happening in Mr. Delgado's classroom and the school that are resulting in what I observed. I will explore those as well.

The Lens of Adult Learning

Understanding adult learning is essential to effective coaching. Many of the ways in which adults and children learn are similar, but there are also some critical ways in which we learn differently, and the conditions for our learning need to be modified in order to support us.

One of the most obvious differences between adults and children is that adults have simply lived longer and have had many life experiences. For those of us guiding adults in learning, it means we have more to work with—more starting points and, perhaps, more things to undo. What is essential is that we understand what we're working with—what previous experiences, knowledge, competencies, beliefs, and interests someone is bringing to a new learning space. Then we can build from those, or be mindful about attending to them. It means that we don't meet our adult learners as if they were blank slates (of course, children are not blank slates either, but they have fewer fixed ideas and they are often more malleable). Most adults have come to believe that "experience is the best teacher." In order for us to extend learning, we need to understand what experiences someone has had, and then we need to create more meaningful experiences for learning. We also have to accept that people can only be where they currently are.

Because they are not blank slates, adults want to be the origin of our learning and want control over the what, who, how, why, and where of our learning. We will commit to learning when we believe that the objectives are realistic and important for our personal and professional needs. We need to see that what we are learning is applicable to our day-to-day activities and problems. When principals, coaches, or professional developers run into conflicts with teachers who seem "resistant" to, for example, a professional development (PD) session or training, it is often because these essential elements of adult learning theory are not being attended to. Adults need to see very clearly the relevance of what they're being asked to learn; they need to have some say in what they're doing. This is exactly why coaching can be an effective strategy to support adult learners: our coachees have a tremendous amount of control over the objectives of the coaching, and the content of the learning is immediately applicable to daily activities and problems. Coaching is a way to guide—not direct—people through learning; that's why it works.

Adults also need direct, concrete ways to apply what we have learned to our work. We do not learn by simply hearing or reading about abstract theory; we need to apply the learnings fairly quickly. But we also do not automatically transfer learning into daily practice. We might attend a three-day workshop on strategies for teaching English language learners, but unless there is coaching and other kinds of ongoing support, the learning may not be sustained. Furthermore, we need feedback on the results of our efforts. Without feedback, we are unlikely to sustain new learning or reach a level of mastery. Again, coaching is an effective strategy because it responds to all of these requisites of adult learning.

Finally, adult learning theory reminds us that adults, like children, need to feel emotionally safe in order to be able to learn. Our emotional states are inextricably tied to our abilities to learn. For those of us who aspire to create learning spaces for adults, we must keep this fact in mind.

The lens of adult learning assumes the following:

- Problems of change are problems of learning
- People can only be where they are
- Every human being is "on a path" from one place to another, and it is important to find out both where people have been and where they're going
- We all enter the work of equity and justice from very different starting points
- If you don't acknowledge progress, you lose people's trust
- Adults have had a lot of life experiences that affect how they continue to learn
- Adults must feel safe to learn
- Adults want to be the origin of their own learning; they want to control certain aspects of it
- Adults want and need feedback

Questions that explore the lens of adult learning include the following:

- What is the goal or objective?
- What came before?

- What is the gap between the goal and what is?
- What progress has been made?
- Is there evidence of prior learning?
- Does the will for learning exist?

Applying the Lens of Adult Learning in Mr. Delgado's Class

Thinking about Mr. Delgado through this lens makes me wonder what Mr. Delgado is bringing to his current role in terms of experiences, beliefs, and capacities about classroom management. I am reminded that he is a man in his late fifties who has lived in two different countries in very different time periods; I am curious about his beliefs around the behavior of young people and how they should be regulated.

I'm also curious about his will to learn. What does he want to work on and improve in his teaching? What might he regard as a realistic goal for himself? What does he need to feel safe in his learning? What does he feel like he's made progress on in his teaching career? Applying this lens makes me curious and also excited to learn more about Mr. Delgado.

The Lens of Systemic (Structural) Oppression

The lens of systemic, or structural, oppression is premised on the assumption that oppression resides in systems and structures (such as our education system and school structures), as well as within our individual consciousness. Social inequality, therefore, is woven throughout our institutions. In order to transform our system, a close examination of the structures that hold oppression must be made along with our examination of the individual consciousness of those within.

A premise of the lens of systemic oppression is that human beings are born without prejudice. Prejudice is a preconceived judgment or opinion that is usually based on limited information. We are continually exposed to misinformation about others—which is how we end up with prejudices. Stereotypes, omissions, and distortions all contribute to the development of prejudice. Given that prejudice is something we acquire, it is something we can unlearn.

Racism is a system of advantage based on race—a personal ideology and a system of institutional policies and practices that manifest in the beliefs and actions of individuals. Racism is prejudice plus power—racial prejudice combined with social power (access to resources and decision making) leads to the institutionalization of racist policies and practices. Racism is more than just individual beliefs and attitudes; it is systemic.

Individual prejudices are different from systematic mistreatment. Entire groups of people have been intentionally disempowered because of their identity in order to maintain an unequal power structure that subjugates one group over another—this is the definition of structural oppression. Racism, sexism, classism, and homophobia, therefore, are not simply individual prejudices, but they have historical antecedents and they manifest in economic, political, social, and cultural systems. Systemic oppression is sometimes blatantly visible and sometimes insidiously obscure.

The lens of systemic oppression assumes the following:

- Oppression and injustice are human creations and can therefore be undone
- Systemic oppression exists and negatively affects relationships and the educational process in multiple ways
- Oppression and systematic mistreatment (such as racism, classism, sexism, and homophobia) are more than just the sum of individual prejudices
- Systemic oppression has historical antecedents; it is an intentional disempowering of groups of people based on their identity to maintain an unequal power structure that subjugates one group over another
- Systemic oppression manifests in economic, political, social, and cultural systems
- Systemic oppression and its effects can be undone through recognition of inequitable patterns and intentional action to interrupt inequity and create more democratic processes and systems supported by multicultural, multilingual alliances and partnerships
- Discussing and addressing oppression and bias will usually be accompanied by strong emotions

Questions that explore the lens of systemic oppression include the following:

- Who is at the table? Who isn't?
- Who has power here? What is that power based on here?
- How are power relations affecting the truth that is told and constructed at any given moment?
- Where and how does each person locate herself in a conversation?
- How are oppression, internalized oppression, and transferred oppression playing out right here, right now? (In this school, group, organization, or district?)
- How safe is it here for different people to share their truths?
- Does the truth telling connect to shared purposes and commitments for action?
- How can I build the alliances here to move forward?
- How is leadership constructed here? What forms does it take? Who is missing?
- What can we do to make room for different cultural constructions of leadership?
- How do I understand my practice as an antiracist, antibias educator, given my differences from and similarities to my colleagues? To the people I am serving?

- How can I build my practice as a leader for equity starting with who I am and what I bring because of who I am?

Applying the Lens of Systemic Oppression in Mr. Delgado's class

I have a feeling that in Mr. Delgado's situation there may be a number of factors that stem from systemic oppression, but it's hard to tease those out. I wonder what it's like for Mr. Delgado—who is a black man from a different culture and country—to teach these African American students. I wonder how the students see him—do they relate to him? Do they feel he is "other" because of his background, accent, and different ways?

When I read over the questions that address the lens of systemic oppression, I pause at the questions about power: Who has power here? What is that power based on? At first glance, I don't feel that anyone has power—the teacher struggles to assert his place in the classroom, the students gain power by being disruptive, and then they lose it. There is an uncomfortable void of power. What does seem to have power, however, is the "behavior management system" that the principal would like Mr. Delgado to use, and that ultimately is the entity determining the student's outcome—suspension. If I consider that this source of power is fraught with the implications of a system that historically has oppressed African American men, then I wonder how Mr. Delgado might feel using it, or not using it.

The lens of systemic oppression infuses my increasing wonderings about Mr. Delgado's classroom with some questions, but also with an awareness. I am reminded to pay attention to the invisible tentacles of a historical system of oppression.

The Lens of Emotional Intelligence

The final lens on the Coach's Optical Refractor is the lens of emotional intelligence. This perspective will tune us in to an individual's ability or skill to identify, assess, and control the emotions of oneself, others, and of groups. We have learned a tremendous amount about this "intelligence" from Daniel Goleman, who pioneered this field. As coaches supporting others in their learning, this field offers us valuable insights.

Particularly useful is Goleman's work on emotional intelligence and leadership. The work he coauthored with Richard Boyatzis and Annie McKee, *Primal Leadership: Learning to Lead with Emotional Intelligence* (2002), is invaluable when coaching principals, administrators, and teachers.

 Administrators: this book is a must-read for leaders!

The lens of emotional intelligence assumes the following:

- We are all born with a certain level of emotional intelligence, and we can also develop these skills and capacities
- The emotional intelligence of a leader is a primary act of leadership
- There are four areas of emotional intelligence: self-awareness, self-management, social awareness, and relationship management
- An effective leader can speak about her emotions, welcomes feedback, and knows when she needs help
- An effective leader manages her emotions by demonstrating self-control and by being clear about her beliefs and actions
- Adaptability and flexibility are indicators of high emotional intelligence
- A high degree of emotional resiliency is an indicator of emotional intelligence; an effective leader sees adversity as opportunity
- Demonstrating empathy is an expression of social awareness
- Organizational awareness and an understanding of power relationships are indicators of emotional intelligence
- Managing relationships between people is the skill of an emotionally intelligent leader

Questions that explore the lens of emotional intelligence include the following:

Self-Awareness

- When does he recognize how his feelings are affecting him at work? How does he speak about his feelings?
- When does he recognize his limits and strengths?
- How does he invite or welcome feedback?
- Is he aware of the times when he needs help?

Self-Management

- How does she respond to disturbing emotions?
- How does she manage high stress?
- Is she clear about her feelings, beliefs, and actions? Can she admit her mistakes or faults?
- How does she adapt to new challenges?
- Does she welcome or create new opportunities? Or does she usually wait for them?
- How does she deal with changes and setbacks?

Social Awareness

- Can he sense the unspoken emotions in a person or group?
- Can he detect social networks and key power relationships? How does he recognize political forces in an organization?
- How does he cultivate an emotional climate that ensures that people are getting what they need? How does he monitor the satisfaction of those he serves?

Relationship Management

- Does she create resonance and move people with a compelling vision or shared mission? If so, how?
- How does she model what she wants from others?
- How does she try to appeal to different stakeholders? How does she try to enroll key people?
- When does she seem to be genuinely interested in developing her people? How does she learn about their goals, strengths, and areas for growth? When does she give feedback? Is it useful and well received?
- When does she recognize the need for a change and aim for transformation? When does she strongly advocate for change, even in the face of opposition? How does she find practical ways to overcome barriers to change?
- When there's a conflict, how does she understand different perspectives? How does she surface the conflicts, acknowledge views from all sides, and then redirect the energy toward a shared ideal?
- In what ways does she model respect, concern, and collaboration? How does she build relationships, identity, and spirit?

Source: Adapted from Goleman, Boyatzis, and McKee, 2002, 253–256.

Applying the Lens of Emotional Intelligence in Mr. Delgado's Class

Because this lens offers so many questions to consider, when I am faced with a situation such as Mr. Delgado's, I skim the list of questions, starring specific ones that immediately jump out as those that might possibly offer insight.

The questions about emotional awareness make me wonder how Mr. Delgado views his emotional experience in the classroom. I wonder if he recognizes his own mounting frustration and whether he has tools to manage these feelings. Within the domain of self-management, I wonder how Mr. Delgado feels about the challenges he's facing in his classroom. Does he see them as opportunities to improve his teaching practice? How has he dealt with challenges like this in the past? Does he feel pessimistic or optimistic about being able to address these issues? I wonder, in general, how Mr. Delgado will respond to my inquiries about his feelings—I am aware that speaking about feelings is more accepted in certain cultural and social groups and often more comfortable for women. I know that some people believe there is no place in our work contexts for discussing feelings. I will need to activate my own emotional intelligence and be attuned to how Mr. Delgado responds to my inquiries in this area.

Within the area of social awareness, I wonder if Mr. Delgado noticed Davontae's increasing agitation. I wonder what tools he has to address the emotional ups and downs that most eighth graders experience. Again, I am aware that there are different cultural assumptions about feelings—and teenagers with feelings—so I will be mindful of the assumptions that I make (that Mr. Delgado *should* notice a student's emotions and should respond) when I speak with him. The purpose of my coaching is not to impose a belief system, but to help my coachee explore his beliefs and actions.

Finally, under the domain of relationship management, I wonder how Mr. Delgado thinks about developing a community of learners. How does he try to get his students to buy into learning Spanish and into the vision that he has for his classroom? How has he explored who his students are and what their goals and aspirations are? And how does Mr. Delgado model the kind of behavior that he wants his students to demonstrate? Does he feel that he needs to?

Planning the Debrief Conversation

After reflecting on how each lens applies to Mr. Delgado's class and situation, the next step for me is to select some questions to ask him—I can't explore all of my wonderings in this first meeting. I also need to think through why I'm asking what I'm asking, and what I'll listen for. Just as teachers create lesson plans, a coach needs to create a plan for a debrief. This plan might change, and we need to be flexible, of course, but we need to go in with a plan. Table 4.1 presents my plan.

Table 4.1. Coaching Conversation: Debrief Plan

Teacher observed: Mr. Delgado

1	**Question: How are you feeling about today?**	
	My Thinking	*Lenses Used*
	This will reveal some information about Mr. Delgado's emotional intelligence: What language does he use to discuss what happened? How does he name his own emotions? Or does he bypass that topic and move into other topics? I want to start our conversation by opening this space because in order to have a discussion about other areas, we often need to clear emotions first. This is what makes coaching unique and effective—we acknowledge the presence and role of emotions, we attend to them, and we support our clients in processing them.	Emotional Intelligence
2	**Question: How do you see the problem or the challenge in that incident? What do you think was going on?**	
	My Thinking	*Lenses Used*
	I want to understand how Mr. Delgado sees "the problem." Is it his own management skills, as the principal believes? Is it the students and the disruptive student, as teachers sometimes feel? Does he feel that someone else (the principal) has defined "the problem" and determined that *Mr. Delgado* is the problem?	Inquiry
	If Mr. Delgado talks about the students' behavior, I may ask if there are groups of students in specific periods that he struggles more with.	Inquiry
	I am curious how Mr. Delgado will speak about the students' emotional expressions—how does he name their feelings? How does he interpret them? Did he recognize Davontae's frustration level when he entered the room? How does Mr. Delgado deal with students' feelings? Did he recognize his own increasing frustration?	Emotional Intelligence
	I will be listening in this conversation for how Mr. Delgado talks about power, if he does at all. Does he see power as residing within the classroom teacher? Does he feel students have "too much power" or none at all? I may ask him directly where he feels that the power lays, if he doesn't address this question.	Systemic Oppression
	I am also wondering if Mr. Delgado makes any connection between his own instructional skills and student behavior. I wonder if there's an entry point here for instructional coaching, which could incorporate everything from instructional objectives to his vision for himself as an instructor.	Inquiry

(continued)

Table 4.1. (*Continued*)

3	Question: What are your strengths as a teacher? What areas would you like to work on?	
	My Thinking	**Lenses Used**
	Although I believe that I'll need to start this conversation by addressing what I observed today, I would like to shift it at some point (fairly early if I can) into a broader conversation about Mr. Delgado's strengths and areas for growth. I really want to know what he feels he's bringing as an educator—I want to start building on these immediately. I also want to know what areas he identifies as areas for growth.	Change Management and Adult Learning
	Based on what he identifies as areas for growth, I will let him know that I'm going to explore what resources there are available to support him. It's important that he not feel that he needs to grow but that there are no supports.	Change Management
	I will also listen carefully throughout our conversation for indicators of his will to change and what areas he seems more willing to work on. When exploring the area of will, I'll pay close attention to the tone of voice he uses, his cadence, the words he chooses, his body language and all nonverbal cues as to how he feels. Will is very tricky to explore.	Change Management and Adult Learning
4	Question: I don't know much about your background. Could you tell me a little story about why you got into teaching and when you've felt successful as a teacher?	
	My Thinking	**Lenses Used**
	These questions will give me some valuable background on Mr. Delgado. If I'm going to coach him I not only need this information but I want him to know that I'm interested in it, that I want to know who he is and what he's done well. In order to get to a goal setting place, we need to get this information on the table first. I also need to understand his perspective—based on his age, gender, ethnicity and life experiences—in order to support him.	Adult Learning Emotional Intelligence
5	Question: I'm also curious about your feelings and beliefs about classroom management—what have you seen that's effective with young people?	
	My Thinking	**Lenses Used**
	This question might allow me to explore how Mr. Delgado views himself within a system of management, or oppression. It will also give me insight into what his knowledge base is, what kinds of skills he has in this area, and what his will to change might be.	Systemic Oppression Change Management

Table 4.1. (*Continued*)

6	Question: I know that you're new to this school this year. Can you tell me a little about how you learned the behavior management system this school uses?	
	My Thinking	*Lenses Used*
	I'm curious about how the administration made their expectations clear for teachers; how was Mr. Delgado brought into a system?	Systems Thinking
7	Question: I'm also wondering about how students are assigned to Spanish. What's your understanding of this process?	
	My Thinking	*Lenses Used*
	Another question to explore the school's systems and Mr. Delgado's understanding of how this system is set up and run.	Systems Thinking
	Depending on his answers and understanding, I want to let him know that I'd like to ask the principal and counselor some questions about how schedules are made and student assignments determined.	Systems Thinking and Inquiry
8	Question: How has it been for you coming to work at this school? What's been challenging? What are you enjoying?	
	My Thinking	*Lenses Used*
	I'm curious whether Mr. Delgado will address any factors around age, race, ethnicity and background. I know they play a role—within a system that is inherently oppressive, they always place a role. Does Mr. Delgado raise any of these issues? If not, I may ask him what it's been like to be a man of African descent teaching African American students, what his relationship is like with his male students—does he think they see him as an ally? Or do they engage in power struggles with him?	Systemic Oppression
	I will also pay attention to how Mr. Delgado describes his emotional experience of being at this school and facing the challenges he's dealing with. Does he feel that he can grow and learn from facing these challenges? Does he want to? Does he seem optimistic?	Emotional Intelligence

A STORY ABOUT A TEACHER WHO SEEMS TO STRUGGLE WITH CLASSROOM MANAGEMENT: PART 2

"Hi, Mr. Delgado," I said, as I let myself into his classroom. Mr. Delgado was sitting at his desk, staring at his computer monitor. "I'm glad we're going to have a chance to work together. I'm looking forward to supporting you."

"Thank you," he replied. "This was a hard day."

"Let's talk about it, then," I said. "I'm wondering if you'd mind sharing what you felt today during the time I was in here observing?"

"OK," he said. "But I really want to hear what you thought. I don't know what to do."

"We'll get to that, but first I'd like to hear about how you experienced today."

"I felt very upset," Mr. Delgado said. "I felt very disappointed in my students and in myself. I do not believe in shouting at children, even when they behave in the way that Davontae behaved. I lost control and I regret that."

"I hear that," I said, nodding. "I'm curious if you noticed that you were losing control?"

"I did. I told myself a few times to ignore their comments and take deep breaths. They are just young people in a difficult situation and I must not take out my anger on them."

"Could you tell me more about how you see the situation or the problem?"

"Well, I will start by saying that I know that the principal thinks the problem is my classroom management. That's why he wants you to coach me, right? He thinks if I was stricter that I wouldn't have these problems in my class." Mr. Delgado's tone is shifting just a bit; I hear irritation.

"It sounds like you disagree," I said. "How do you see the situation?"

"I am not sure that anyone wants to hear my perspective of the situation," he responded.

"I'd like to hear it. I'm here to support you."

Mr. Delgado looked at me for a few seconds. He exhaled loudly. "Maybe you could help me to understand this management plan I'm supposed to use," he said.

"Sure. What parts are working for you?"

"One of the problems is that I don't even know what I'm supposed to do. I was hired two days before school started and so I missed the training that everyone went to. The principal said he was going to schedule a makeup session for me, but that hasn't happened. So I don't really know what this plan is or how I'm supposed to use it."

"Oh," I said. "Well, I can see how that would make it hard to implement! That seems like it is one of the challenges in this situation."

"Yes, and it's frustrating when people keep coming to me, and they are upset by my management, and yet I haven't had the training."

"That would be very frustrating."

Mr. Delgado leaned closer to me. "The assistant principal even insinuated that I could lose my job if I don't improve. I told her I'd missed the training and that I wanted to learn this program. And then she told me that she'd talk to you about meeting with me."

"That seems unfair."

"It is. And she made it seem like if I didn't meet with you I'd be fired. I guess I was a little annoyed by that, and that's why I missed some of our meetings."

"I understand. That's not what coaching is about—I'm not here to fix you or make you use a program. I'm really here to support you. I'm wondering if you could tell me a little about your background. I don't know much about your teaching experiences. Maybe you could share what brought you into teaching and what you feel are your strengths?"

Mr. Delgado spoke at length and with enthusiasm about his teaching background. In Cuba, as a young man, he'd taught English at the university. After he immigrated to the United States, he taught in various after-school programs as well as at the high school level. He felt that his strengths were in developing relationships with students and in understanding their lives. When he shared this, I found a way to connect it back to what I'd observed in his class that day.

"Mr. Delgado, it's fantastic that you feel confident about being able to connect with students. I'm curious what you know about Davontae."

"I have worked hard to get to know Davontae in the last two weeks. You know he's a Katrina refugee?"

"No," I said. I did know that hundreds of displaced families from New Orleans had come to Oakland in the weeks since the devastating hurricane.

"His mother sent him here because they are homeless. He's living with his great-uncle, who is disabled. Davontae can barely read in English. I think he may have learning difficulties. I don't know why they put him in a Spanish class."

"Wow, poor kid," I said. "I can see you have really started to get to know him."

"I have. I care about that boy. I can relate to him—being a refugee, not being able to go home. I have tried to work hard with him, but I can't reach him. He needs more help."

"That seems like something we should advocate for. I wonder if he can get counseling and other support."

"I've been trying to get that to happen, but the system at this school is very slow, and I don't really understand it."

"I can try to help with that," I said. "I'm wondering about something you mentioned—I'm curious what the process is for determining who takes Spanish and why Davontae was put in your class."

"That is a very good question," Mr. Delgado said, sitting up, his face looking animated. "That is another thing I have been asking about. I asked the school counselor why she'd assigned Davontae to my class. She said, 'You had space.' I said, 'It's Spanish 2, and he's never had Spanish.' She explained that the only other elective for eighth graders at that time was advanced band and that the music teacher selects students who are in that class. They are students who have been in band since they were in elementary school—so they are a very special, select group. Have you ever been in that class?" Mr. Delgado asked me.

I had observed advanced band. The students were quite talented. I had also noticed that the band students did not represent the racial demographics of the school—these students, who had been in band since early elementary, drew from our city's middle class and predominantly white elementary schools. Those were the schools that, because of the fundraising efforts of the PTA, still had a music program. The middle school they now attended drew from both the city's poorest neighborhoods, which were almost exclusively African American, and from its upper-middle-class neighborhoods—which were predominantly white. The result was that although the school was 80 percent African American, advanced band had only two black students (out of thirty students total). The effect of that scheduling decision was that advanced band dictated the school's master schedule and created a de facto tracking system that cut across racial lines.

Mr. Delgado and I talked about this for a while. I was starting to get a picture of the complicated set of factors that were entwined in Mr. Delgado's "classroom management issue." I told Mr. Delgado that I'd raise some of the systemic issues with the administration—issues of how new teachers are brought into a school's program such as the behavior management program, how students are assigned to classes, and what kinds of social and emotional support could be provided to Davontae. Then I shifted the conversation back to what Mr. Delgado might be in control of and what he could do in his classroom.

"I hear that you really care about Davontae and understand him. I'm wondering what you noticed about him when he entered your classroom today?," I asked.

"I could tell he was angry," Mr. Delgado said, nodding. "I noticed that."

"I'm wondering if there's anything you think you could have tried to help him calm down?"

"I was just trying to get my lesson off the ground. I want my students to just come in, take their seats, and start working. I want them to care about their learning and be responsible for it."

"I hear that, and that's great. You want them to be intrinsically motivated. I'm wondering, however, when a student comes into class and you can tell he's emotionally upset, if you there are things you could try in order to get him to settle into learning?"

"I'd like to try something. Do you have some ideas?"

We spoke for a while about different strategies that teachers use to defuse student behavior or help a student calm down. Mr. Delgado was open and interested. When I broached the subject of the behavior management plan that the school was using, Mr. Delgado became less engaged. He seemed resistant or reluctant to use a plan. "I just want them to care about their learning and get into it without me having to tell them to," he said several times. I validated this feeling and suggested that his role was to help students bridge the world of the lunchroom, the hallway, or wherever they were coming from, and the learning that was possible if they settled into it.

We ended our conversation with an agreement to meet weekly. Mr. Delgado was receptive to support on lesson planning and instructional strategies. He also agreed that he'd like to learn some ways to calm himself down and not explode when students pushed his buttons (he admitted that this had happened before). But he remained apprehensive about support on the specific topic of classroom management. He agreed to attend the training that the principal would set up, but dismissed coaching in this area.

Using the Coach's Optical Refractor and the six lenses to view what I'd observed in Mr. Delgado's class raised many questions and opened many paths for exploration. Although my debrief that day revealed some of the answers and some of the factors, I knew there was still more to what was going on with Mr. Delgado. Had I not used the lenses, I might have approached Mr. Delgado and focused my conversation exclusively on management. He may not have engaged as openly with me, he may not have taken up the offer of more coaching, and I may not have been able to see the systemic implications of the situation.

As I coached Mr. Delgado that year, I continued to apply this set of lenses and questions to what I noticed in his classroom. Management continued to be an issue—students were often out of control in his room and getting into fights, and Mr. Delgado seemed unwilling to manage them. A couple months into our coaching work together, I asked Mr. Delgado one of the questions I'd wondered about after my initial visit: I asked him how he experienced being a black man teaching mostly African American children. "What's that like for you?" I asked. It was this question that finally revealed some of the core issues at play.

"I love teaching these children," Mr. Delgado said. "My heart and soul is with them. I was like them once—perceived as someone who would not make anything of himself, viewed as a second-class citizen, as someone who would become a criminal. It is this that makes my job so difficult. I refuse to be another person in their lives who oppresses them. I refuse to be a policeman or a prison guard. I refuse to be a part of this racist system. This is what I feel I am being asked to do."

Once he trusted me, and once I asked the questions, Mr. Delgado was very clear about why he was not invested in using a classroom management plan that he felt resulted predominantly in the suspension of African American boys. But because he was also committed to helping students learn, he struggled with this contradiction in what his job required. Over the year, he instituted some structures and learned to manage some of his students' behaviors, but at the end of the year he decided that given the current conditions in schools, he could better serve African American youth outside of the classroom. Through coaching, he had been able to explore the contradiction he experienced between wanting to serve children by being a teacher, and the personal and systemic factors that made this hard to do. He resigned from teaching and went on to work with a restorative justice organization where his work was appreciated and he felt effective.

The issues that Mr. Delgado raised about how students' schedules are determined, how new teachers are brought into a school's program, and how students receive additional support services were large ones to tackle. Within my role as a coach, I was able to raise these and draw connections between the challenges faced by classroom teachers and the larger system issues. Some of these issues were addressed immediately (Davontae's schedule was changed so that he didn't have to take Spanish 2, and he was referred to a mental health provider for services), some other issues were changed the following year, and certain other issues were not addressed. But what was essential was that the various complicated and entangled issues that manifested when Davontae stormed into Mr. Delgado's class and was eventually suspended, and the administration's perception that Mr. Delgado simply struggled with classroom management, were deconstructed.

WHEN WILL I USE THESE LENSES?

As coaches, we can use the lenses when planning coaching work, when confronted with dilemmas, and in reflection on our work. They can be used as they were in this chapter to analyze a complex situation. As I described, applying the lenses to guide my work helped support a teacher to find an effective place from which to serve children, helped shift a system, and helped one student have a better eighth-grade year.

The lenses are woven throughout the chapters that follow, and here's a quick map to what you'll find where. In Part Two of this book, we'll look at how these lenses can be applied as the foundation is set for a coaching assignment. As we *develop trust* with a client, we want to specifically look through the lenses of emotional intelligence and adult learning (Chapter Five). As we engage in the stage of exploration and *learn about a client and his context*, we'll take a careful look through the lenses of systemic oppression, inquiry, and systems thinking (Chapter Six). Finally, as we *develop a work plan* with a client, we'll look through the lens of change management, and again through the lenses of inquiry and adult learning (Chapter Seven).

In Part Three, which describes the "coaching dance"—the conversations and activities that make up the bulk of coaching work—the lenses are integrated into *a coach's analysis and decision making*. In this final part, each chapter concludes with a section on common challenges. These common challenges explore the lenses that yield insight into the dilemma presented.

In Chapter Fourteen, on reflection and assessment, I return to the lens of systems thinking to analyze *how coaching has affected systems change*.

On my website http://www.elenaaguilar.com/ there are many additional examples of common challenges that arise in coaching and descriptions of how to apply the lenses to resolve the challenges.

PART TWO

Establishing Coaching with a Client

CHAPTER 5

Beginning a Coaching Relationship: How Do I Develop Trust with a Coachee?

Read this chapter when:

- You're about to start working with a new client.
- You sense that your client doesn't trust you.
- You've broken a client's trust and want to rebuild it.
- You're a principal interested in strategies for developing trust with a staff member.

"WITHOUT TRUST THERE CAN BE NO COACHING"

Most coaches know that this statement by Rafael Echeverría and Julio Olalla (1993) is true, but what does it mean in a practical sense? How do we develop trust? How do we know if our coachee trusts us? And what do we do when trust breaks down?

Anytime someone engages in coaching, they are bound to feel vulnerable at some point. Learning, reflecting, and taking risks are all scary. Furthermore, coaches are sometimes assigned to educators who might be struggling. Although I believe that no one should be mandated to work with a coach, some teachers or principals are just apprehensive or distrusting of coaching and we can still win them over to it.

At the beginning of a coaching relationship, a coach needs to help a client get excited about and buy into a coaching relationship, to become open to what coaching can offer; we call this "enrolling." Enrollment doesn't necessarily happen in one meeting—it can take months, or a client might already begin the work partially enrolled. Clients often need to be reenrolled—we must not take it for granted that we have someone's trust and engagement. While this is an ongoing process, the first meeting is critical. It can be very hard to return from a less-than-positive first meeting.

A STORY ABOUT TRUST

Jackie was a middle school principal I'd been assigned to coach. I knew she'd been at two other schools and struggled at both, I'd heard that she felt like the district had mistreated her, and I knew that she was told that if she didn't agree to work with a coach, she would lose her job. "She's going to be a tough nut to crack," my manager told me. A colleague who knew Jackie said, "It's going to take you a year to gain her trust," she said. "I don't have a year," I said.

I developed a plan for our first meeting and carried it out. I asked questions that allowed Jackie to reveal her strengths. I asked how she'd gotten into education and where her passions lay. I allowed her to lead the conversation into the areas that she wanted to work on. I shared that I was moved by her commitment to children and to her school, that I heard that her will was strong. I emphasized the confidentiality agreements that would frame our work. While we were speaking, I repeated a mantra-like statement in my mind: *I'm here for you, Jackie. I care about you.* I felt this and wanted to make sure that it was louder than anything else in my mind. I needed her to sense this from me the whole time. I had to put my own judgmental doubts and concerns out of my mind and focus only on the person sitting in front of me, who was scared and frustrated and dedicated to serving students.

A month later, and after many coaching sessions, Jackie ran into my manager. She thanked her profusely for assigning me as her coach and praised my work. That year, though Jackie had many areas in which she wanted to grow and her progress was slow, she made a significant impact on her teachers and students. Her school's test scores skyrocketed, her leadership with the parent community was publicly recognized, and her contract was renewed.

At the end of the two years that I coached her, Jackie shared that of the three coaches she'd worked with, I was the first whom she really trusted.

"What was different?" I asked.

"I think I just felt from the beginning that you really cared about me," she said, "that you didn't believe all the rumors you'd heard, and you were really invested in my success. I felt like you saw me as a human being and not just a principal."

WHAT IS TRUST?

In the enrollment stage the goal is to determine the work that the coach will do with the client, which is articulated in the work plan (see Chapter Seven). But the greater goal is to gain the client's trust. This is a challenging end point to evaluate, as it resides almost exclusively in the subjective and volatile realms of emotions and beliefs.

What is trust? Exploring a definition can provide insight into how we develop this elusive but essential quality. Stephen M. R. Covey, author of *The Speed of Trust* (2008), defines trust as the feeling of confidence we have in another's character and competence. Character comprises integrity, which in turn includes how honest we are and how aligned our actions are with what we say. It also encompasses intent: What is our agenda? Are we really here to help or serve another, or do we have hidden agendas? The confidence we have in another's competence will also build or decrease our trust. Does the other person have the skills, abilities, attitudes, and knowledge that we need? Can he produce the results he says he will? Distrust, therefore, arises from suspicion of integrity and capabilities (Covey, 2008).

Another definition proposes that "distrust is not merely the absence of trust, but is an active negative expectation regarding another" (Lewicki and Wiethoff, 2000, p. 87). This definition yields insights for those of us working in contexts in which "active negative expectations regarding another" can be a part of a school's history and culture, as well as in the experiences of anyone who has spent any time—including as a child—in schools. Therefore, as a coach, we might encounter a first-year teacher who already has an active negative expectation of those in positions of authority in a school because of her own experience as a student, or we might work in a school that has had a great deal of turnover in administration or that feels that the district's central office has made decisions that negatively affect them. These negative experiences can contribute to a distrusting institutional memory.

Gaining and maintaining a client's trust is paramount; this is a key moment for coaching to be practiced as an art. Coaching is not just a technical application of tools; following a step-by-step routine will not necessarily gain someone's trust. A coach's emotional intelligence will be essential: How well does he know himself? How aware is he of the impact of his verbal and nonverbal communication? Does he notice the subtle shifts in a client's emotional states, and can he adjust to meet those? Is he aware of his own judgment and opinions about a client? A coach needs to be able to reflect on his integrity, intentions, and communication skills in order to effectively build a relationship. Because so much hinges on a coach's ability to gain trust, it is critical that a coach has a reflective practice and, ideally, a space where he can engage with coach-colleagues and be supported. We'll return to this topic in Chapter Fifteen.

USEFUL LENSES FOR THIS STAGE

The lens of emotional intelligence and the lens of adult learning can be very useful at this point. They remind us to pay attention to how a client is experiencing emotions and to how she expresses (or doesn't express) her emotions. In initial meetings with clients, we need to carefully attend to body language, verbal expression, and choice of words. As we engage in conversations, we need to tune in to emotional subcurrents.

The lens of adult learning reminds us that as coaches, it is our job is to determine where someone is on their path to learning. We are reminded that everyone is on a journey, and we must accept people wherever they are at this moment. This lens pushes us to find out where our client is on her learning journey, where she has been, and where she wants to go. Our agenda—or the one we are sent in to implement—is put on hold while we explore who we are sitting with and her concerns as an adult learner.

It's also important to acknowledge that levels of trust can be affected by differences between a coach's gender, race, age, cultural background, or sexual orientation and those of the client. This is simply a reality to be aware of and to possibly explore.

TEN STEPS TO BUILDING TRUST

The following ten suggestions are very relevant to the initial period of working together, what we call the "enrollment process," the stage of ensuring that the client buys into coaching. But trust is not simply built and left standing; it needs to be maintained and occasionally patched up. These steps are relevant across the duration of a coaching relationship.

 Administrator: these ten steps will also be useful to address issues of trust at a site.

Plan and Prepare

The first meetings with a client, or a potential client, should be carefully planned. Write up the questions you want to ask and anticipate the questions you might receive. Visualize the first meetings and the outcomes that you want to achieve. If you have a coach colleague, you can role-play or rehearse meetings. It's imperative that you feel confident, clear, and prepared. Your client will be watching you and listening to you very, very carefully. She will be looking for indicators of your competence, credibility, integrity, and character.

Exhibit 5.1 presents some questions you might want to include in your plan for your first meeting.

Cautiously Gather Background Information

Before meeting a new client, you might be tempted to speak to others who know this person, but this should be done with caution. While it can be helpful to gather impressions of the person you might coach, and some of that information can be instructive on how to gain that person's trust, it is also possible that what you hear could influence your feelings and beliefs about the individual. It is essential that you go into your first meetings with as many positive feelings about the client as possible. Therefore, if you hear things that plant seeds of doubt in your mind, it might be harder to listen deeply. Furthermore, do not underestimate the other person's ability to subconsciously pick up on what's lurking right beneath your coach-surface.

For my own integrity, and so that I can best get to know my client, I try to know as little as possible about a potential client before I meet him. I suggest that you don't gather information in advance unless you have a very trusted colleague who understands the work of coaching. If that person exists, you might want to ask questions such as these:

- What do you think are his strengths as a teacher or leader?
- What might be important for me to know in order to build trust with him?
- Are there any specific words or phrases that I could use that might resonate with him or be a trigger?
- Is there anything in my own background that you think might be worth sharing with him?

Exhibit 5.1. Questions to Pose in Your First Meeting with a New Client

The following questions should be incorporated in such a way that the meeting proceeds more like a conversation than an interview or an interrogation. Not all of them need to be asked at every meeting. You can also return to this list in your second or third meeting with a new coachee.

Background

1. Can you tell me about why you went into teaching and/or administration? What drew you to this field?
2. What do you enjoy about your position?
3. What is challenging about it?
4. What do you think are your strengths?
5. What do you think are your areas for growth?
6. Outside of work, what are your interests and passions?

Relationships

1. How would you describe your relationship with your principal?
2. How would you describe your relationship with your colleagues?
3. How would you describe your relationship with your students?
4. How would you describe your relationship with your students' parents?
5. Do you have colleagues (on-site or off-site) that you trust? That you feel good about collaborating with?

Professional Development and Coaching Experience

1. How do you feel that you learn best? Can you tell me about a powerful learning experience you've had over your time as an educator?
2. Have you worked with a coach before? Describe that experience. What worked well? Were there things that didn't work for you?
3. What's prompted you to explore coaching now?
4. What is your understanding of what coaching is? Of my role?
5. What are your hopes and fears for our work?

6. What do you need from me as a coach?
7. Is there anything I should know that would help me in my work with you? That would make our work together more effective?
8. Is there anything you'd like to know about me that would help make our work more effective?
9. What do you anticipate might be a challenge or get in the way of our working together?
10. How can I support you when those challenges arise?
11. What would you like me to hold you to, as far as your engagement with coaching?

Additional Questions for Administrators

1. What grade level(s) and content area(s) did you teach?
2. What other roles have you held?
3. What's surprised you about being a leader?
4. What are this school's or network's strengths? What does it have going for it?
5. What are the big issues and challenges for this school or network right now?
6. Are there any other big issues that you anticipate might come up this year?
7. How would you describe your relationship with teachers? With other staff? With your colleagues? With your students and their parents?

Remember that in order to gain trust, you will need to establish credibility. One way of doing this is by demonstrating that you know what you're doing, which is particularly hard to do when you're a new coach! You can show that you know what you're doing by coming to a first conversation with some knowledge about what your client is dealing with. If you are coaching a principal, for example, you might be able to do some online research into the site's history, test scores, and so on. However, in a first meeting you also need to allow your client to be the expert and the one supplying the context. Many people who receive coaching feel vulnerable about what has been said about them or their school, so in some cases you can gain trust by *not* coming in with information from external sources. When in doubt, my advice is to start with as little information in your mind as possible. This will allow you to be more completely focused on the person in front of you and to be authentically curious about who he is, where he's been on his learning journey, and where he wants to go.

This is not to say, however, that you won't do some research later. In order to better support your client and to effect systemic change, you'll need to do some research (more on this in Chapter Six). But first you need to enroll your client—and this is harder to do if you've heard that he's been bounced around from school to school, that parents hate him, or that he's dismissive of students with learning disabilities. Proceed into the realm of research with caution.

Establish Confidentiality

In your first conversation with a client—or, better yet, in an e-mail before you even meet—establish confidentiality. Repeat this several times during the first few conversations. For most clients, this will be extremely important and you will need to be absolutely true to your word. Be warned: if you violate the confidentiality agreement, you may never be able to regain a client's trust.

Here's what I usually say, immediately after sitting down for the first conversation:

"Before we get started, I want to return to what I shared in my e-mail about the confidentiality of our conversations. Our conversations are absolutely confidential. I will not discuss what we talk about with your supervisor or anyone else. If I ever need to e-mail your principal or supervisor about something we talked about, I will CC you on it. I would speak to him or her in person about you only if you are present."

Although complete confidentiality is necessary for coaching to work, there may be times when principals and supervisors want to know about the work. In that case, it is important that the client is also aware of exactly what will and won't be communicated and how it will be communicated. Supervisors also need to know that a confidentiality agreement exists between the coach and client. Staff development experts Joeleen Killion and Cindy Harrison (2006) suggest that coaches share the four Ts: teacher, time, topics, and tasks. The first T identifies the person receiving coaching support (the teacher, in their framework). If you are working at a school, or within a network, then the principal or supervisor is informed about which *teacher* is receiving coaching. Second, a coach shares how much *time* is spent with the coachee each week or month. Third, a coach names the *topics* that are being worked on. For example, "Mr. Smith and I are looking at formative assessment strategies for academic vocabulary." Finally, a coach describes the *tasks* that she is doing with the coachee. For example: "I am observing Mr. Smith and offering feedback. We read an article together."

The coaching log shown in Exhibit 5.2 is a tool that can be used to report to supervisors (and a blank version can be found on my website). This can be completed

Exhibit 5.2. Coaching Log

Coach _____

Coachee _____

Date	Time	Topic	Activity
9/15/11	12:00–1:00 p.m.	Classroom management: entry procedures	Coaching conversation
9/21/11	9:00–9:30 a.m. and 3:30–4:30 p.m.	Classroom management: entry procedures	Classroom observation and debrief of observation

by the coach and client at the end of each meeting and given to the supervisor or stored on an online platform that all parties can access. The only exception is when the coach hears anything that puts the safety of another person—adult or child—at risk. And, of course, if we hear or see our client doing something illegal, we are obligated to report it.

As coaches, we must be careful to share only information that is nonevaluatory. This information is best communicated in a monthly report (see Chapter Fourteen) that is e-mailed to both the coachee's supervisor and the coachee. The more formalized, the better.

For coaching to be most effective, the client must feel confident that you will not share any information with his supervisor. You will need to state this intention when you first meet, you will need to repeat it, and you will need to be very careful when you're in the same room with your coachee and his evaluator—your client will be watching you closely to see if you reveal anything. And again, be warned: if you break the confidentiality agreement, you may never be able to regain your client's trust and, as a result, there will be no coaching. And if you violate the trust of a teacher, for example, you can be fairly certain that that teacher will speak to his colleagues about you and they will not trust you or be receptive to your coaching. Be very, very careful. On the other hand, after you've established yourself as a trustworthy coach, positive word of mouth will get around. When you are enrolling a client and discussing confidentiality, you can refer your new client to others who may vouch for your trustworthiness. This can make the enrollment process quicker and easier.

Listen

From the very first time you meet with a client, you'll want to demonstrate your listening skills. A client will be very attuned—consciously or unconsciously—to your capacity to listen deeply. The purpose of deep listening is for you to truly perceive and understand where the client is coming from and his deeper desires and fears, so that you can guide him into territory that he may not even be aware he needs to explore. A big step toward building trust with a client is your ability to listen.

In coaching, we listen deeply, without ego or attachment; we are listening with acceptance. When clients experience this, they develop confidence in you and in your integrity. Give your coachee this experience the first time you meet: it is a way for you to demonstrate your intent to create a reflective learning space, and it will help him begin to trust you.

Active listening is a useful strategy for a first meeting. Active listening requires us to restate or paraphrase what the client has said, both to check our own understanding and let the client know that he's been heard. Furthermore, when a coach says, "I'm hearing . . . Is that accurate?" it invites the client to build on what he has shared.

Chapter Eight is all about listening; there's lots more to say. You might want to read that chapter before engaging in first meetings with new clients.

Ask Questions

Your initial meetings with a client are an opportunity for you to demonstrate your skill. Coaching questions can shift a client's perceptions, deepen learning, move actions, and transform practice. But given that so much is at stake in the first meetings, and that you can't anticipate and plan for everything that someone else will say, what can you ask? Clarifying questions are usually safe and often productive. Simply asking for more information—*Could you tell me more about that?*—can be revealing. Your client can experience it as an invitation to go deeper in her thinking, to share a next layer of reflection. It is a way for you to express interest in the other person. It is often surprising what another person will share when you simply ask for more. While you don't want the first meetings to feel like interrogations, asking clarifying questions is generally a safe route.

While you might have a list of questions to ask (such as those in Exhibit 5.1), you also need to respond to what you hear your client saying. If you are able to ask a few questions that give your client a glimpse of your capacity as a coach, you will gain ground in building trust. Even those who are suspicious of coaching often suspect that probing questions might be helpful. They yearn for a question that will give them new insight or offer a new perspective. Try to ask one of these if you can.

Connect

As you start getting to know a new coachee, try to uncover personal connections. I go into a first meeting like a ravenous animal on the hunt, my eyes scanning the office or classroom for a family photo, a postcard, a certificate, or anything that I might be able to connect with. I also try to surface connections through the questions I ask. General questions—such as: How was your summer (or vacation or weekend)? Where did you grow up? and How long have you been teaching?—can open doors. You can also try the specific questions in Exhibit 5.1.

I intentionally look for connections for a couple of reasons. First, sometimes they allow me to share a snippet of personal information ("I have a toddler too"), which helps personalize me for my client—they need this too, but I only share tiny tidbits of personal information. Second, the personal details I learn help me care more about my client; they help me see beyond the teacher or principal label, and then my heart opens and my compassion expands.

This coaching strategy was critical with Susan, a central office administrator. My manager told me, "She's old school, has very little background as an instructional leader, and she's going to be intimidated by your experience, but she does want coaching." Knowing this, I wondered if during our first conversation I could find a way to elicit Susan's knowledge and skills. As I sat down in her office the first time we met, I noticed a number of prominently displayed photos of a young man who I guessed was her son. He looked to be of a similar multiracial mix to my own child, who had just started kindergarten that week. Susan was more than eager to talk about her son, and we spent two hours discussing our children, the challenges of raising boys of color in Oakland, and the difficult decisions that mothers must make. I asked questions, asked for advice, and shared my fears about my boy entering public school. As I left her office, she hugged me and said, "Next time we'll talk business, but sometimes it's good to just get to know someone before you start working with them."

This was what Susan needed in that first meeting—to have her expertise authentically recognized and appreciated and to see me as a learner as well. The connection we made also informed my coaching moves as we worked together that year. As challenges arose, I recalled the bigger picture of Susan and her strength as a mother, and I was able to help her transfer that knowledge and strength to her role as an administrator.

Validate

A transformational coach is a master at uncovering a client's assets. It is almost as if we wear glasses that make a person's strengths pop out in Technicolor while everything else fades into shades of gray. These glasses are an essential accessory for first meetings with a client. Remember that most clients feel vulnerable as they begin coaching—after all, coaching is a way to improve, grow, change, or transform. Put on those glasses and share your observations.

Validating another's experiences is powerful. A simple and sincere, "Wow. That sounds really hard," or "Congratulations! That's great!" communicates validation. A key rule for praise is to be specific and acknowledge the action. For example, "I hear that in the last week you moved across country, set up your house, got your kids into a new school, and started this teaching job, and you still seem energetic! That's amazing!"

Sadly, people who work in schools are rarely validated for what they do. Think back to your time in the classroom. How often did you feel appreciated or recognized for the multitude of things that you did every day? Just echoing what you've heard and observed a client doing can build trust. It shows that you listen carefully and recognize the struggles and triumphs of the profession.

As with everything else you say, your validation and praise must be completely sincere. Don't compliment something that you don't truly appreciate; your client will pick up on that inauthenticity and trust will plummet. But also, don't overpraise—that's not what you're there to do. Your role as a coach is not necessarily to praise, but to hold a mirror up to your client and help him see his strengths reflecting back. In the beginning, he may not see them—that's why you'll call them out. Eventually, you need to be able to walk away and let the client hold up the mirror himself.

Be Open about Who You Are and What You Do

Most teachers and principals I've coached have been less interested in who I am and what I've done than in *why* I do what I do. I offer a very basic professional-biographical sketch and then ask, "Is there anything else you'd like to know about me?" Usually they aren't interested in me, which is helpful, as we want to keep the focus on them.

Proactively demonstrating an awareness about the role that your gender, ethnicity, or cultural background might play in a particular coaching situation can be a way of developing trust with a client. Thoughtfully naming the differences between you and your client can reflect your awareness of these dynamics. When I was assigned to coach an older African American male principal in a community that was 100 percent African American, I raised this point in an early conversation. I asked, "I'm wondering how you feel about working with me, given the differences in our age, gender, and ethnicity. What comes up for you?" We had an honest conversation that helped me understand this principal much better, and he expressed appreciation that I'd named the differences and initiated a discussion.

What I never do with clients when I'm raising gender, race, and other background differences is make assumptions that my own knowledge or experience is directly transferable to their situation. I don't say, "My best friend is also a _____," or "I'm married to a _____." My job is to get to know the person standing in front of me, to understand what it's like to be him in the context he is in. I don't want to suggest that I know things because of my prior experiences.

What new clients do wonder about is *why* I'm doing what I'm doing. Even if they've willingly engaged in coaching, there's always a bit of curiosity around this practice. Some have asked, "What's your agenda?" I address these concerns by sharing my coaching vision, what I believe coaching is and can do, and what my agenda is (see Chapter Three).

Here's an example of what I've said:

> I know you don't really want to work with a coach, and I appreciate your honesty in sharing that. I hear that you've been working really hard to turn your school around and that you feel misunderstood by your supervisor. I want to repeat that everything we talk about is confidential. I know that you've been put on an improvement plan, but I'm here to support you in anything you want to work on, in whatever area you'd like support in. I'm not attached to that plan, it's not my agenda—my agenda is to help you help your school and community. Can we talk about what that might look like for you?

If I do have an agenda—if I've been asked to address something specific—then I state that:

> I'm here to support you in using this classroom management plan. I know you asked for some help as a first-year teacher, and I know that if we focus on a few areas you'll make progress quickly. I'm not evaluating you in any way, however, and I don't share our work with your principal. How does that sound?

Ask for Permission to Coach

Frequently asking for permission to coach can build and increase a client's trust. Our job as a transformational coach is to help someone explore her behavior, beliefs, and being. Even after a client is enrolled, we need to remember that sometimes it can be tiring to have someone gently nudging you to reflect and grow. If we frequently and explicitly ask for permission to coach, we remind the client that she is in control of the process and can put the brakes on whenever she needs to.

The following questions are ways to ask for permission:

- I'm wondering if you'd mind sharing some of the challenges you're dealing with?

- Would it be OK if I came to your staff meeting? It might help our work if I could observe the dynamics between teachers.

- Next time we meet, would it be OK to look at some student work?
- I hear that you're really frustrated with your assistant principal. Would you like some coaching on that issue?
- What role would you like me to play at the meeting?
- I'm noticing that you seem upset by my last question. Can we check in on what's coming up for you?

By asking for permission, a coach demonstrates her respect and knowledge of adult learning and emotional intelligence. When we demonstrate our professional competency, a client's trust increases. We can damage our client's trust when we don't have permission and we push too hard. As a coaching relationship deepens and develops, we want to be careful not to overstep trust levels in this area.

Keep Commitments

It can be very tempting early in a relationship with a coachee to make too many promises. Sure, you say, I'll meet for a 7:00 a.m. planning session, then gather materials, do a demonstration lesson, give feedback on a dozen unit plans, make copies, and make calls all by the end of tomorrow. Not only will it be hard to keep this up, but some of these tasks are not really your job.

Clients who are apprehensive about coaching often ask for a coach to prepare or provide tangible things (books, materials, lessons, and the like), perhaps unconsciously testing your trustworthiness and credibility. They explore boundaries—how much can they ask you for? What are you *really* willing to do for them? While these feelings are understandable, a coach needs to be careful that she doesn't accept too many requests, especially the kind along the margins of what a coach's role should be (such as making copies and making phone calls). Doing those things for people does not change their practice. In addition, when they ask a coach to undertake tasks such as these, some clients feel they are making good use of the coach, but this is actually a way to keep the coach at a distance.

At the same time, gathering materials, curriculum, assessments, and so on can be a way for a coach to demonstrate her usefulness. We often have piles of resources at our fingertips and are eager to share. When we volunteer to be the note taker at a meeting, our value is apparent. However, we have to be careful not to take on too much and end up unable to meet our commitments. It is extremely important that we fulfill the promises we make. It's much better to underpromise and overdeliver than the reverse.

One way to ensure that you can meet your commitments is by writing up a formal agreement with your client. It's always helpful to put things in writing. See Exhibit 5.3 at the end of the chapter for a sample.

ASSESSING LEVELS OF TRUST

At this stage of the coaching cycle, your goal is to gain your client's trust, a quality that is hard to measure. Over the course of your work together, your client's trust may fluctuate. So how can you know if your client trusts you?

One of the first steps in a coaching relationship is to engage your client in developing a work plan (see Chapter Seven). While this document does not necessarily reflect the presence of deep trust, it does reflect a client's willingness to proceed with coaching. It's a solid indicator of trust developing.

Trust is also reflected in what a client says—how open and vulnerable he is and what kind of support he asks for. For example, being observed teaching and leading a staff meeting are far riskier activities than sitting with you alone in an office. Pay attention to your client's nonverbal communication as well: Are his arms crossed over his chest? Are his shoulders pulled up toward his ears? Other nonverbal indicators of a person's emotional state include sighs, long exhales, changes in volume or tone of speech, leaning forward into the conversation, reclining backwards, and fluctuations in eye contact. Notice how your client holds his body, how much and at what points he moves, shifts weight, fidgets, checks his phone, and so on. Hone your observation skills as you get to know a client and then pay attention to changes.

When you notice changes in body language—perhaps a big sigh or the dropping of shoulders, try to identify what led to those changes. What did you say? What did he say? Sometimes you can ask, "I'm noticing that your face suddenly looks more relaxed. Are you feeling better about the situation? What allowed that shift to happen?"

If you notice changes that might indicate emotional distress (sudden stiffening of the body or abrupt, one-word responses to questions, for example) it can be useful to voice what you noticed and ask if the client would like to share what's going on. Sometimes just saying, "I noticed that after I asked you that question you crossed your arms and leaned away from me. Can I ask what feelings were coming up for you?"

There are many ways that we can damage a client's trust. Because the people we coach are engaged in their own learning and exploration of behavior, beliefs, and being, the coaching session can be a very vulnerable experience. Their trust can be diminished when we don't listen well, when we don't validate their growth, when we don't show enough compassion, when we don't ask for permission to coach, when we push them in directions they're not ready to go, if we speak to their supervisor without honoring the agreements we made, and so on. A coach needs to develop a keen awareness of her client's emotions and notice all fluctuations. Then she needs to learn the language and gain the confidence to address them. She also needs to take responsibility for her actions and be accepting of anything the client expresses. It can be hard to hear someone say, "I just feel like you weren't really listening to how hard it is to do this job and you keep pushing me to do more." A coach who thanks a client for his honesty and reflects on this feedback will be more likely to repair the damaged trust.

A coach who can accurately assess a client's levels of trust has strong emotional intelligence and intuition. These are skills that we can develop. The questions listed in Exhibit 5.1 can yield insights into what's going on with a client. A coach can also develop his intuition by engaging in some of the practices suggested in Chapter Fifteen to remain grounded and present.

COMMON CHALLENGES AND HELPFUL RESPONSES

Challenge: My client seems to really distrust me. I don't know what I've done, but she always seems standoffish and keeps our conversations on a superficial level.

Lens of Inquiry. It sounds like this client has come to you with some "active negative expectation." There's a potential for a big breakthrough here, which could happen immediately or over time, or this client might not be coachable. Applying the lens of inquiry might open up some conversations.

Distrust is usually a suspicion of integrity and motives, which can come from previous experiences or a lack of knowledge and information about who someone is and what she does. Does your coachee have a good understanding of what you do? Have you shared your vision for coaching and described your role? Is there someone else with whom you've worked who might be willing to speak with this reluctant client about your work?

Ask the client about previous experiences with coaches or what she's heard about coaching, as she may have heard false information. In addition, ask general questions about what kind of professional development she's experienced, what she's found helpful, how she learns best, and so on.

Finally, your client might be bringing her own fear and experiences of betrayal to your relationship. If others have seriously violated her trust or lied to her, then your chances of enrolling her in coaching might be slim. This is not necessarily something you need to explore; it's just worth remembering that sometimes when someone doesn't seem to trust us, it has nothing to do with us at all. Don't take it personally.

Challenge: I'm coaching a teacher, and her principal is constantly asking me about our work. She wants to know if the teacher is improving, if we've addressed this or that yet, if I've seen the teacher shouting at students, etc. When I started working at this school, I spoke with the principal about our confidentiality agreements, but she doesn't seem to remember them.

Lens of Adult Learning. The principal is on her own learning trajectory as far as understanding what coaching is, what conditions are necessary for it to be effective, and how she can best support her teachers and students. It can help to think of the principal as an unofficial client.

Start by printing out and reviewing the confidentiality agreement and your coaching logs. Within this conversation, be explicit about why these formalities are in place—why coaching must be a protected learning space. You can also shift the conversation into the principal's role—how is she working on changing her teacher's practice? Help her see that your role is professional developer; her role is professional developer and evaluator. You cannot play any role in evaluation. You might also suggest that the principal have some conversations with the teacher about the growth that she's been making in coaching, and that the principal observe her and gather her own data on the teacher's progress.

Finally, just smile and repeat, as many times as necessary, "I can't share that information with you. I'm sorry, but as a coach, I can't share that. I can share the information that's in our coaching log, and that's all. Thank you for understanding."

"THE THIN CORD OF TRUST"

Rafael Echeverría and Julio Olalla, experts in the field of coaching, offer provocative words on trust:

> Trust will always be at stake during the process of coaching. Trust can increase and become more solid, and it can be taken away. It can be initially gained,

then lost and afterwards recovered. Or it can be lost for good. The coach always moves along the thin cord of the coachee's trust. To take for granted the coachee's trust is one of the big mistakes a coach can make. (1993)

These words are a reminder that coaches have a tremendous responsibility to clients. We invite people into what can be a scary journey of reflection where the aspects of themselves that they are most ashamed of might be brought to light. This is precisely the power of coaching—in bringing these areas to light, we diminish their ability to disempower us, and we move on to consider other ways of being that lead to different actions. We support our clients along the arduous journey of change, encouraging them when they tire, cheering for them when they succeed. When we can invite teachers, principals, vice-principals, and others who work in schools into the vulnerable space of growth, when we elicit trust and maintain our integrity, our coachees will join us eagerly on the journey to transform schools. The success of this endeavor hinges on trust.

Exhibit 5.3. Coaching Agreement

Coach _____

Client _____

Coaching will begin on _____ and will end on _____.

The Work Plan

- The work plan will be created by the coach and client and will be finalized by

  _____.

- The coach will reflect monthly on our work plan. This reflection will be shared with the coach's manager. (Documents written by the coach are shared with the coach's manager *only if* that manager is not *also* the client's supervisor.)

- A separate document, the coach's monthly report, will be completed by the coach, approved by the client, and shared with the client's supervisor every month.

- We will review our work plan midway through our work together on _____. The coach will write a reflection on this work and will share it with his or her manager.

- We will reflect on our work plan at the end of our designated time together. The coach will write a reflection on this work and will share it with his or her manager.

Meeting Logistics

- We will meet for ___ hours per month.

- Our meetings will take place on _____, from _____ to

  _____.

- The location for our meetings will be _____.

- Our time will be documented on the coaching log, which can be shared with our supervisors or kept on an online platform that our supervisors can view.

- If one of us has to cancel a meeting, whenever possible we will give the other person at least twenty-four hours' notice. We also recognize that unexpected things come up and that sometimes we are forced to cancel without notice.

- If the coach cancels a meeting, he or she will make every possible effort to reschedule as soon as possible.

- If the client cancels a meeting, the coach will make an effort to reschedule, but cannot always promise that this will happen due to his or her other commitments.
- If cancellations become a pattern, the coach and client agree to review the coaching agreement.

Feedback

- The coach welcomes feedback from the client at any time. The client is encouraged to share feedback.
- The coach will ask the client for formal feedback midway through the coaching contract and at the end of their work together. If possible, the coach will also provide an online link for an anonymous survey on his or her services.

We agree to work together under the above-described conditions. We understand that doing so will increase the likelihood of serving children and transforming our schools.

Coach signature _____

Client signature _____

Date _____

CHAPTER 6

The Exploration Stage: What Do I Need to Know at the Outset?

Read this when:

- You're beginning a coaching assignment and you need to learn as much as possible about the context for coaching
- You want to clearly delineate the equity issues at play
- You want to intentionally examine systems and direct your coaching toward systems change

FROM THE EDGE OF THE FIELD

Imagine this: you are a farmer invited to cultivate a plot of land that has lain fallow for some years. You stand on the edge of the acre, leaning on a shovel, surveying the space. You notice the tall trees on the east side that block the sun from hitting the soil until late morning. Tunnels indicate the presence of gophers, and deer droppings are numerous along a side where blackberry vines are encroaching on the field. You kneel to touch the soil and roll it between your fingers. It is loamy and dark. You dig deeper and see an earthworm—a good sign. Moving a few feet away, however, the soil is compact and rocky.

From your pocket you pull out the shiny black seeds that you hope will become watermelons. You know that if they do become fruit, it will be a product of a number of factors: sun, water, soil quality, and your attention. You know that you can't do much about the sun, but you can remove the weeds, erect a fence to keep the deer out, water, and use a nontoxic method to keep slugs from devouring the seedlings. You won't plant the watermelons in the area that is shaded, rocky and invaded by a thistly weed, but because you eventually want to make full use of this field, you will start to look at what's going on there and what might need to happen in order for it to be arable.

There's a lot that as a farmer you can do — and there's a lot that's out of your hands. The potential in the seed itself, for example, is unknown, and ultimately it's all about the almost magical energy of the seed. Most seeds sprout, but some don't. The seed has a lot of work to do by itself. In the end, you'll know that that beautiful melon is the result of a number of factors, many of which were beyond your immediate influence, but many others were not.

We can chart our future clearly and wisely only when we know the path which has led to the present.

ADLAI E. STEVENSON (1952)

Farming is an apt metaphor for coaching. Just as the farmer would never simply walk into a field and drop a seed in the soil, a coach cannot walk into a school and start delivering professional development (PD). We must know what we're working with, the history of the environment, and the health of various elements. We must also be aware of the different systems that we're working within: just as a farmer needs a comprehensive understanding of her ecosystem, a coach needs to identify the various systems at play in the site or context in which she will work. Ultimately, we engage in all this exploration and understanding to determine where and how we can get some results: we want to remove the obstacles that are easy to remove, direct our coaching toward the most fertile areas, be responsive to the climate and work with it, and then be patient, gentle, and attentive to what emerges.

THE STAGE OF EXPLORATION

This might be obvious, but it's worth stating: in order to be effective as a coach, you're going to want as much information about a client and his context as possible. This, therefore, is the stage of exploration. Once you're equipped with the tools and checklists offered in this chapter, as well as an insatiable curiosity, exploration is essential: the underlying root causes of challenges must be surfaced in order for transformation and systemic change to occur. Don't rush through this stage—it can start even before you meet a client and can continue simultaneously with the relationship-building phase described in Chapter Five. I have usually felt that I needed a couple of months to get to know a new site, even in a district in which I've worked for seventeen years.

So what's to explore? There's the history of the school or district where you'll be coaching, its successes and struggles, the history of leadership, the demographics and changes in demographics of communities served, and so on. You'll also want to know as much as possible about the individuals you'll coach, as well as about the teams to which they belong. Think of these as stories that you'll gather, not necessarily truths. Finally, you'll strive to surface the formal and informal systems that are at play at a site—you need to know what is connected to what and how decisions and actions in the past and in other spheres influence what your client is experiencing.

An Abundance of Data

This stage of coaching will be marked by moments in which you may feel overwhelmed by the complexity of the picture that's developing—that's a good sign! It means you're gathering a lot of data. Your exploration should reveal the equity issues that your client is facing as well as those that are systemic in the site and/or district. You'll also uncover the site's and client's assets and have enough information to create a work plan (see Chapter Seven). You'll also expand your awareness about who you need to be and what you need to be mindful of in order to be an effective coach with this client.

At this stage, work on gathering information to respond to the questions in Exhibit 6.3 (the data-gathering tool at the end of the chapter). This might take a month or two. At the end of the stage of exploration, I offer a Coach Reflection: Stage of Exploration (also in Exhibit 6.3) to process the data you've gathered and the information you've learned.

USEFUL LENSES FOR THIS STAGE

The lens of systemic oppression raises questions of power, presence, position, and patterns. We explore who holds positions of power in a classroom or school and how power is held. We look at how different groups—teachers, students, girls, boys, African Americans, Latinos, and so on—are positioned in relationship to power and whether they are present or not present in a variety of conversations. We examine leadership positions and explore how those were created and who holds them. We look and listen for a multiplicity of voices, particularly voices that represent the community that the school serves. We look at who is present and who is absent from positions of leadership, on lists of honor students and suspensions, in special education classes, in student government, and so on. Finally, we look for patterns — we look at the data we've surfaced and consider how it reflects historical patterns of oppression; we consider whether systemic oppression is replicated or ruptured in the context we're investigating.

The lens of systems thinking is indispensable at this stage and also a tricky thing to use. It'll take some practice to see the complex webs of systems that exist at the present moment and throughout time in order to determine the most effective place to work from. As you explore and ask questions, follow the leads that come up and ask more questions — with the teacher who is frustrated because her students aren't doing well on the English language development tests, ask what curriculum she uses, who determined that curriculum, how she was trained in it, how it is differentiated, and so on. You are unraveling complex problems, and your inquiry will take you into the domains of resources, PD and capacity development, communication and information, national education policy and legislation, and so on. These are systems, and the first step is to identify them.

The lens of inquiry is essential, because we'll be asking a lot of questions at this stage. In order to gather the data I'll need, I must be mindful of how I ask questions and explore many perspectives. The lens of inquiry will also remind me that I'll never have all the information I want and at some point I'll need to start acting.

Gathering data is not a dry emotional experience, however. As coaches start to see painful situations and hear disturbing stories, a range of feelings can surface — sadness, anger, frustration, and impatience — and conflicting feelings can emerge about the clients we're supposed to coach. It's essential that coaches have places and people with whom they can process these emotions so that we can help clients explore their behaviors and beliefs and impact the experience of children in schools.

TEN STEPS IN EXPLORATION

The following ten steps can surface a pile of information about your client and his context and provide suggestions for how to document your discoveries and record your reflections. As in all aspects of coaching, the coach needs to use her judgment about the order or sequence of these activities and what the impact of engaging in them might be on her client's emerging trust of the coach. Finally, what's described here reflects the ideal situation for a coach; however, it's not always the case that a coach can do this much research and reflection before being asked to "start."

 Administrators: these ten steps can also be useful for an administrator new to a site.

1. Gather Relevant Documents

Create a binder for all the relevant documents you'll gather about a classroom, school, and district. You'll want the type of things a teacher or principal might use to guide decision making: calendars, schedules, organizational maps, descriptors of roles and responsibilities, professional development plans and calendars, curriculum maps, pacing guides, power standards, assessment tools, report cards, site plans, vision and mission statements, strategic district plans, and so on. You want to note what exists and what doesn't exist, what parameters for decision making are in place and, if possible, who determined those.

It is also important that you explore your client's understandings and feelings about these documents. Does the new teacher you are coaching know that curriculum maps exist at her site? Does the principal agree with the district's strategic plan? Did he have any input into it, or is he being asked to implement something that's not aligned to his site's needs? Does the site have a vision and/or mission statement that directs the work of the staff? Are there pacing guides for the math and English departments, but nothing to guide the instruction of history and science teachers? Does the principal expect that all teachers fully adopt the new curriculum, or is there flexibility? You'll need to explore what these documents mean to various stakeholders, how they feel about them, and how they're actually implemented.

What all of these documents should yield is insight into systems, structures, and decision making. You'll need this big picture. Knowing it will increase your credibility, ability to support and guide your client, and alignment with larger site and district goals and initiatives.

2. Gather and Analyze Formal Data

Coaches should not necessarily be "driven by data," but coaches need to be aware of data. Gather as much data as possible: data on graduation rates, the percentage of students promoted to the following grade, attendance data, suspension and expulsion reports, standardized test score data, internal district assessment data, English language competency data, reports on special education populations, data on socioeconomic status of students, neighborhood and city demographics, and so on. Search national, state, and county databases, ask for access to a site's printed reports (probably in those dusty binders in the principal's office),and ask teachers for access to grading systems, behavior tracking systems, and so on. You want to be inundated with multiple forms of data.

Once the data is piled on your desk (or computer desktop), do some analysis. Read through the data looking for patterns, outliers, and surprises. Compile the questions that arise. Follow the leads that surface. Data analysis is a puzzle to organize—keep sorting and sifting and thinking as the picture comes together.

You also need to explore how your clients think and feel about the data, and how they use it. Is your coachee driven by data? Does she display it on her classroom door? What kinds of data does she gather? How does she communicate data to her students and their parents? How does she explain and interpret the data? How does it inform her teaching? How often does she gather data?

Given that data is at the crux of the battle over how to reform, fix, or transform schools, and given that some think of a data as a four-letter word while others hold it as a Bible, coaches need to be very attuned to their client's data-related beliefs and behaviors. Without this understanding, you won't be clear on how to use data—not what you've gathered and analyzed or the data you will continue to gather. You'll need to make some agreements with your client about what kinds of data to gather and how often, and how these data will be used. This topic is addressed in Chapter 7.

3. Initiate Informal Conversations

You'll want to become familiar with the school grounds where you'll coach, and as you wander around you can initiate conversations with parents, staff members, and students. Ask general, open-ended questions such as: How are things going for you this year? How's that new reading program working for your students? How have you dealt with the latest budget cuts? How's your child doing in third grade? You want to hear from a variety of stakeholders.

Whether you coach a teacher or principal, you'll want to hear from students. Ultimately, your efforts are going to affect them. Let your client know you'll be doing this, and then ask students what they appreciate most about their school, teachers, and principal, what they are learning, what concerns they have about their school, and so on. Get really curious about the experience for children, and ask as many questions as you can.

The purpose for doing this is to build relationships and expand your understanding of the site. Furthermore, because you are perceived as an "outsider," sometimes people will share information that they won't share elsewhere. As long as you use these data to help you better understand your client's context, it's okay. Just be careful not to engage in gossip or share what you heard elsewhere.

4. Uncover Knowledge, Skills, and Passions

In addition to getting to know your client as a professional and understanding his personality and psychological profile, you also want to know who your client is outside of school. What are his additional interests, passions, areas of expertise, skills, and abilities? Some of these may have surfaced if you asked the suggested questions in Exhibit 6.1.

This information allows you to do several things. Hopefully, you'll find some connections to your client, which can be really helpful to have on tap when coaching gets tough. They remind us that our clients have many sides to them — they are also parents, world travelers, musicians — people with a variety of dreams and aspirations and passions. As coaches, we will need these reminders if we become frustrated with our clients.

This information also opens another set of coaching tools. One principal I coached felt very uncomfortable having hard conversations with her staff, though in high school and college she had been an actress. Because I knew this about her, when she expressed anxiety about delivering difficult news to her staff, I reminded her of the skills she already had. I asked how she'd prepared for performances, how she'd managed nervousness, what specific actions she took before and during shows to manage her discomfort. Had I not taken the time and been intentional about figuring out who this principal was outside of school, I would not have been able to build this bridge to her prior knowledge.

As a coach, you can help people see the parallels between what they already know how to do and what they are trying to do better. You can help them transfer knowledge, understanding, skills, and beliefs. If you're working with a teacher who runs marathons, then in November, when that teacher is exhausted, overwhelmed, and doesn't know how she'll make it through the year, you can remind her that she already knows a lot about perseverance. You can instantly shift her thinking because of what you know about her. Everyone we work with knows a lot more and can do a lot more than we think. It's our job as coaches to find out what it is that they know, care about, can do, and are committed to, and then to use that information to help them move their practice.

One way to elicit your client's history, skills, and passions is to ask for stories. Simply framing a question as "Tell me a story about . . ." is very inviting.

Exhibit 6.1. Storytelling Prompts for the Exploration Stage

- What's been your favorite place to live, and why?
- Where was the most difficult place you lived and why?
- Where is home to you?
- What's the most significant thing that's happened in the last month in your life?
- What's the best thing about your life right now? What's one thing you'd love to change?
- Tell me a story from your life that would give me a picture of who you really are. What is an event that shaped you as a person?
- Tell me about someone who has helped you become the person you are today. Who has really influenced your life, and how?
- If you could go back in time and meet any historical figure, who would it be, and why?

5. Explore Beliefs about Change

In an early conversation with a new client, I ask many of the following questions. I need to know as soon as possible how my client thinks and feels about change. As you read these questions over, you might reflect on your own experiences—as coaches, we also need to be aware of our own beliefs about change.

- Tell me about a positive change you've made in your life as an adult, something that you felt good about, such as a change in how you eat, manage time, or exercise.

How did this change come about? What prompted it? What were the bumps and obstacles along the way? How did you negotiate them? At what point did you realize: "I've changed!"? How does it feel to have accomplished this change? What did you learn about yourself in the process?

- Tell me about a new skill you learned as an adult—maybe it was how to bake bread, surf, or create PowerPoint presentations? What the process was like for you? What feelings came up? What was challenging? What did you learn about yourself as a learner?

The ways clients tell these stories expose beliefs and feelings that help me be an effective coach. Do the stories reveal that change was painful, relentless, and difficult to attain? Was it something they charged right into, eager and enthusiastic, or where they dragged off, perhaps pressured to change when their blood pressure skyrocketed? Were there key people in the client's life who supported her and encouraged her? Is she driven by goals, and does she approach change analytically?

I also listen carefully for how a client goes about learning. Did he seek specific, precise instructions on a new skill? Did he learn to bake bread by attending a class, reading a book, watching a friend, or did he just start mixing up ingredients and throw them in the oven? And how did he feel about the challenges? How does he communicate and celebrate his success?

After inviting personal stories of change and learning, I ask a few questions to explore my client's intellectual and theoretical beliefs about how social change happens. Underneath our daily activities are deeply held beliefs about justice and power. As a coach, one of my primary tasks is to surface those beliefs, because sometimes they are beneficial, but other times they hinder our efforts. I begin to excavate these beliefs with these questions:

- What are your thoughts about how social change happens?
- How do you think transformation happens?
- Name a historical leader whom you admire and would follow.
- Can you share an example of a historical social change that you find inspiring?

I listen for how a client perceives a power structure, how he understands the role or agency of an individual, and how he feels about the rate of change ("Change is so slow!" or "Change can happen overnight"). I listen for beliefs about relationships among groups of people working together and those who hold power.

A primary goal in coaching is to bring belief systems to the surface of our consciousness. Beliefs are powerful things — at their worst, they hold us back when they live in the shadows; at their best, they can propel us forward. In coaching we look at how beliefs are working, examine the results we're getting from holding them, consider tweaking one or two, giving up a few, or we think about how to use them as fuel to keep on going. We look at our actions and consider how our beliefs align with what we actually do, and we consider whether there are areas of misalignment. Beliefs about change are instrumental to draw out as you begin engaging with a client on a change effort.

6. Offer Personality and Psychological Self-Assessments

A number of valuable tools are available for free that can help us get a deeper insight into our client's personality and psychology.

 Administrators: These assessments are useful tools for understanding a staff. The Compass Points activity is invaluable when developing a team.

The Myers-Briggs Type Indicator (MBTI) is a widely used personality assessment that helps us understand how we perceive the world, make sense of it, and make decisions. There are several free online questionnaires to identify your type, and many articles available to help interpret the results. When a client is willing to share his type, it can be very insightful for a coach. The more we know about a client's personality, the better we can coach.

Another quick personality inventory is the North, South, East, and West: Compass Points activity (which can be downloaded from the National School Reform Faculty website at www.nsrfharmony.org or found on my website.) This is an invaluable tool to use when working with a team and can also be used with individuals. Ask your client what direction she is most like when at work, at home, with friends, and so forth. Then you can ask the questions to prompt reflection on how your client's personality affects the way she works with others.

The field of positive psychology has influenced coaching and has much to offer our practice. It focuses on what is working in our emotional lives and how things ended up going well for us (as opposed to psychology's traditional approach of studying pathology and treating mental illness). One of the founders of this movement, Dr. Martin Seligman, offers over a dozen free well-being questionnaires on his website (www.authentichappiness.sas.upenn.edu) that help people identify their strengths, what makes them happy, what gives them satisfaction, and so on. I often refer clients to these questionnaires and suggest specific ones such as the VIA Signature Strengths Questionnaire, the Grit Survey, and the Work-Life Questionnaire. I let them know that they might gain new perspectives on who they are and that if they'd like to share the results or their reflections on what they learned, they're welcome to. I have never had a client who did not want to share his results and reflections; they have always experienced these surveys as extremely helpful, as yielding new insights, and as generating ideas for how to improve their lives.

7. Observe the Client

First, ask your client for permission and then observe him in a variety of contexts—greeting parents in the morning, escorting students to lunch, talking with colleagues in the staff room, and so on. As you observe your client, stay in the mind-set of an explorer. Look for strengths, try to get to know who he is and what his work is about, and be mindful of your own lapses in judgment about what you're uncovering.

If you're coaching a teacher, you want to observe her teaching, but this is a tricky to negotiate. You want to make sure you have permission—dropping by unannounced and uninvited can be damaging to an emerging coaching relationship. You also want to establish some agreements with your coachee about what you will observe for and when you will talk about the observation. For the majority of educators, regardless of how long they've been in this profession, being observed is scary. Our professional culture is not one in which we have been regularly observed, nor do we agree on what constitutes "good" teaching. Therefore, it's critical that your observations—especially the first ones—are planned, structured, and focused. (Chapter 12 discusses observations in greater detail.)

If you're coaching a principal, observe him interacting with as many different stakeholders as possible—with teachers, custodians, secretaries, parents, students, and so on. Pay attention to who he engages with, what he says to people, how he says it, how people relate to him, and how he moves through different spaces. It also helps to observe a principal with his supervisors and colleagues. You might ask a principal-client if you can shadow him for a day. Your empathy will increase tremendously, especially if you've never been in this role. If you have been a principal, it will be useful to get a deeper understanding of his unique context so that you don't use assumptions in your coaching from your own experiences.

Within every context that you observe your client, there are power dynamics at play. Looking through a lens of systemic oppression can help clarify these. As your understanding of the equity issues in the classroom or school become clearer, look for information about how your client manages those: Does she actively interrupt them? Does she seem to be oblivious to them? Does she unconsciously play into them and uphold them? Does she notice them but feel powerless?

Whether you're coaching one teacher at a site, multiple teachers, or a principal, you'll also want to get a sense of the staff culture. Meetings are a key to observe—whole staff, grade level, department, leadership team meetings, professional development sessions, and so on. You'll want an understanding of the social context in which your clients work and how they engage with their colleagues. As you get to know your client, you'll look for alignment between who they say they want to be and how they show up in various contexts. To coach for transformation, we need to coach our clients as they move through different spheres.

8. Conduct Formal Interviews and Surveys

If you are coaching a principal and you get permission, it can be very helpful to conduct a few interviews with key stakeholders. Frame it as something like: "It can really be helpful for me to get some additional perspectives on your site. Are there a couple of staff members who you feel would be useful for me to speak with in order to understand this school's history, assets, or challenges? Or someone on-site who you feel knows you well and supports you?" This is essential if you do whole-school coaching and work with teachers, administrators, and teams. Establish explicit agreements about confidentiality, and be very clear with the person you interview and your client about whether the data will be shared with anyone else.

As you engage in interviews, remember that what you hear is one person's perspective, one person's story of events and characters. Their story is their reality, and it might be a reality shared by many, but as you are gathering data you need to remember that it's only one story. It can be hard if you hear a teacher say, "The principal is a dictator. We all want him removed. He is destroying our community," and you are coaching that principal. Chapter 8, on listening, addresses these challenges.

Surveys can be a powerful way for a coach and teacher or principal to gather data and feedback. If given in the beginning of coaching work, they can be used as baseline data and can be repeated three or six months later to compare results.

The purpose for doing surveys is two-fold: the coach gets more data about the site (classroom or school) and about relationships between people (teachers and students or teachers and staff). Second, the relationship between coach and client deepens as they process the data together and use it to make decisions about a work plan. One reason surveys can be useful is that if done though an online tool, the responses can be anonymous. This can allow data to surface that might not arise in conversations or interviews. Surveys also enable everyone's voice and perspective on an issue to be heard.

Exhibit 6.2 offers a short list of general, simple questions that can be given to a school's staff if you are coaching a principal. Chapter 11 offers other sample surveys and discusses their use in more depth.

Exhibit 6.2. Survey for Staff (When a Principal Is the Client)

1. What do you appreciate most about your principal?
2. What do you think are his or her strengths? What does he or she do best?
3. When have you felt appreciated by your principal? How does he or she show his or her appreciation?
4. What would you like to see your principal do more of?
5. What do you enjoy most about your job?
6. What would you like to do more of in your job?

---

9. Look for the Fires

As you talk to stakeholders, gather data and documents, and get to know a site, look and listen for the "fires" that teachers and administrators are frantically trying to put out. Fires are clues about systems that are breaking down. We'll hear them expressed by administrators in comments like these:

"My teachers gossip so much!"

"Parents don't come for report card conferences."

"I never eat lunch because I'm always on yard supervision."

"Teachers are supposed to turn in lesson plans, and only about 20 percent do so."

"We bought thousands of books for guided reading, and no one is using them."

In a classroom, common fires might include the following:

The teacher who looks like she's playing whack-a-mole, managing student behavior as it pops up and disrupts class, bouncing around the room.

The teacher is looking for materials, rifling through piles on his desk, in his bag, in the boxes on the counters, mumbling "I know your tests are here somewhere," as students get restless.

The new teacher who is informed that "grades are due next Monday." She confesses to her coach that she'd completely forgotten she'd need to do grades and she hasn't really given her students any tests and is behind on grading homework and isn't sure she's seen the report card anyway.

The teacher who is frantically cutting out construction paper triangles as students come in after recess.

Underneath these fires and complaints are systems that are breaking down, failing, or don't exist. In the stage of exploration we take notice of them and document them, we listen for those that are recurring and expressed by many, and we might start asking a few questions to start exploring root causes.

The first step in coaching for systemic change is to identify the current reality at a site. It helps to have an understanding of the common systems in use in schools, such as resource allocation, professional development, onboarding of new students and staff, communication and information, discipline and school culture, assessment, and data.

The authors of *Blended Coaching* write, "The coach's job is to help the client get out of the habit of putting out fires and instead to invest time and energy into installing automatic sprinkler systems and removing fuel and sources of ignition" (Bloom, Castagna, Warren, and Moir, 2005, p. 106). To coach for system change, we must start by cataloguing the fires.

10. Engage in Self-Awareness Exercises for Coaches

This last step will have the greatest impact if taken up simultaneously with data gathering and also if used as a reflection tool at the end.

First, I highly recommend that coaches explore the self-awareness tools, survey, and questionnaires referenced in step 8, earlier in this chapter. They're exceptionally helpful to increase our self-awareness, and if we're going to suggest that clients use them, we need to try them first.

I also encourage coaches to keep a reflective journal. While I'm aware that writing is my preferred way of processing my experiences, I also believe it's a key element of a reflective practice. If you keep a coaching journal, then as you gather the data described in this chapter, record your thoughts, feelings, questions, wonderings, fears, hopes, anxieties, and excitement as you gather data. Just notice — and name — your responses.

Once you've reached a level of saturation in what you've gathered — perhaps you recognize that you have enough to be able to move on to the work plan (Chapter Seven) — then you might respond to the questions in Coach Reflection: Stage of Exploration in Exhibit 6.3 at the end of this chapter.

MOVING ON TO PLANNING

At some point, you will recognize that you have enough information to construct a work plan — maybe not all the information you would like, but enough. In the process of gathering data, you've also been developing trust with your client, and at some point you may feel that your client is ready to focus and deepen the work. The process of constructing the work plan will continue to surface information about your client and build trust.

COMMON CHALLENGES AND HELPFUL RESPONSES

The biggest challenges in the exploration stage are often how we as coaches respond to the data we discover. There are rare occasions when the things a coach uncovers present such challenges that she needs to request a different coaching assignment. However, most of the time the challenges indicate an area of growth for the coach, and provided there is support for the development of the coach, these can be worked on.

Challenge: I'm assigned to coach a principal who seems to single out African American boys. The site's suspension data confirm this, performance indicators show that African American males are failing at twice the rate of other students of color, and I've seen the principal respond to the behavior of black boys far more aggressively and severely than any other group. When I see the way this principal behaves, I feel outraged. As the mother of an African American boy, I just don't know if I can coach this client. I don't think I have the patience.

Lens of Emotional Intelligence. This is a difficult situation, and thinking about it through the lens of *the coach's* emotional intelligence can help. Each coach brings his personal experience and current realities into the work. While most coaches have emotional responses to the inequities they see in schools, when the children affected by them are this close to home, it's going to be even more painful. The anger that we feel can act in two ways: it can make us ineffective, or it can be fuel for our commitment to transformation. In order for it to serve us, we need to find ways to process and release the emotions that arise. Coaches must have support—from another coach, a team of coaches, or a manager.

There is a tremendous opportunity here. If you develop a trusting relationship with this client, if he is open and receptive to coaching, then you might be uniquely positioned to work on these challenging areas with him and perhaps improve the experience for African American boys. Everyone is capable of reflection and change when the conditions are right for learning. However, you definitely need to build a support network if one doesn't already exist and explore ways to process these feelings. This won't be an easy assignment. You might consider using the lenses of emotional intelligence to reflect on your own capacity to manage this client.

That said, I don't believe we have to prioritize our work over our role as a parent and our maternal inclinations. You don't have to be a martyr, and perhaps there's another coach who could work more productively with this client.

Challenge: I don't think my client should be a teacher. What should I do?

Lens of Inquiry and Lens of Systems Thinking. Actually, you don't really get to do much of anything. A coach is not positioned to make decisions about what someone should do or engage in a conversation with anyone who does make decisions. In some ways, a coach doesn't get to have opinions or judgments. Who are we to decide what someone should or shouldn't do?

Using the lens of inquiry can help us manage this situation: Who is defining the problem? Just you? What data do you have on the problem? From what perspective are you seeing this? How is it connected to other things? The lens of inquiry can open up other directions for you to explore your own judgment.

This scenario also raises a number of systems issues that a coach might be able to play a role in addressing. Applying the lens of systems thinking can surface questions about how teachers are observed and evaluated, how expectations for teaching are communicated, how and when conversations around teaching happen, and how peers give each other feedback. These questions can be raised in conversations with site administrators or leadership teams and can invite a broad inquiry into what happens in classrooms.

Unfortunately, this situation is not uncommon. I have worked with a number of educators who were very unhappy in their roles and who weren't very effective at meeting the expectations laid out for them. Under their care, students were not thriving. I didn't question whether they "should" be a principal or teacher, but rather, whether the job was a good fit for their interests, skills, personality, and needs. I'd invite them into a conversation on why they went into teaching, how they felt about it now, and what they wanted in their lives. I made sure to have this conversation without overlaying my own judgment and personal desire that they'd just quit (I did have those) so that the client could honestly engage in this reflection. I have coached a handful of teachers and principals who have left the field of education; their conversations with me led them to this decision, which ultimately was the best thing for them and for their students. That was about all I could do.

Exhibit 6.3. Data-Gathering Tool for a Teacher or a Principal Client

This information can be gathered from state, district, or site databases, if available, as well as by interviewing and/or surveying staff members.

Data on Students

Student enrollment data for previous five to ten years
- How many students were enrolled ten years ago?
- How many students are enrolled this year?
- Have there been any changes in where the student population is coming from?
- What explanations are there for these changes?

Student enrollment data by ethnicity, socioeconomic status, and language fluency for the previous five to ten years

- Have there been significant changes in any of these areas in the last five to ten years?

Student attendance data for previous three to five years

- Are there any grades that struggle with chronic absences—less than 90 percent attendance over the year?
- Are absence rates higher for boys or girls? For any racial/ethnic subgroup or other student population?

Student suspension and expulsion data

- Have there been any significant changes in these data over the last three to five years?
- Are suspensions or expulsions higher in any grade level?
- Are rates disproportionate for boys or girls, for any racial and ethnic subgroup, or for any other student population?

Annual test scores for previous five to ten years

- Annual test scores for previous five to ten years disaggregated by race and ethnicity, gender, socioeconomic status, language fluency, and special education designation

Data on Staff

Teacher assignments and demographics for past five to ten years

- What is the site's annual turnover rate?
- How many teachers have been at the site for over seven years? For over four years? For less than two years?
- How often have those who have been at the site for over four years changed grade level or subject area? Do teachers frequently change positions?
- What is the racial and ethnic composition of the teaching staff? Gender composition? Age breakdown?
- What percentage of the teaching staff has a background similar, in some way, to the student population?

Administrative—principal, assistant principal, dean, and other—assignments and demographics for the past five to ten years

- How long have the current principal and assistant principal been in their roles?
- What is the site's history with respect to administrators? Do administrators turn over often? Have staff played a role in selecting their administrators?
- What is the racial and ethnic and gender breakdown of the administrators at the site? Do any of them share similar backgrounds with the student population?

Collaboration

- How do teachers collaborate with each other? How often? In what configurations?
- What happens during collaboration time?
- How often and for what purpose do administrators meet with teachers?

Documents and Artifacts

Any of the following will help construct a deeper understanding of the site:

School's vision and mission statements

School site plan

School's goals: student achievement, attendance, culture, and climate

Instructional areas of focus for year and goals

School's master schedule and bell schedule

School's discipline policy and behavior expectations

School calendar

Professional development plan and calendar; professional development providers
    and partners

Staff roster or staff roles and responsibilities document

Staff organization chart

Descriptions of different teams that exist at the site—leadership teams, parent organiza-
    tions, and so forth

Also ask: Are there any other documents that would help me develop a deeper understand-
    ing of your school?

Reflection on Data Gathering: Stage of Exploration

Observations of Client

1. When and where have you observed your client? What did you notice?
2. What strengths and positive qualities did you notice?
3. What kinds of power dynamics did you notice?
4. What questions are coming up for you about your client?

Observations of Meetings

1. What kinds of meetings have you observed?

2. What stage of team formation have you observed in different teams?
3. Where are the bright spots in teams and meetings?

Informal Conversations

1. Who have you had informal conversations with?
2. What kinds of things have you asked and heard?

Interviews

1. Who have you formally interviewed?
2. What are some patterns in the comments you have heard?
3. What surprised you, what questions came up for you, and what do you want more information about?

Surveys

1. What are some patterns in survey responses?
2. What surprised you, what questions came up for you, and what do you want more information about?

Formal Data

1. How does your client feel about data?
2. What kinds of data are used at this site? How are they used?

Documents

1. What kinds of documents did you gather? Were they readily available?
2. What were you surprised by?
3. Were there any notable gaps in documents?
4. Does your client seem to use these documents for guidance and decision making?

Personality and Psychological Assessments

1. What did you learn about your client's personality and psychological profile from the suggested tools?
2. Which of these learnings might be useful to remember and access during coaching?

Knowledge, Skills, Passions

1. What kinds of knowledge, skills, and passions does your client have outside of his or her professional life?
2. What does she or he already know how to do well?

Coach Reflection: Stage of Exploration

1. What am I looking forward to in coaching this client?
2. What might be challenging about working with this client?
3. Which coaching skills might I need to develop in order to be effective with this client?
4. What additional knowledge do I need to bone up on in order to support this client?
5. On a scale of 1 to 10, how willing am I to coach this client? What is it that is keeping my motivation below a 10? What could I do to increase my motivation?
6. What is it about me—my background, experiences, race/ethnicity, gender, age, or other—that might be an asset in my coaching with this client?
7. What is it about me—my background, experiences, race/ethnicity, gender, age, or other—that might present a challenge in my coaching with this client?
8. Is this client likely to push any of my buttons?
9. Who does this client need me to be? What would that look like, sound like, feel like—to me and the client? Can I visualize being this person? Am I willing to be this person?
10. Who does this school-community need me to be? What would that look like, sound like, feel like to me and the school-community? Am I willing to be this person?
11. Are there any contradictions between who my client needs me to be and who the school-community needs me to be? How might I deal with these contradictions?

Coach Self-Reflection

Complete the Coach Reflection: Stage of Exploration in the next section.

1. Judging by the self-reflection you did during and after gathering data, what will be the most important things for you to remain aware of as you proceed with coaching?
2. What are your two biggest take-aways from this reflection?

CHAPTER 7

Developing a Work Plan: How Do I Determine What to Do?

Read this when:

- You've completed many, if not all, of the suggested inventories and activities in Chapter Six, which helped you understand your client and his site
- You're a little overwhelmed by what you've heard, observed, and learned and are unsure how to proceed
- You're an administrator guiding others in focusing work assignments

WHAT ROLE DOES A WORK PLAN PLAY?

What distinguishes effective coaching from other kinds of professional development activities is that coaching is an ongoing effort focused on developing a specific and agreed-on set of skills or practices. Though a client might experience coaching as a series of meaningful conversations, the coach is consciously working within a structure and toward an end. The work plan is the structure that holds the conversations, questions, and actions that make up coaching. It is a foundational element of the intentional and directed nature of professional development. Without a work plan, a coach can feel lost and overwhelmed.

I've occasionally heard teachers reflecting on previous experiences with coaches: "We just sat around and talked," or "Every time we met, we talked about something different. I got feedback on every area of teaching." When coaching is unfocused, or when the purpose for coaching is unclear, both the coach and client can feel unsatisfied.

When a teacher or principal agrees to receive coaching, she expects growth or change in her practice. Some clients might be clear about what they want to work on—such as classroom management, authentic assessment, or communication skills—but many will know only that they want to improve. The coach's task is to listen carefully and engage in a process of exploration and assessment, so that together with the new client you can create a learning or work plan.

A good work plan makes both the coach and the client feel excited, energized, and focused. It includes a vision—a compelling picture of the success and accomplishment that can become a reality in the near future, as well as an action plan—the specific steps that they anticipate will get them there. This document brings the coach and client together: it is the project they embark on through their partnership. It allows each of them to identify her specific roles and contributions. This plan becomes the external entity to which they are both accountable. Above all, a good work plan makes coach and client eager to dive in and begin coaching.

Throughout the stage of exploration we engaged in exercises and activities to better understand the client we'll be working with and the site he is connected to. Although the coach should come to discussions about a work plan having analyzed and reflected on qualitative and quantitative data that might indicate areas for the client's development, we don't determine the work plan alone. It should be co-constructed with the client.

The plan is developed through a number of conversations exploring the gaps in the client's will, skill, knowledge, and capacity. As we engage in this process, we are still enrolling the client and getting him to buy in to coaching. Creating the work plan is a vehicle to do this and therefore shouldn't be rushed. This chapter will describe the components of a good work plan and the steps to create it, then will offer examples of coaching conversations at this stage. There is a sample work plan in Exhibit 7.1 at the end of this chapter.

Coaching Journal, 9/17/08

Teresa seems thrilled to have a coach. She's invited me into her class to observe several times, and she says she's in this profession for the long haul. I'm excited to work with her. But when I go into her class, I have no idea where to start. She's good with the kids, but she's all over the place. Her lessons are disjointed, she doesn't have materials prepared, she does direct instruction and then releases the kids without checking their understanding, she crams way too much into a lesson, she does little formative assessment, she diverges into speeches that keep the kids' attention but take her way off her plans. Last week I saw two kids dozing in the back rows, and she never noticed. Her desk is a disaster zone. The office staff are frustrated because she never does attendance on time. She grossly mispronounces the Arab students' names. She's teaching a novel that's not even recommended for this grade level; in fact, it's used with next year's curriculum and that teacher is going to be irritated that the kids already read it. I have no idea where to start coaching her.

USEFUL LENSES FOR THIS STAGE

At this stage of coaching, there are three specific lenses that are worth taking a long look through. The first is the lens of change management. We use the questions for this lens to guide our own thinking and to guide our clients toward goal areas. While it can be tempting for clients to take on a massive challenge, and while we want to encourage them to push themselves, we also need to be mindful of the conditions for change. We're responsible for making sure we can guide our clients to meet their goals. The lens of change management helps us ensure that the goals are realistic and attainable.

The lens of inquiry helps clients identify a goal area that they truly own and is not the result of

When we exercise the courage to set and act on goals that are connected to principles and conscience, we tend to achieve positive results. Over time, we create an upward spiral of confidence and courage. Our commitment becomes stronger than our moods. We build the courage to set increasingly challenging, even heroic goals.

O'NEILL AND CONZEMIUS
(2006, P. 152)

external pressure. The questions for this lens can contribute to a goal that is strategic, meaningful, and relevant to the client.

The lens of adult learning is essential to determine a client's zone of proximal development (see Glossary). If we don't identify where a client is in her learning, we can't plan for and design the kinds of learning experiences that will help her meet her goals. This lens is invaluable.

As you create a work plan it can help to keep these three lenses at close reach and reflect on them as you move through the following steps.

DEVELOPING A WORK PLAN

Ten Steps to Developing a Work Plan

1. Identify areas for coaching: what's the big picture?

2. Identify standards and criteria

3. Determine a SMARTE goal

4. Identify high-leverage activities

5. Break down the learning

6. Determine indicators of progress

7. Develop coaching theories of action

8. Determine coach's goals

9. Compile resources

10. Present and celebrate the plan

Before I describe what happens at each step and offer examples of these conversations, I want to name an essential understanding when developing a work plan: although it is described as a sequential process, it is not. It is presented this way in order to explain each component of the plan's creation, but the process must also be flexible and circular. For example, you may guide a client through the steps of creating goals, first identifying high-leverage activities, and then while discussing the indicators of progress with the client, you might both realize that the goals need to be modified. In fact, at each stage of creating the work plan, the coach should reflect on earlier steps and consider whether the emerging plan makes sense. Finally, once the plan is created, there are many potential reasons for it to need revising, narrowing, or amending as the work with the client develops. Exhibit 7.1 at the end of this chapter is an example of a coaching work plan.

1. Identify Areas for Coaching: What's the Big Picture?

First we identify a couple of broad areas of pedagogical or leadership practice that our client wants to work on. For example, for a teacher, these could be within one of the following domains: lesson or unit design, teaching the Common Core State Standards, classroom management, academic language, checking for understanding, data analysis, classroom culture, routines and procedures, or others. A principal might want to work on distributing leadership, communication, professional development, resource management, building teams, accountability, inspiring and motivating staff, or his own emotional intelligence.

Coaches also need to take into account schoolwide initiatives or expectations about what clients work on. If, for example, a school is focusing on cooperative learning structures and all teachers are expected to use these strategies, we'll raise this matter with our client as a possible area of focus. A coach can also help bridge an external mandate with a client's authentic area of need or interest. For example, if we're working with a first-year teacher who is concerned about her classroom management skills, but who has been told to focus on cooperative learning structures, we can coach the teacher on the management strategies that will allow her to effectively implement cooperative learning structures.

If coaching is connected to broader school- or district-level efforts, there is a greater possibility that coaching will be reinforced in professional development sessions, peer observations, and the like, and that we can better support our clients. This can also focus and narrow the scope of our work—and, in general, the narrower the better. However, if clients feel forced by their principal or district to implement practices or policies that they don't believe in, this can be challenging. In that case, a coach should probably start with a goal area that the client is authentically invested in.

When we're helping clients identify these areas, we also want to ensure that they are high-leverage areas to work in. A *high-leverage area* is one that has great potential for improving the experience and outcomes of students, particularly those who are struggling the most; it is also an area that, if addressed, would positively spill over into other areas—it would leverage other improvements. Improvements in many areas of teaching and leading can point to this end, and a coach needs to use her own knowledge to ensure this alignment and also make this explicit with a client. We always ask, "And what would that mean for students if your work improves in that area?"

The "Areas for Coaching" Conversation

Coach: It's been really helpful for me to learn about your school over the last month. I hear how much growth you made as a first-year principal, and I better understand the challenges you're facing this year. What are some of the leadership areas you'd like to continue working on that I might be able to support you in?

Principal: I don't know. There are so many, I don't know where to start. I need to get better at managing my school's budget, I need to do more classroom walkthroughs, our professional development is not what I want it to be, and I think I need to find a way to manage my stress better. I also feel like I don't hold people accountable in the way I should. And my supervisor has told me that I take on too much and need to distribute leadership. Ah! What should I focus on—can you just tell me?

Coach: This is an overwhelming job, I know. We're going to start with a couple bites at a time, and we'll determine some high-leverage areas to focus on. Answer this question without thinking too long: If you could develop your skills and grow in one of the areas you just named, which do you think would help you significantly as an individual?

Principal: Oh, managing my stress, no doubt.

Coach: OK—let's consider that one possible area for us to work on. From my experience coaching leaders, building capacity in managing stress does make a huge difference. Now what about your students? If you were to develop your capacities in another area that you named, which might make a big impact on students?

Principal: I can see how my leadership in all those areas affects kids, but I think if I were able to do more classroom walkthroughs, instruction would improve and that would benefit kids.

Coach: Tell me a little more about that.

Principal: Well, I think part of the problem is that I just don't know what's going on in classrooms. I'm embarrassed to admit that. If I had a better sense of what my teachers were struggling with, I'd also be able to deliver better professional development and I could give them more feedback. I feel confident in my ability to give teachers feedback. I think I've also been reluctant to distribute leadership because I'm not sure who is a strong teacher. I think I definitely need to get into classrooms more.

Coach: That's great to hear that you feel confident in giving feedback. And gathering more data on what's going on in classrooms is definitely a high-leverage area to work on. Let's hold those two general areas as possibilities for our work this year.

2. Identify Standards and Criteria

In conjunction with the conversation about goal areas, we'll need to determine if there are external standards and criteria that we could, or should, use — standards or rubrics of effective teaching, evaluation tools, administrator's leadership standards, or externally mandated improvement plans. These tools can be useful if they are developmental and growth-oriented, if the criteria are clear and concrete, and if the client feels they are authentic. However, if the client does not feel that the tools are valid or feels that they could be used for punitive measures, then we should use them only to the extent that we must. This can be a tricky negotiation. Coaches will need to explore how to make something like an improvement plan that has been handed down from the central office as meaningful and relevant as possible.

If measurement tools for teaching or administration don't exist, then a coach can select a tool with the client or create a new tool. Measurement tools can be helpful for framing a goal around practice, but are not essential.

3. Determine a SMARTE Goal

 Administrators: SMARTE goals are useful to guide the work of teachers, teams, and other staff working in schools.

Once we have identified one or two high-leverage areas the client would like to focus on — and whether we can use measurement tools such as standards or rubrics — then we'll work toward developing a goal. Unfortunately, teachers and principals may have had negative experiences with goal setting. For example, educators are often asked to create annual goals, which are submitted to a supervisor in the fall and are filed away and never discussed. Coaches need to know if the client has any distrust or cynicism about goals, and if he does, you need to address it. Creating goals with a coach should be invigorating. It's another step in supporting clients to envision and describe the improved-self they'll work toward. In the process of creating the goals, we also want to foreshadow how goals will be used and how often we'll reflect on them; this is important to get the client's buy-in.

> *SMART goals are gap-closing goals: We use them to attain a result that is different from what currently exists.*
>
> O'NEILL AND CONZEMIUS
> (2006, P. 43)

In order for a goal to be an effective tool in a client's transformation, the goal needs to be a good goal—a "SMART" goal. Jan O'Neill's and Anne Conzemius's (2006) book, *The Power of SMART Goals*, is an essential resource at this stage of coaching. While the term *SMART goal* has been around for a long time, these authors define the acronym as strategic and specific, measurable, attainable, results-based, and time-bound. Some organizations have added an E to represent equitable, thus the SMART*E* goal.

Strategic and Specific: A strategic goal is aligned, when possible, to larger efforts—to a school or district's goals. A strategic goal is also one that, if reached, will make a significant difference to students. In order to help a teacher or leader determine a strategic goal, a coach needs to apply his knowledge of content and instructional practice or of leadership practice.

A specific goal is focused, narrow, and targeted. It is the difference between "I will teach reading comprehension" and "I will teach students how to summarize nonfiction text."

It's essential that the goal be articulated as *a change in teacher or administrator practice*—not as improvement in student learning. We want to create goals that are fully within the sphere of influence where our own learning and growth are found. We want to articulate the connection between how our growth in practice will affect students' growth—and it's fine to include goals about our hopes for students' results when we meet our goals—but our client's goal always needs to be about her own practice as a teacher or leader.

Measurable: A measurable goal is critical. When our goals are not measurable, they can feel frustrating and unreachable. Many people have made goals to "get healthier," but without any specific, measurable ends, we often fail. In schools, it can be equally hard for teachers and leaders to recognize their growth and success because this element of a goal has not been articulated. When writing a measurable goal, be sure not to use any adjectives or adverbs as descriptors—those words create judgment- and opinion-based goals, and fact-based goals will be much more helpful here.

Attainable: Goals need to motivate and make us stretch, but they also need to be attainable. In order to support clients to create an attainable goal, a coach needs to have a good sense of where a client is in terms of skill development—we need to have ascertained his zone of proximal development, and we need to help him see what's just a few leaps out of reach. A coach must understand the dimensions of the gap between where our client is in a strategic area of practice and where he wants to get to. It's our responsibility to determine what it'll take to close this gap and to identify how much focus, time, energy, and resources we can put into helping our client close the gap. This is a tricky balance: we don't want to aim too low—we must have high expectations and believe that our client can make remarkable accomplishments, but we also don't want to set someone up for failure. This is why creating a SMARTE goal is much easier if there's a rubric and criteria to use; then a teacher can self-assess and identify an attainable stage that she'd like to reach.

Results-Based: A results-based goal compels us to explore the impact the goal could have. We can ask our client, "Imagine you've met the goal. What is the result?" This can help us distinguish between a process goal—"I will teach a unit on persuasive writing," and a goal that has a clear result—"I will give feedback to my students on a weekly basis that results in 95 percent of my students producing a persuasive essay that scores at least a 4 out of 5 on our rubric." A results-based goal means something to children, it can't be accomplished without teacher learning, and it is motivating.

Time-Bound: A time-bound goal is framed within a specific time period. A teacher, for example, may decide to improve relationships with families by having parent-teacher conferences. The difference between a time-bound goal is clear when we compare these two goals: "I will have parent-teacher conferences with all of my students," and "I will have one parent-teacher conference with the parent(s) of each of my students within the next two months." A time frame builds accountability and commitment. It helps us determine exactly what we need to do in order to be successful.

Equitable: An equitable goal is one that addresses the needs of students who are not succeeding, whose needs are not being met, or who traditionally have been outside the sphere of success. The entire goal itself might be aimed at supporting a population of students who are struggling—for example, English language learners or students who have learning disabilities or African American males—or there can be an element of the goal that specifically focuses on a segment of the population. The purpose of including this element in the goal is to bring focus and awareness to students who need additional support. A transformational coach is intentional about interrupting patterns of inequity and supporting the students whom our system has failed. This is another moment when a coach might apply her own knowledge about the experience of children at a site or in a district to guide a client through this process.

The most effective goals are those that focus on a clear change in practice. Some clients may want to focus, for example, on increasing their emotional intelligence, developing better relationships with colleagues, or managing stress. While these are worthy aspirations, when establishing a goal it is more effective to settle on an instructional or leadership practice that can be measured precisely. Emotional intelligence, stress, and relationships will arise in conversations about goals—most likely these will be key areas of growth to address *in order to meet goals*—but they should not be identified as the end goal.

A client can also create subgoals under the main goal. For example, a principal may decide that his end goal is a highly functioning leadership team. In order to meet this goal, the principal may need to set a subgoal about communication. He may recognize that he needs to communicate in a way that invites others to take leadership and expresses his receptivity to other ideas. This principal may know that he won't achieve his larger goal without working on these areas, and in that case he should formulate a subgoal. This kind of subgoal, however, is hard to measure—it is very subjective, but it is worth naming because this can be the zone in which transformational change happens. Subgoals about emotional intelligence and relationships are also hard to measure. Naming these areas as subgoals gives us an entry point into these conversations while also saving us from gathering hard evidence to prove that the goal was met.

The "Goal-Setting" Conversation

Creating a goal is done in collaboration with a client. Like all coaching conversations, it is also an opportunity to coach and continue building trust and, like all conversations, it helps to prepare beforehand (see Chapter Thirteen).

The following is part of my goal-setting conversation with Teresa, a first-year teacher. (We didn't have a specific performance rubric to use.)

Coach: Today we're going to try to determine a couple of goals for our work together this year.

Teacher: I need to be more organized. That's my goal. I'm a disaster all the time.

Coach: Teresa, if you were to meet this goal and become more organized, what would that look like?

Teacher: I'd always be able to find my papers. I'd have file folders set up, systems to track information, and the surfaces in my room would always be clear. I'd feel so much better.

Coach: How would that affect students?

Teacher: Well, I'd be calmer. I'd be able to find things fast and could give them back all the work they've turned in.

Coach: How would that affect their learning?

Teacher: I often lose work they've turned in or sometimes their tests. I don't have a good system to keep track of how they're doing. So if I was more organized, I'd be able to give them more timely and accurate information about how they are doing in my class.

Coach: That would be really high leverage! We know how important regular assessment data is for students. I'm wondering if that should be the goal area that we work on—tracking student learning and communicating assessment data to students?

Teacher: Yes, that is so important. I know assessment is my biggest area of growth.

Coach: And as you recognized, in order for you to reach this goal, you'll need to develop some organizational systems and routines.

Teacher: I agree. And that sounds much more exciting.

Coach: Of your school's instructional foci this year, which feels most relevant to you in connection with this goal?

Teacher: I think our writing goal. We're aiming to have more than 10 percent growth on our district's writing exam, and I want to see 15 percent growth for my English language learners (ELLs). I really care about that goal, and I think I'm already doing a pretty good job at teaching writing. It's just the feedback, the assessment piece I'm not great at. I need to just do it I don't know why I don't.

Coach: Great! Let's build on what you're already doing well. In terms of assessment, what might have a significant impact on your students?

Teacher: Sit down with them and talk about their writing more often, as well as give them more written feedback. And keep track of how they are doing.

Coach: Great. That's getting really specific. So far I hear that you want to provide verbal and written feedback to students on their writing assignments. Let's think about the time frame. How often do you want to do this?

Teacher: Every week. Definitely. I want to give them the feedback within two days of the time they turn in their assignments.

Coach: OK. How long do you think it'll take you to read and respond to all their assignments?

Teacher: Probably six hours.

Coach: So is doing that every week realistic?

Teacher: Probably not.

Coach: OK. What might be more realistic?

Teacher: I think every other week. I could do that.

Coach: Is this something you want to do all year? Provide feedback every other week?

Teacher: Definitely. But wait—if I miss one time, then have I failed my goal?

Coach: Our work is to make this possible—so that the systems and structures and routines are in place and you can meet this goal. I believe you can do it. What might be a realistic time frame for you to set up systems to track their progress?

Teacher: I think I need a couple months to get that figured out. I'm going to say after the first marking period.

Coach: OK—here's what I'm hearing so far. It sounds like we have two goals: (1) I provide verbal and written feedback to all of my students on their writing assignments every other week within two days of submission of their assignment for the entire school year. (2) By the end of the first marking period, I have created systems to track their progress on the writing standards. I use these systems for the entire school year. As a result of the feedback I provide students and the assessment systems that help me track their progress, all students make 10 percent growth on the writing exam, and the ELLs make 15 percent growth. Does that sound like what we've been talking about?

Teacher: It does. But now I'm getting nervous—that seems like a big goal.

Coach: It is. What other feelings are coming up for you?

Teacher: I guess it's exciting too. I know it would make a significant difference for kids. What do you think?

Coach: This is a focused, narrow goal. You've already started thinking about how you'll realize it. I believe you can meet it. Let's go for it! Let's start thinking through the action steps. OK?

Teacher: OK. If you're really going to help me meet it, then yes, let's go for it. And I'll get organized along the way, right?

Coach: Well, that's the next thing we're going to talk about: What are the actions you're going to need to take in order to meet these goals? Organization sounds like one of them.

---

4. Identify High-Leverage Activities

The next step is to identify the activities that will guide a client toward his goal. This happens in two parts—first, in a brainstorming conversation with the client, and then you can reflect on the work thus far and add other activities that might be helpful.

The "High-Leverage Activities" Conversation

Coach: Teresa, I'm really excited about working with you on this SMARTE goal. I know it has the potential to make a big difference for your students. Today we'll brainstorm activities that can lead to meeting this goal. Many of these are the coaching activities we'll do together, some you'll do alone, and some I'll do alone. I'll take notes today. What are your first thoughts about the kinds of activities that will help you meet this goal?

Teacher: As I said, I need to get organized.

Coach: Great. Let's start with that: develop systems of organization. What else, Teresa?

Teacher: Then I just need to do it—sit down and read their papers and give them feedback.

Coach: What needs to happen first to help you do that?

Teacher: I need to make the time.

Coach: OK. How about if we capture that as "create time management systems"?

Teacher: That sounds good. I definitely could improve my time management. Is that something you know about?

Coach: I can gather some resources that we can look over together. I'll add that to my column of things to do. What else might be challenging about giving feedback?

Teacher: OK—here's the truth. Sometimes I'm a little vague about what I'm giving feedback on. I read their essays and I'm a little stumped about how to respond—I'm overwhelmed by how much improvement they need to make, and I don't know where to start.

Coach: What if we were to read some student papers and analyze them together? Would that help?

Teacher: Yes, I'd love to get your perspective on their writing.

Coach: Great. Let's add "Identify what kind of feedback you want to give."

Teacher: Right—and I want to give both written and verbal, remember?

Coach: Yes. Would it be OK if at some point I observe you giving a student feedback? Could I sit on the side and just observe the interaction? Sometimes it can be really helpful to have another set of eyes on a high-leverage exchange like that—I might notice things in the student's reaction that might be helpful.

Teacher: That would be great. Sometimes I wonder if I'm really clear when I give kids feedback.

Coach: Sure. Are there any other moments when you think it might be helpful to have me observe?

Teacher: I'm not sure. I can't think of any.

Coach: I was thinking about when you explain an assignment and give instructions. I could observe those lessons.

Teacher: That might be helpful. Maybe I'm not clear at that point either. Yes, that would be great.

Coach: OK, so we've identified some moments when I will observe and then we can debrief. Going back to what you said when we identified this goal—that you know you need to "just do it"—I'm wondering what other things might have gotten in the way of doing it before? Beyond the absence of organizational systems?

Teacher: I think part of the problem might be with how I'm assessing or what I'm assessing for. I realize that sometimes my rubric isn't clear. I think the kids don't really know what's expected or what to do. I'm afraid I'm vague about this too. I didn't learn enough about assessment when I got my teaching credential.

Coaching: That's really insightful. How about if we spend some time looking at the rubric together and thinking about this question you identified of how you can clarify what you're expecting?

Teacher: Definitely. I don't know how to go about that alone, so I could use your support.

Coaching: That's what I'm here for. Now let's think about one specific element of this goal: the needs of English language learners . . .

This conversation continues until coach and client have exhausted their ideas about what actions might lead to meeting the goal—this is a first start at exploring the gaps in the client's skills, knowledge, and capacity. This list can be added to or modified as coaching plays out. It provides immediate ideas of what happens within coaching; it should be instructive, inspiring, and exciting.

5. Break Down the Learning

At this point, after eliciting the client's perception of the actions that will lead her to accomplish her goals, the coach retreats to think and plan alone. It is essential that coaches determine where a client is in her learning; we can only coach within the ZPD, and the parameters of this zone can be murky. It takes a while to know our clients as learners and we can roughly identify a ZPD by listening, observing, and asking questions. Coaching challenges often stem from the coach's inaccurate assessment of the client's ZPD. As we get to know them, we also anticipate the scaffolding we need to construct in order to help the client build her skills.

For example, let's say the teacher we're coaching wants to use literature circles in her classroom and has never done so. She has identified some actions that she thinks will help her reach a goal around developing this structure, but she can't gauge how much she doesn't know. Using knowledge of this instructional practice, a coach can identify the skills, knowledge, ability, and capacities that the teacher needs to have in order to successfully implement literature circles. The coach knows that the teacher will need to understand the students' reading levels and interests, identify appropriate texts, order or gather materials, group students, communicate expectations and procedures, delineate roles for discussions, and so on.

For each of these teacher actions, the coach must assess her client's capacity to implement them. The coach may know, for example, that the teacher has a database for tracking student's reading levels, but that she struggles to communicate procedures. Literature circles are procedure-heavy; the coach recognizes this as an area for focused coaching.

At this stage the coach works alone to plot a course of coaching actions. When we show up to a coaching session, we navigate between letting the client direct the conversation where he needs to go and steering the conversation toward the ends the client has determined. But in order to steer effectively (as we often need to do), we must have thought through the learning chunks. When we haven't done this planning, we are likely to forget components of knowledge and skill that the client needs in order to be successful.

After reflecting on the chunks of learning that a client must engage in, we add to the list of high-leverage activities. When we review the plan with the client, we'll point out the activities that we added and explain our reasoning.

6. Determine Indicators of Progress

In the next step, we return to a conversation with the client to agree on the data and evidence we'll gather along the way to demonstrate progress toward goals. This conversation is another opportunity to identify the changes the client is hoping to make and how those changes will be evident.

For a goal like Teresa's (the teacher), the evidence will be easy to collect: documents that track student performance, feedback forms and copies of feedback to students, and the coach's direct observations of the conferences with students are all relevant data that will show that the teacher met her goals. However, when the goals are more subjective, then data are a little trickier to gather.

The "Indicators of Progress" Conversation

Here's what this type of conversation might sound like with the aforementioned principal who wants to improve his communication.

Coach: I hear that you want to improve your communication with your leadership team. You want them to feel that you believe in them, that you want to hear their ideas, and you want them to take leadership. How might we know when that has happened?

Principal: Right now I think they're apprehensive about sharing their thoughts. I'm so opinionated and I'm concerned that I might have shut people down. So I think if I heard my team sharing their ideas and even disagreeing with me I'd feel like I'd met this goal.

Coach: Great. That's something I can definitely take note of when I'm observing leadership team meetings. I'll be sure to listen for those moments and document them. What else?

Principal: I guess if members of this team volunteered to take on different roles or tasks, then I'd feel like they were taking a lead.

Coach: OK, I'll be sure to note that as well.

Principal: But I don't want them to only volunteer for things. I really want them to feel that they can do what I ask—I want to make sure I build their capacity to take on leadership roles so that they feel good about it.

Coach: Definitely. That's really important to distinguish—it's not just about doing the role, but doing it well. So what might we look for?

Principal: For them to volunteer for something and then be effective. Then I'll feel like I'm meeting my goal.

Coach: OK—how are we going to know if they're effective?

Principal: I'm going to have to carefully monitor what they do and the result. I'll talk to them about it and get their perspective.

Coach: It might be helpful to give some surveys about how they feel, their confidence level, even how much they feel you believe in them. If we did one now, we could do another in a few months and then at the end of the year so we'd have a few sets of data. What do you think?

Principal: That would be helpful.

Coach: What else might be evidence, perhaps during leadership team meetings, that you've improved your communication?

Principal: I really want to talk less and listen more. I want to get them thinking and talking about the issues facing our school.

Coach: So I could script some leadership team meetings and take notes of what you say—how many times you ask questions or share your opinions, how many times other members ask questions or share their opinions. That could be interesting data to collect now and in a few months.

Principal: That would be good. I'm afraid to see what it's like now. I dominate every discussion, I already know.

Coach: Well, if we start documenting it, we can see the change. Let's think of this as another type of data that we'll collect.

7. Develop Coaching Theories of Action

A theory of action is an articulated rationale behind a strategy that's meant to improve student learning. It's expressed in a simple if-then statement, but it also needs to be specific and explicit in its reasoning. This helps us to be clear on what each element of our plan is intended to result in. Although it may need to be revised once it's in play, your theory of action is your best thinking made explicit.

This stage of planning is done alone by the coach and doesn't need to be shared with the client—it's the equivalent of a teacher's lesson plans. This is when the coach thinks through what *she* needs to do in order for the client to meet his goals. We consider the coaching strategies we'll try and anticipate how our client's practice will shift. We also take time to consider and articulate the strategies that could result in systems change.

Here are theories of actions that I developed to help Teresa meet her goals:

If I scaffold Teresa's learning and apply a gradual release of responsibility model

And if I coach Teresa on time management

And if I help her explore her beliefs about giving students feedback consistently and systematically

And if I engage Teresa in a range of facilitative and directive coaching activities

Then she will stay committed to these goals all year and receive the support she needs in order to meet her goals

And then there is a greater likelihood that student performance in her class will improve.

And these were my strategies to work toward systems change at Teresa's school:

If I coach Teresa to develop effective systems for assessment in her classroom

And if we can document these and gather data on their impact

Then we can present these systems and findings to her ELA department and propose their usage schoolwide

And then there is a greater likelihood that student performance across the school will improve.

8. Determine Coach's Goals

This step is also done alone by the coach or with coach-colleagues. Ideally, the coach has a set of standards by which to guide and assess her coaching. The transformational coaching rubric (in Appendix C) is such a tool. In light of the client's goals and her theories of action, the coach determines which coaching practices she needs to focus on and hone in order to reach these ends. For example, a coach might reflect on the development of her coaching skills and then look at her emerging plan and decide that with this client, she'll need to refine her observation and feedback skills. Or the coach may recognize that she's inconsistent in her application of adult learning theories and determine that her client would benefit if she were more systematic and intentional in this area.

What's essential is that the coach look at her own practice and consider where she'll need to grow and develop in order to meet the needs of her client.

9. Compile Resources

At this stage, the coach identifies key texts or resources she might use, such as books, articles, curriculum guides, other teachers or specialists, trainings, workshops, and online resources. These are primarily for the coach to access and draw from, but they can also be shared with the client. There are inevitably some areas of teaching and leading that coaches aren't deeply knowledgeable about; we can't be experts on everything. To me this aspect of the work is very appealing, because I can continue to learn. Furthermore, we want to make sure that the strategies we offer educators or the suggestions we make about whole-school change are grounded in best practices and reflect recent thinking about education.

10. Present and Celebrate the Plan

The final step in this stage of coaching is for the coach to write up the plan and present a copy to the client. A teacher might want to select sections of the plan such as her goals to share with the principal, or she might be expected to share them. It can be useful for principals or supervisors to know what kind of work is happening with a coach—it can build their support for coaching and demystify the process. Supportive principals can also be a resource for a teacher and can reinforce, encourage, and help deepen the coaching work. The client, however, always has the final say about whether anyone other than the coach's supervisor sees the work plan—as long as that person is not *also* the client's supervisor.

When presenting the plan, the coach's attitude and energy need to be infectiously positive. Clients can feel overwhelmed, apprehensive, and intimidated by a challenging work plan—they are taking a big risk in trusting you to guide them through a long series of activities that will hopefully help them meet their goals. This moment—when you lay that printed copy of the work plan on a teacher's desk—is an opportunity for you to express confidence in the teacher's ability to learn and grow, to communicate excitement about the journey you are both embarking on, and to recall the connection between the client's goal and how children will be affected.

The "Work Plan Presentation" Conversation

Here's what part of the work plan conversation with Teresa sounded like:

Coach: Teresa, how are you feeling about this work plan?

Teacher: It's exciting, but I'm also nervous. It seems like so much work and I'm afraid I won't be able to do it all.

Coach: I hear that, and it makes me think we've set a good goal—it should feel a little challenging. If you meet this goal, what would it mean for your English language learners? For Guadalupe and Felipe?

Teacher: If I met this and gave them regular feedback, and their writing improved by 15 percent, it would be huge. They'd almost be on grade level. It means that in two years when they first take the high school exit exam, they'd probably be able to pass it. I'd feel really good sending them on to high school if I met this goal.

Coach: Great. Stay connected to that vision of Guadalupe and Felipe going to high school and passing the exam. Their chances of going to college and determining a career path will be much greater if their writing is on grade level. We'll return to this image when the work gets hard, but I know you can do this—I know that together we can do this. I'm going to be using this plan every week when I prepare for our coaching work, and we'll review it in January to see how we're doing. What's really exciting is that now we're headed in a clear direction, and we have a strong plan for how to get there.

Coaching Journal, 6/12/09

I met with Teresa to reflect on our coaching work this year. She was so excited to see that she'd met the goals she'd laid out. She recognizes that she has a lot more growth to make, but felt good that we'd stayed focused on a couple areas. I can also see how by focusing on the areas of writing feedback, the skills she developed were incorporated into other aspects of her teaching. When I go into her room now, I still see many things she needs to work on, but it's not overwhelming and I see how I can prioritize and scaffold those skills.

COMMON CHALLENGES AND HELPFUL RESPONSES

Challenge: My client really wants to work on *X* goal area, but I think she should address *Y* goal area.

Lens of Adult Learning and Lens of Change Management. This kind of dilemma arises frequently—our knowledge might suggest that a teacher should focus on classroom management, for example, whereas he wants to explore cooperative learning structures. We know that if a teacher is not strong in basic management, then implementing cooperative learning structures will be challenging. However, a core principle of adult learning is that the client's desires and needs drive the work—if he does not own his goals and is not fully invested in them, then transformational change cannot occur. We might try coaching our client toward a different goal area—discussing the conditions in which cooperative learning can be effective, attempting to sway his opinion—but we might also need to go in the direction he's excited about and coach other skills along the way.

The lens of change management can also shed some light on this dilemma. What are the conditions for change here? What are the strengths that can be built on? Where is the will for change? At this point you can see the intersection with the lens of adult learning. If the client is really excited to work on X area, he has the will to change that practice, and because he needs to drive his own learning, you should go with it.

Challenge: I've been asked to coach a teacher who refuses to implement any of the school's new curriculum or use any of the school's best instructional practices. These were the goals, and they were set for us. I don't want to be an enforcer, and I don't know what to do.

Lens of Change Management and Lens of Systems Thinking. Let's look at this dilemma through a change management lens. Consider these questions: Who made the decision for you to coach this teacher? How was it made? What does that decision maker hope that you will do? Who is defining the work of coaching? What is that person's understanding and assumption(s) about what coaching can do? What is the teacher's understanding of what you are supposed to do?

Now take a step back and look through the lens of systems thinking: What is the state of the school's vision and mission? What is the state of leadership at the school? How have decisions about the curriculum and best instructional practices been made? What resources were available to teachers to implement the new curriculum or instructional practices? How have expectations around curriculum, instructional mandates, and coaching been communicated?

Now focus back in on the teacher: How does he see and understand the school's vision and mission? What is his relationship to them? Which skills does the teacher have? What indicators are there of his will to change? What knowledge does he need to make changes in his practice? Why should he improve his practice? What are the incentives? What will happen if he doesn't?

The purpose of exploring all these different angles is for you to talk with someone who has decision-making power. While there might be a possibility that you can change the teacher's practice, you might need administrative support, and it might not be the best way for you to spend your time and energy.

If we think about everyone as being on a continuum of openness to coaching and improving their practice, a coach shouldn't be used to work with those at the low end of that range. If someone is really closed down to being reflective or making change, it's a waste of a coach's energy to work there. Usually, in any school, there are dozens of other educators who are eager and grateful for support.

HOW DO I USE THIS WORK PLAN?

Individual professional goals are also powerful sources of motivation. When teachers set professional learning goals based on self-identified professional growth challenges, the goals are more compelling. When teachers can relate their goals to better outcomes for the children whose faces they see every day, the goals are more meaningful. And finally, when teachers develop individual professional goals that take them incrementally to a personal career vision, the likelihood of remaining committed to the goal over the long term is enhanced. In this way, professional development designed to achieve these motivating goals becomes an exciting opportunity as opposed to an imposed mandate.

O'NEILL AND CONZEMIUS
(2006, PP. 126–127)

Coaching is the professional development that can help teachers or administrators achieve their goals; the work plan is a road map toward that end. A coach will reference work plans when preparing for a coaching session, and she'll reflect on them monthly, always looking for indicators of progress. Periodically, she'll engage her client in reflecting on how they are working toward meeting the goals, and they'll collect evidence to document this growth. Chapter Fourteen goes into depth on this process.

Finally, work plans *can* and *should* be flexible. They often change as coaching develops. What originally felt like the goal may end up being less important than something else that emerges in coaching, and sometimes goals are narrowed or trimmed down. Often they need to be modified because we inaccurately assessed our client's ZPD when we created them. Work plans are a tool and should always serve the journey of transformation. See Exhibit 7.1, next, for a sample work plan.

Exhibit 7.1. Coaching Work Plan

Teacher: Teresa Phillips, eighth-grade English Language Arts

School: Harriet Tubman Learning Academy

Coach: Elena Aguilar

Coach's Personal Vision

I coach to heal and transform the world. I coach teachers and leaders to discover ways of working and being that are joyful and rewarding, that bring communities together, and that result in positive outcomes for children. I coach people to find their own power and to empower others so that we can transform our education system, our society, and our world.

Schoolwide Student Achievement Goals

- English Language Arts: 60 percent of students overall and in each subgroup score proficient or above in ELA
- English Language Development: 100 percent of English language learners will improve their writing scores by 15 percent.

Client's Goals

SMARTE Goal 1

I, Teresa Phillips, will provide verbal and written feedback to all of my students on their writing assignments every other week, within two days of submission of the assignment, for the entire school year.

SMARTE Goal 2

By the end of the first marking period, I, Teresa Phillips, will have created systems to track students' progress toward mastery on the writing standards. I will use these systems for the entire school year.

Rationale

These goals are connected to the school's goal on improving student writing, as measured in part by the district's annual writing assessment. Our school aims at improving scores by 10 percent for all students and by 15 percent for English language learners. I will help meet this goal by focusing on how I give students feedback on their writing and how I track student progress.

Strategic Activities

Teacher and Coach Together

- Research systems of organization and determine most useful ones to put in place.
- Determine useful time management systems; work together to put those in place.
- Analyze student writing.
- Analyze writing rubric and identify lessons that can demonstrate the elements that students are struggling with.
- Coach will model writing lessons on rubric elements that students struggle with. Teacher will observe. Debrief together.
- Cocreate tool to use when giving students feedback.
- Prepare for feedback session with students; role-play one feedback conversation.
- Coach will observe teacher giving student feedback; debrief and reflect.
- Coach will model giving student feedback; teacher will observe; debrief and reflect.
- Coach will observe teacher giving writing assignments; debrief and reflect.

Teacher

- Engage in all coaching activities.
- Set up organization systems and use them consistently.

Coach

- Gather resources on time management.
- Gather resources on teaching writing to English language learners. Determine most useful tools based on analysis of writing.
- Look for conferences and external workshops that Teresa could attend.
- Find teachers at other sites who have strong practices in teaching writing whom Teresa could observe.

Indicators of Progress

- Assessment tracking systems and evidence of their use
- Coach observations of feedback conferences with students
- Evidence of student growth from one writing assignment to another, based on specific feedback given by teacher during conference
- Teacher-created documents and tools used in feedback conferences

Dates for Plan Review

- January 28
- June 14

The following portion of the work plan should not be shared with the client.

Coach's Theories of Action

To Meet Teresa's Goals

If I scaffold Teresa's learning and apply a gradual release of responsibility model
And if I coach Teresa on time management
And if I help her explore her beliefs about giving students feedback consistently and systematically
And if I engage Teresa in a range of facilitative and directive coaching activities
Then she will stay committed to these goals all year and receive the support she needs to meet her goals
And then there is a greater likelihood that student performance in her class will improve

To Effect Systems Change

If I coach Teresa to develop effective systems for assessment in her classroom
And if we can document these and gather data on their impact
Then we can present these systems and findings to her ELA department and propose their usage schoolwide
And then there is a greater likelihood that student performance across the school will improve

Rationale

Systems of authentic formative assessment are almost nonexistent at this school, so this approach could be a way to support the development of methods to assess student growth beyond the annual standardized tests.

Coach's Goals (as Measured on the Transformational Coaching Rubric)

By June 2012, I will reach the indicated levels on the following elements:

1.C. Adult learning theory: Refining
4.D. A range of conversational approaches: Refining
5.F. Gradual release of responsibility: Developing
6.A. Gathering data on coaching: Developing

Rationale

1.C. I apply adult learning theories in my coaching, but I am inconsistent. I want to be more intentional about applying them and reflect on what that means exactly with Teresa. I think it will be most important to remember and use when applying a gradual release of responsibility model.

4.D. I use a range of conversational approaches, but I still feel that I do so only when I plan for them and am very intentional. I don't feel that I've internalized them, and that's what I'd like to get to this year.

5.F. I think I often inaccurately assess a client's ZPD, so I want to be very thoughtful about how I assess Teresa's and how I coach at the edge of it. I also want to be systematic and intentional about using a gradual release model. I want to think about what that means in terms of an adult learner, how I check to see that she's ready for the next level, and how I scaffold her learning.

6.A. I want to be much more systematic about gathering data on my coaching. I want to record a conversation at least twice a month—this is something I haven't done consistently enough. I want to record those that I don't plan for, so I can see how I'm internalizing coaching conversation approaches. I also want to bring transcripts of these conversations to our coaching team meetings and have other coaches give me feedback.

PART THREE

The Coaching Dance

CHAPTER 8

Listening and Questioning

Read this when:

- You want to hone your listening skills
- You want to refine your questioning skills
- You are supporting others to develop their listening and questioning skills

THE THREE MOVEMENTS IN THE COACHING DANCE

Imagine that coaching is a dance with three movements. In the first step a coach listens, a subtly complex skill. At some point a coach takes a step and responds to what she's heard—primarily with questions to promote deeper learning and reflection. In the third step, the coach might suggest an action or learning activity for the client to do alongside the coach or alone.

While there are three basic moves in this dance, the choreography is flexible and improvised. The coach often takes the lead, as she holds the expertise around the adult learning process, but if, or when, the coachee suggests a new direction, the coach eagerly follows. The order of the steps will also change with each client and in different phases in coaching. However, the basic movements—listen, respond, engage in activity—have elements that can be delineated and intentionally applied. The art of coaching is the ability to apply a tremendous range of skills in response to a particular situation in a way that appears seamless, effortless, and, at times, even beautiful.

Listening is a magnetic and strange thing, a creative force. The friends who listen to us are the ones we move toward. When we are listened to, it creates us, makes us unfold and expand.

DR. KARL MENNINGER
(1942, PP. 275–276)

This chapter explores the first step in this coaching dance, a hard but foundational skill to learn: listening. Author and coach Lettecia Kratz explains it this way: "Deep listening is essential in transformational coaching, because only when we are getting an understanding of the whole of it can we cause a major transformational shift. If a coach listens only at a surface level, she can assist only in shifting smaller, surface-level things. The deeper we listen, the broader our understanding, and the greater our chances are for finding an access point to cause profound transformation" (personal e-mail communication with Lettecia Kratz, 2012).

LISTENING IN TRANSFORMATIONAL COACHING

Take a moment to reflect on listening. When was the last time you felt really, truly listened to? Who was listening to you? How did you know you were being listened to? What did it feel like? What did this allow you to think and feel and do?

Now think about a time when you were sharing something and were not listened to. What was that like? What was the effect on the relationship?

And now, take a moment to reflect on how you listen to others. Do you listen in order to find a connection and be able to share some information about yourself? Do you listen in order to find a point with which you can argue? When you listen, do you notice yourself feeling judgmental about what the other person shares? Do you listen to offer suggestions for fixing a problem? Do you find your attention wandering or drifting toward other ideas? Of course, we all do this at times. Listening is a skill; you can train yourself to do this, and you will get better with practice. Deep listening is hard to do. At first, it can feel very strange, uncomfortably empty and quiet, unlike anything you've ever experienced. But it is the most effective tool you'll use in coaching. When you are listening deeply, you stop thinking—your own mental chatter is quiet. When you are listening very deeply to another person, your own thoughts and concerns quiet down and your ego naps in a corner of your mind. This creates a tremendous space for your client to explore her own issues. You can support and guide that exploration through the questions you ask. Once you've created a clear, safe, nonjudgmental field, there is plenty of space for clients to wander around their own mind, exploring their beliefs, their blocks, and their goals and how to fulfill them.

How can we learn to listen well? We can start by noticing our own listening. Listen to your listening—what's going on in your mind? Try this activity: listen to a friend, colleague, family member, or client while you listen to your own listening—pay attention to what is happening in your own mind in your own listening. Then go and write down what you heard your own mind saying.

Here's what I heard in my mind some years ago during a coaching conversation:

> She's really going to complain about that again? I thought we'd discussed this and come to some agreements and now she's back here? How can we ever make progress on the real work if she's always going back to this whining and complaining about something she can't do anything about?

Becoming aware of what your mind is doing when you're supposed to be listening is very useful, because then you can make a choice about what you will do. My mind used to lapse into this judgmental place a great deal. I was not a very effective or artful coach. But once I started to notice this chatter, I began to make a change. I'd ask myself to stop. I'd remind myself that I couldn't be a good coach and couldn't transform education from a place of judgment. I'd say to myself, "Please put the judgments aside while I'm sitting here talking to this person." Sometimes I'd yell at myself—in my own head, of course, or I'd visualize going into my mind and hitting the mute button. By persistently returning my focus away from myself, back to the client, to what she is saying, what she is experiencing, I can create a space for transformation. After a while, I noticed that I didn't have that soundtrack playing in the background when I was listening. This took practice—and it took time. It was hard, and I still have relapses. But it is something that as a coach we can do and we need to do.

After you've paid attention to your mental chatter while you're listening, notice what happens when someone you are speaking with stops speaking. Are you inclined to jump in right away and ask a question or say something? Just as teachers need to provide several seconds of "wait time" with students after posing a question, a coach can also practice wait time. After the person you are speaking with stops, wait a few seconds. You can nod, smile, indicate nonverbally that you're present and alive, but don't say anything. If you need to jot down a note or two so that you are not distracted by trying to remember what the client said, jot it down. This frees up your mind to continue listening to the other things the client needs to share. You'll be surprised at how often the other person will continue talking without a prompt. This is good — it's usually good for your client to speak a lot. They will often reveal juicier, more important information when they are assured that you are listening to them and honoring their experience.

After you have deeply listened, allow yourself a few moments to formulate what you are going to say. If need be, you can even say something like "OK, let me think for a moment," so that the response that comes out of your mouth will be the best you can offer in that moment.

Quiet Listening

When I feel really listened to, it seems like time slows down. There's a stillness and quietness that I perceive from the person who has created a protected space for me. I don't feel that he brings an agenda, is bursting to share something with me, or needs anything from me. I feel drawn in and empowered to explore my own thoughts, feelings, and experiences. When I am really listened to, I feel acknowledged, recognized, and validated on a fundamental level. This can actually be a transcendent experience. In that space, when someone listens to me deeply, I find that my most brilliant insights and solutions appear to me and then come out of my mouth because when someone deeply listens, I can better understand myself.

Sometimes as a coach, it's very effective to hold a space like the one I just described — a wide-open invitation for clients to explore their thinking. We listen so that people can unravel what's going on for them. Often all they need is a place to start. We listen from the point of view that people don't need answers, advice, or wisdom. They can do their own thinking, discover solutions, and figure out their next steps. It demonstrates respect when we listen to someone from this space, believing they will come to their own understanding, and that my own understanding is not necessarily better than theirs. This is a quiet place for a coach to work from — with our bodies, minds, and energy we communicate that a client can enter the exploration and we'll be there if necessary. We may occasionally ask a probing question, but in this kind of listening we don't say much. Listening in this way can be very useful if a client is processing difficult emotions or sorting through something that happened. It can also be very useful when someone is trying to articulate a new idea, a path forward, or a possibility that other people have not been able to hear without skepticism or shutting the person down. Many people relish this kind of space to speak and be heard, and the results can be very productive.

When we as coaches hold this kind of a listening space, we don't share our opinions, experiences, or feelings. We don't give advice or suggestions. We never interrupt. Furthermore, a coach refrains from asking a lot of questions, particularly clarifying questions. A clarifying question is usually a request for information for our own needs—so that we can get clear on details. We might ask questions to support the client in digging deeper into his thoughts, but these are carefully selected. It can be more effective to simply ask, "Can you say more about that?" Often this invitation is all that people need to keep exploring.

At times someone might start speaking and diving deep into his thoughts or feelings, but then suddenly just stop. It can be powerful to sit in silence for a few moments—while it might feel uncomfortable, it extends another invitation for the client to keep speaking. Frequently, the speaker will pick up again and continue talking, going far deeper into his thinking. As coaches, we welcome and hold quiet pauses.

Silence is essential for deep transformation ... like still water that reflects things as they are, the calming silence helps us to see things more clearly, and therefore, to be in deeper contact with ourselves and those around us.

THICH NHAT HANH (2011)

Intentional Listening

When a coach listens deeply, her mind is not blank and vacuous. She listens for what the client is saying as well as assumptions, interpretations, and underlying beliefs. For example, a teacher might say, "My principal came into my room when I was teaching. He looked around, scowled, and left without saying anything. I know he's trying to get rid of me." A coach could form an opinion like "She's paranoid" or could think something like "I hear an assumption and interpretation to explore. I'm going to note that comment and come back to it."

We also listen for what is *not* said: for what lurks below the surface—feelings, thoughts and beliefs, and for the gaps in a story. A client might withhold something not because he doesn't trust the coach, but because he's not aware of these holes. When we listen deeply, closely, and over a period of time, those holes become glaring. Frequently, they are areas or concerns that as coaches, because of our experience working in schools, we know others in similar situations often have. When we address them, clients can experience great relief, perhaps even a breakthrough.

> *Courage is what it takes to stand up and speak; courage is also what it takes to sit down and listen.*
>
> WINSTON CHURCHILL (N.D.)

In order to help a client change beliefs and behaviors, a coach must listen carefully to understand the client's patterns of thinking. In order for this to happen, we need to let people talk and talk and talk. Initially, this experience can feel overwhelming, but if we just sit back, empty our minds, and let it all in, there will come a time when we start to notice the patterns, hear the unintentional meanings behind words, see the distortions, and, most important, understand where our client is on his learning trajectory and where he is emotionally. We cannot be effective as coaches if we don't have a clear picture of this terrain. A coach's action and speech should emerge after a period of stillness and silence.

Collecting Stories

Another way of thinking about how we listen, starting from the very beginning, is to remember that we are collecting stories. A coach gathers a client's stories, mentally filing away chapter after chapter every time we meet. Our clients speak in narratives, they will tell the stories of their struggles and successes, interspersed with stories of who they are and where they are from. We collect these stories, including seemingly irrelevant anecdotes or comments, and we store them in our mental archive.

> *Everything is held together with stories. That is all that is holding us together, stories and compassion.*
>
> BARRY LOPEZ (EVANS, 1994)

After a while, we will notice patterns running through the narratives; we'll see clues to who someone is and why they do what they do. Our role as a coach then becomes to help a client connect the dots—to see the themes in what they have shared with us. This can sound like "A few months ago you talked about how you have a hard time managing teachers who are older than you. Could that be why you're apprehensive about giving this teacher difficult feedback?" When we return to these stories, our clients feel heard and validated. They also have the option of looking at these connections as a "data set" and an opportunity to begin shifting their thinking or behaviors.

What Does Listening Look Like, Feel Like, and Sound Like?

Next time you are in conversation with someone, pay attention to your own listening: What is the chatter in your mind saying? Mine often sounds like this: "Oh, that's a good point ... I agree with that ... When that happened to me ... Why did you say that? I never would have said that ... OK, that makes sense ..."

When we are listening deeply, it is like we have joined the coachee in her own world, and are sitting next to her, listening from her perspective. We understand or "get" what it is like for her, where she is coming from. We might say: "I hear that ... That sounds really hard ... I'm sorry you experienced that ... Do you want to say more about that?" At some point we'll begin to ask more questions to push the coachee's thinking, but broad, open-ended listening often comes first—this builds the client's trust, ensures that we're hearing and understanding what our client is saying, and helps us identify the questions we might ask to provoke deeper reflection.

Active listening is a strategy for a speaker to convey that she's listening, and also to ensure that she's hearing precisely what the other person wants to share. We can repeat back or paraphrase what the other person says. It can sound like this:

- In other words ...
- What I'm hearing then ...
- It sounds like you are saying ... Is that correct? Did I miss anything?
- I'm hearing many things ...
- As I listen to you, I'm hearing ...

Although it can feel awkward at first to paraphrase, it is a surprisingly effective way to build trust with a client and demonstrate your intention to listen deeply.

How can we show that we're listening? Recall a time when you were sharing something personal and you felt that the other person was not listening to you. What did you notice? Often the clues are subtle, but when we're taking a risk by sharing something important, we are supremely attuned to the other person's every movement. We will notice a glance at a clock, a comment that feels slightly disconnected, a question about something that we already shared, squirmy feet, or a stifled yawn. A coach must be mindful about how her body and words demonstrate attention by maintaining eye contact and inclining slightly toward the listener or mirroring his posture. Start paying attention to what your body does when you are engaged in conversation or listening—you might be unconsciously moving or positioning yourself in a way that communicates an emotion or judgment that you were unaware of.

Refining Our Listening

When you are listening to somebody, completely, attentively, then you are listening not only to the words, but also to the feeling of what is being conveyed, to the whole of it, not part of it.

J. KRISHNAMURTI (1969)

Chapter Fifteen offers suggestions for how to improve our listening as coaches and how to be fully in the present moment. My favorite activity is one that everyone can start practicing right away (it's also one that I frequently ask clients to engage in). It's called listening to your own listening. Listening is a practice; we all have wandering, disagreeable minds at times. The first step is to notice what's going on in there while we're coaching.

A Story about Listening to Silences

James was an experienced African American high school principal whom I was assigned to coach. For the first semester, his attention focused on improving instruction, but he became increasingly distressed by data showing that a disproportionate number of African American males were sent out to the office for "defiant" behavior. When I asked James if he wanted to find a way to share these data with his staff and explore some ways to address it, he seemed reluctant and wanted to continue focusing on instruction. However, when he did walkthrough observations, his feedback to teachers addressed how they interacted with students. Teachers pushed back: "I thought you said you were coming in to observe how I'm teaching vocabulary," they responded. "This feedback is not fair."

"How do they think they're going to teach vocabulary if they keep throwing kids out?" James said to me in a coaching session. "And that lesson was horrible. It was too slow and confusing and there were no opportunities for students to apply their knowledge." Together we had just visited a classroom where three African American sixteen-year-old boys were in the "reflection corner" with their heads down for the twenty minutes we were there. James had a long list of negative comments about the lesson we'd observed; he planned on delivering another professional development session for teachers on vocabulary instruction. He spoke at length about the teachers' poor application of the professional development (PD) they'd already received, about how their lesson plans were weak, and about how he wanted to hire an entire new faculty.

"James, could I ask you something?" I said when we were sitting back in his office. "I'm wondering what it's like for you, as an African American man, to see this suspension data and those three boys sitting in the corner. What does that feel like?"

James dropped his head into his hands. He was silent for several minutes and then looked up at me, his eyes wet. "I think if I go into the feelings I might not come out. I might not be able to do my job. Those boys are me, my brothers, my dad, my childhood friends. I feel powerless. I'd rather just focus on vocabulary instruction."

"I hear the pain you're in," I said. "I see it in your face when we go into those classrooms."

"It eats away at me," he said. "But what can I do?"

"You say you'd rather focus on instruction, but you can't. You're focused on the ways teachers interact with their students and you mull over this suspension data for hours, as you should. You're right — those kids can't learn if they're constantly being kicked out of class. I think you might want to do something."

For the following five months, James shifted the school's focus to explore teacher-student relationships, ways of managing behavior, and alternatives to suspension. While he acknowledged emotions that he wanted to work out, our coaching focused on his responses as a leader to the data he was gathering. What he needed from me as a coach was not to help him process the feelings, but to have listened deeply, collecting his stories along the way, and then to raise the emotional experience as one that may have been blocking him from taking action that would make a significant difference. Simply by bringing that to the surface, James was able to take action in a way that was empowered and clear and that allowed him to be effective.

LISTENING AS A VEHICLE FOR WHOLE-SCHOOL TRANSFORMATION

Margaret Wheatley is a visionary leader, writer, and activist whose work deeply moves me. In her book *Turning to One Another: Simple Conversations to Restore Hope to the Future* (2009), she encourages us to take the time to sit together, listen to each other, worry, and dream together. She calls on us to talk to people we know, those we don't know, and those we never talk to.

I believe we can change the world if we start listening to one another again ... Simple, truthful conversation where we each have a chance to speak, we each feel heard, and we each listen well.

MARGARET WHEATLEY (2009, P. 7)

There are many people working in our education system who have suffered — both as adults and children. In order for us to move forward, many wounds need healing. Wheatley suggests that being heard is deeply healing, because listening creates relationships: "Listening moves us closer, it helps us become more whole, more healthy, more holy. Not listening creates fragmentation, and fragmentation always causes more suffering" (2009, p. 94).

Think about the school where you work: Which groups of people have not been heard, perhaps ever? As coaches, we are uniquely positioned to bring listening into our schools as a vehicle for transformation. First, we need to refine our own abilities to listen, then we can invite others in to be heard. Frequently, when our clients experience deep listening and the kind of reflection and change that is possible as a result, they are inspired to create a similar experience for those with whom they work. We can coach individuals to listen to others — to listen to their students, to parents, and to colleagues. We can also create conditions within organizations and teams for people to speak and be heard; coaches can facilitate this process. This is why listening is the core, elemental, foundational skill for a coach to practice: with this skill, we can connect with others and foster healing and transformation.

Using Dyads to Practice Listening

 Administrators: dyads can have a powerful impact on people's work together. They can be used to open meetings, to help educators integrate what they hear in meetings, and to close and reflect on meetings.

Teachers and administrators often ask me to share tips on how to listen well; they suspect that the communication techniques I use in coaching could be very useful in their work as leaders. This request for support moves us into the stage of the coaching dance where we are instructive and learning alongside our client. I share lists of question stems and language that can reflect listening, we practice these in role-plays, and I observe their conversations and give them feedback on their listening.

In addition to coaching individuals, coaches in schools often work with teams of teachers, administrators, and staff. Sometimes coaches are asked to lead or facilitate this work, giving us an opportunity to directly affect how a group of individuals interact with each other. If we are invited into the process in this way, we can introduce listening structures that can become routines for a team—this establishes the possibility of making sustainable change.

Dyads are a listening structure that is fairly easy to set up, takes minimal time, and can yield profound results. Dyads are a form of "constructivist listening," a kind of listening described by professor Julian Weissglass in which the speaker constructs his own understandings of self and emotions. Weissglass insists that schools must attend to the feelings of the adults who work in them—that without helping teachers, administrators, and parents work through their feelings about education and change, we won't make the kinds of changes we are striving for (1990, p. 352).

A dyad is a formal structure in which two people take turns agreeing to listen to each other for a fixed amount of time. The talker has the opportunity to talk about her feelings, thoughts, and experiences; the listener does not interrupt, paraphrase, analyze, give advice, or break in with his own stories. The premise is that people can solve their own problems, and the role of a listener is to hold a space for that to happen. Often a facilitator will offer a prompt for the dyad, but the time belongs to the speaker, so the speaker can go off topic if she pleases.

Another essential element in a dyad is confidentiality. The listener does not talk about what she has heard, ever—not with other people nor with the speaker herself, because feelings change, and we might feel different about what we say five minutes after we say it. What is said stays encapsulated within that moment of time and space.

Dyads can be a part of a regular team meeting, often placed at the beginning of a meeting to allow participants to process anything they are coming in with and transition to the intended work. A two- or three-minute dyad can be effective at doing this, and it takes very little time. While the primary purpose for a dyad is to create some space for someone to speak and be heard, they also serve to bring people together as we listen to each other. Dyads are a fairly easy structure for coaches to implement in the schools they work in. However, to make them truly effective, I highly recommend reading the work of Julian Weissglass. Dyads are just one of a number of structures that he suggests can help groups of people listen to each other. More information about dyads can be found online and on my website.

QUESTIONING IN TRANSFORMATIONAL COACHING

Some coaching models offer lists of questions that coaches can use. Lists of questions are useful, and you'll find some in Appendix B of this book, but they must be used intentionally and with awareness. A coach needs to know when to use a particular kind of question and when another would be more appropriate or effective. Questions are technical tools; the art of coaching is about applying judgment and discretion and about making intentional decisions after careful listening and analysis. Chapters Nine and Eleven explore different kinds of conversational and questioning approaches, but first, here is a quick overview of clarifying and probing questions, the two most general categories of questions that we use.

Clarifying Questions

Clarifying questions elicit details, specifics, clarification, or examples. A coach can ask clarifying questions for different purposes. First, consider who needs clarity. Does the coach need more information so that she can understand a situation that the client is describing? Would the information help her determine the appropriate stance to take? Or is the purpose of asking a clarifying question to provoke the client to articulate an event, his thinking, or his experience? It's important to consider who needs the clarity, because often when a coach wants to ask a clarifying question, it's for her own purpose. Sometimes this is critical; other times it's not necessary. For example, if a client is describing a painful experience and his emotions are tumbling out and he's talking in a nonlinear way, a coach shouldn't interrupt with a question like, "How many people did you say were in the room again?" As with everything else that a coach says, we want to be intentional with our clarifying questions.

Clarifying Questions

Would you tell me a little more about ... ?

Let me see if I understand ...

I'd be interested in hearing more about ...

It would help me understand if you'd give me an example of ...

So, are you saying (or suggesting) that ... ?

Tell me what you mean when you ...

Tell me how that idea is like (or different from) . . .

To what extent were you . . . ?

I'm curious to know more about . . .

I'm intrigued by . . . I'm interested in . . . I wonder . . .

When did this happen? Where were you? How long did it take? Who was there?

As you read over these questions, perhaps you thought some of them were of the "probing" variety or that they suggested an interest in more than just factual information. Questions can be offered and received in different ways.

Probing Questions

The purpose of asking a probing question is to help a client uncover thinking or beliefs—not necessarily to find an immediate answer or solution. The great majority of the questions we ask in coaching should be probing questions, given that, at its broadest, our work is to help another person deepen reflective capacities and become more self-aware. Therefore, a probing question is for the client, not the coach.

A probing question also should never contain a hidden suggestion that we want our client to get to. For example, let's say you observed your teacher-client deliver a lesson that left many students confused. Perhaps, given your instructional expertise, you suspect that the reason for the confusion was the teacher's directions. They were rushed, only communicated orally, and she didn't check for understanding. You might be tempted to say, "I think they were lost because you . . . " But that would be handing the answers directly to the teacher, and she could shut down because she's being told what she did wrong, and this isn't coaching. So perhaps you frame a question such as, "What did you notice about the way you gave directions?" This is a leading-probing question, a question that is directing the teacher toward the answer you think she should give.

Perhaps this dilemma could be explored by starting with a question like, "What did you hope would happen in today's lesson?" And then, "Tell me about what actually happened from your perspective?" And then, "What do you think your students understood about what you expected to happen?" And perhaps finally, if the teacher doesn't get here by herself, "Can you describe how you expressed your expectations for this lesson? What did you notice about how your students understood those directions?"

Probing questions take many different forms. Chapters Nine and Eleven explore how probing questions can be framed through different coaching stances.

As coaches pay more attention to our questioning strategies, we might notice that some of our questions don't yield the kinds of responses we hope for: some could even be "questioning mistakes," as coach and author Tony Stoltzfus (2008) describes. If we ask too many *why* questions, we can make a client feel defensive. At times we may ask rambling questions, layering one question on top of another as we work through the phrasing. Or we might become aware that we interrupt clients and try to finish their thoughts. A description of common questioning mistakes and how to address them is available on my website.

COMMON CHALLENGES AND HELPFUL RESPONSES

Challenge: When I'm coaching, my head starts swimming with all this information about questioning and listening. The client stops talking and I don't know what to say. I can't figure out the right response.

Lens of Adult Learning. As a new coach, I experienced this kind of thing often. There'd be long awkward pauses as I tried to figure out the best question to ask and the conversation stalled. What we need to learn is that there's no perfect question. Find a couple of prompts that feel comfortable and keep moving the conversation forward: "Tell me more" usually works. You'll also want to find coach-colleagues with whom you can role-play coaching conversations. This dilemma surfaces your learning needs.

Challenge: Sometimes a client says something that I really disagree with or that I find offensive. Then I don't want to paraphrase or ask probing questions; I just want to say what I think. Is this ever OK for me to do?

Lens of Emotional Intelligence. Looking through the lens of emotional intelligence, you might consider how "just saying what you think" will affect the relationship with your client, how you can manage your own uncomfortable emotions, and how you try to appeal to a listener. From your position as a coach, if you just speak your truth, how will the client receive it? What possibilities could close down because you've moved out of the coaching role and into that of an individual? What's the point of just saying what you think? Are you wanting the client to agree with you and see what you're saying, or perhaps are you wanting to shut your client down?

As coaches, we often hear disturbing opinions. Because we show up as nonjudgmental listeners, people share all kinds of thoughts and feelings. We have to learn how to manage the emotions that come up for us and then learn skillful ways to respond.

I coached a principal who, after getting to know and trust me, shared her feelings about the growing Arab community in her school. "I don't like anything about them," she confessed as she launched into a tirade against their religious practices, the way they dress, how they treat women, their attitudes about school, even the way they smelled. "And how do I know they aren't forming terrorist cells right here in Oakland?" she concluded.

I was shocked and offended, but I recognized that I could affect her thinking only if I stayed engaged in my stance as a coach in the conversation she'd opened. I decided to see what could happen if I used an inquiry lens. First, I asked for permission: "Would it be OK if we explored some of these feelings?" She agreed. I used a lot of sentence prompts that began with "I'm curious about ... ? Can you tell me more about ... ? What led you to believe that? How did you learn about ... ? What might be another way to look at ...?" We also discussed what the effect had been for her when other people held certain beliefs about her gender and ethnicity. We spent months unraveling these beliefs—the principal repeatedly made provocative statements, which I suspected was her way of initiating a conversation that she wanted to have. I chose to believe that underneath her bigotry was fear, misunderstanding, and a good, caring person who wanted to sort out these feelings.

As we explored her beliefs, I invited her to learn more about the Arab community. I looked for every possible entry point to help her find connections and appreciation—I knew she liked lamb, for example, so we ate at a local Yemeni restaurant that was owned by parents of her students. She loved the meal and admitted that she'd never tried their food. We read a biography of a female Muslim activist to get insight on women's experience in that culture. At the end of the year, I coached the principal in hosting an event for the Arab community to share their stories and culture because the tension and misunderstandings between different cultural groups was increasing throughout the neighborhood. As dozens of parents from all ethnicities thanked her for organizing the evening, she turned to me and said, "I know I had some prejudices about the Arabs, but I think I'm changing. Thanks for being patient with me."

There had been numerous times when this principal had made statements that I wanted to shoot down, but I knew that I had to stay in a coaching relationship with her to have any hope of helping her grow. This is a common dilemma that coaches face, but it also presents an opportunity that may not open elsewhere when a coach can learn to manage her emotions and find ways to engage in conversations that can shift beliefs.

CHAPTER 9

Facilitative Coaching
Conversations

Read this when:

- You need strategies to gently elicit a client's thinking or help a client release emotions

- You feel stuck in your coaching and want different ways of engaging in conversation with a client

COACHING CONVERSATIONS

When I first started coaching, I had a hard time describing what I did with clients. "We just talk," I'd say, "Mostly, we have conversations." While it's true that coaching happens in conversations, there's a lot that's gone on in order to arrive at the conversation, a lot that a coach does during the conversation, and a lot to do after a conversation. For a coach, the conversations themselves can be cognitively, emotionally, and even physically exhausting, because *a lot* happens in conversation. As our intention is to impact behavior, beliefs, and being, it is our job to artfully guide a coaching conversation in a way that produces results in these areas. It is at this point, during a conversation, that we'll apply different kinds of questioning strategies. Chapters Nine and Eleven deconstruct the coaching conversation in order to illuminate the dozens of moves that a coach makes when in dialogue with a client.

The process of coaching requires both backbone and compassion. The coach must be courageous enough to be gently irreverent with the client to test the client's view of the world. However, coaching can work only when the coach cares deeply about the client and is able to cast aside his own ego to support the client's efforts.

PATRICIA MCNEIL AND
STEVE KLINK (2004, p. 185)

A word of caution: As a coach starts pushing and probing into behaviors, beliefs, and being, clients can feel uncomfortable. Some have described this as feeling that their whole brain is being re-wired as they go through a process of unlearning. Clients return to the place of feeling like a beginner—they don't want to engage in the old behavior patterns, but they haven't quite mastered new strategies consistent with the values they want to embody (Schwarz and Davidson, 2008, p. 82). As we engage in conversations, while our clients make this shift from old patterns to new ones, our support is critical. Coaches must be very patient and compassionate and constantly check that our client is willing to engage in coaching. If we don't, we risk losing trust and therefore, the possibility of transformation.

Essential Framework 3: Coaching Stances

One way that I became clearer about what was happening in coaching conversations, and one way in which I improved my coaching practice, was to apply an analytical framework to the talking that happened with clients. A framework for conversation does three things:

1. It provides a metacognitive structure to guide my questions and statements.
2. It helps me strategically plan a coaching conversation (see Chapter 13).
3. It offers ways to think and act during a session, especially when I'm unsure how to move my client forward.

There are a number of frameworks that can be applied in coaching. After experimenting with different models, I've found that for me, John Heron's is the most effective.

John Heron, a pioneer in counseling, facilitation, and personal and professional development delineates two broad approaches we take in the helping professions: a "facilitative" and an "authoritative" stance. From the facilitative stance, a coach pulls and helps the client to be autonomous by using what Heron identifies as a cathartic, catalytic, or supportive approach. From an authoritative stance, a coach takes an instructive or directive role on behalf of the client and we might use what Heron calls a prescriptive, informative, or confrontational approach from this stance. When referring to Heron's "authoritative stance," I usually use the term "directive" as a synonym.

When I'm coaching, I sometimes imagine that I am shifting my body back and forth between two large, flat river stones—the "facilitative stone" and the "directive stone." Based on where my feet are planted, I behave differently—I say different things and ask different questions. I move between these two stances in response to who my client is, where my client is, and what I hear from my client. Usually, in a coaching conversation, I use most, if not all, of these approaches—I shift my feet often. Visualizing the stones helps me stay anchored in a specific approach and be intentional.

Conversations in which a coach uses a facilitative or directive approach are reflective: either about something that has happened, on thoughts, feelings, beliefs, and being, or on something that a client would like to do. Interspersed with reflective conversation are activities—sometimes even occurring during a coaching conversation itself. For example, a coach might engage a teacher in a reflective conversation on a lesson that didn't go well, and then immediately support the teacher to design a new lesson. Or a coach could help a principal process a difficult conversation that he had with a staff member, and then role-play the principal's follow-up conversation.

The following chapters dissect coaching conversations and activities to illustrate the various components: facilitative coaching conversations are explored in this chapter, followed by a chapter on facilitative coaching activities. Chapter Eleven dives into directive coaching conversations, followed by a chapter on directive coaching activities. In reality, in the coaching dance, we integrate all these strategies.

Masterful coaches inspire people by helping them recognize the previously unseen possibilities that lay embedded in their existing circumstances.

ROBERT HARGROVE (2003)

FACILITATIVE COACHING

From the facilitative stance, a coach guides, helps, and pulls the client's learning. Heron names three ways in which we do this: from what he calls a cathartic approach, a catalytic approach, or a supportive approach.

The Cathartic Approach

Think back to your first year teaching. What are your predominant memories of that time? Perhaps you remember the exhaustion, the responsibility, or the joy. For me it was: "This is *so* hard! I'm overwhelmed by what I am learning about my students' lives, and the daunting task before me. I'm afraid I'm not competent, that I'll fail them." My memory is of the emotions. This didn't really change after the first year because working in underfunded public schools located in communities in crisis and engaging in transformation is, by definition, an emotional experience. It's an unstated part of the job description of being an educator: you will have many emotions in this work.

Julian Weissglass, who developed the constructivist listening structure called the dyad (discussed in Chapter Eight) insists that educators deserve support in processing emotions. He writes, "Reform programs that address only the cognitive and behavioral aspects of educators' professional lives neglect an important part of their humanness and fall short of fully attending to the empowerment of teachers" (Weissglass, 1990, p. 351). Our feelings affect our actions and we need to attend to them.

Coaching is one structure within which emotions can be expressed. When we take a cathartic stance, we intend to help the client release emotions which block her progress. Sometimes, as a coach, it can feel frustrating to work from this stance, especially if our clients have a lot of emotions to process or often want this kind of support. However, we need to remember that without clearing emotions or working through them we often can't impact real behavioral change.

A cathartic approach allows the client to release and express painful emotions. This can be useful if a client is afraid of risk or failure, if he feels incompetent, or if he is frustrated or unmotivated. Emotions can also be a powerful source of energy — we can use them to move forward into what we want to be. One of the most powerful questions to offer a client a cathartic space is simply to invite emotions into the conversation. For example, let's say a principal is describing a staff professional development session that he planned all weekend that did not go well. He's relayed every step he took and wants to plan next week's meeting together. Before moving on, it can be helpful to ask, "I'm wondering what that felt like for you. Is that something we could talk about for a minute?" The client may exhale loudly, sigh, drop his shoulders, or communicate some other kind of relief at the invitation, and then he'll talk. In this case, without processing the emotional experience, the feelings of embarrassment, frustration, or annoyance at his staff might emerge at the next meeting and result in unintended consequences.

Cathartic questions can sound like:

I'm noticing that you're experiencing some feelings. Would it be OK to explore those for a few minutes?

What's coming up for you right now? Would you like to talk about your feelings?

Wow. I imagine I'd have some emotions if that happened to me. Are you experiencing strong feelings?

In Appendix B, you'll find a compiled list of questions organized by coaching stance.

In order for a coach to invite emotions we need to be attuned to nonverbal cues. We could be talking about an upcoming unit plan or workshop and notice that the client seems distracted, fidgety, or tired; the expression on his face, the movement of his hands, or his distant tone indicates that something is off. A transformational coach is acutely observant of nonverbal communication and listens to her intuition. Sometimes we need to ask, "Is something coming up for you that you'd like to talk about?" That can be all a client needs in order to share some of the feelings that might be getting in the way of engaging in reflective conversations and learning activities. Following you'll find an exercise that I adapted from *Facilitative Coaching* (Schwarz and Davidson, 2008, p. 135) to help clients process emotions.

Echo Processing: A Cathartic Exercise

Identify an issue that might be helpful for the client to clarify, release, or celebrate and for permission to address it. For example, "It sounds like you're really having a hard time with your partner teacher. Do you want to explore that a little more?" Or, "It sounds like you had a powerful experience with your students' parents. It can be really helpful to articulate those feelings. Would that be okay?"

Ask the client to tell you as much about the issue as possible: "Don't think about what you're saying, don't filter or pause or monitor your words. Just talk as fast as possible." Most clients love this invitation.

As the client speaks, jot down key phrases and ideas. Nod and indicate that you're listening but don't interrupt, ask clarifying questions, or say anything. If you do this exercise repeatedly with a client, this stream of consciousness talking gets longer and deeper. When the client is done, pause for a few seconds. Take a deep breath and invite your client to take a few deep breaths. Then read back the items you noted, asking the client to just listen to what you recorded. Read your notes back as the client stated them in the first person, for example, "It felt amazing to see my students present their work," or "I felt humiliated."

Finally, discuss the client's reactions to the list. Ask any of the following questions:

- Was there anything you said that surprised you?
- Do you feel like anything was missing?
- How did it feel to hear me read what you said?
- Did you come to any new awareness or make any new connections?
- What needs to happen for you to process these feelings?
- Would you like to release any of the feelings you described?
- What do you want to take away or make sure you remember?

The authors of *Facilitative Coaching* suggest that this process works because often we don't know what we think or feel until we hear ourselves say it out loud (Schwarz and Davidson, 2008, p. 136). When we give clients an opportunity to talk through an issue in this way, their understanding can deepen, they feel affirmed hearing a coach echo their experience, and negative emotions can be identified and often released.

It's important to remember that we want to help our clients fully absorb their positive feelings as well as release the ones that might be blocks. The positive experiences—successes, accomplishments—are the ones that give us the strength to go on. However, there are few venues in which these get a chance to be expressed. Using this exercise to share positive feelings can be powerful—and be warned—the tears can flow just as fast hearing a coach echo back, "It felt amazing ... I was so happy ... I am proud of myself ... I never thought I could do that."

Tips for Using a Cathartic Approach

- Ask permission to invite feelings in—always!
- Acknowledge the role that emotions play.
- Affirm the value in processing and releasing emotions.

The Catalytic Approach

A catalyst is a stimulus to change. In science terminology, it is a substance that speeds up the rate of a chemical reaction without being consumed by the reaction. As coaches, it can be very effective to use a catalytic approach with our clients—we offer questions to stimulate change, not to force, push, or mandate. We design questions based on our understanding of where a client is and where he can go, and if we're right with our assessment, and if the question is offered with care, transformation is possible.

A catalytic approach is most useful to help another person reflect, work through feelings and thoughts, and learn for herself. From this stance, a coach elicits self-discovery and problem-solving, encouraging the client to take responsibility for her learning and future actions. Clarifying questions can help a client make sense of something that happened, but probing questions are our basic tools when using a catalytic approach.

Catalytic questions can sound like these:

Tell me about a previous time when you worked with a challenging person. How did you deal with that?

I hear you're really struggling with organizing your classroom. How do you intend to start?

It sounds like you're unsatisfied with the way that parent conference went. What would you do differently next time?

You've just talked about five different things you want to work on this week. The last thing you mentioned is your grading system. How important is this to you?

A catalytic approach can be used to explore the systemic issues that might be at play when a challenge presents itself. An exercise called The Five Whys can be used with an individual or a team as a catalyst for surfacing root causes to recurring problems. This exercise can be found on the National School Reform Faculty website (www.nsrfharmony.org).

Here's what the strategy might sound like when coaching a teacher who is frustrated by low parent turnout at report card conferences.

Coach: I hear that you're really frustrated by how few parents showed up to report card conferences. Can we explore what might be going on and see if we can figure out what you might be able to do? I'll use a questioning strategy called The Five Whys and I'm going to jot down some of your responses on your dry erase board, OK?

Teacher: Sure.

Coach: So why do you think parents aren't showing up?

Teacher: They don't think report card conferences are important.

Coach: Why do you think they think that?

Teacher: Because they don't understand our grading system.

Coach: Why don't you think they understand it?

Teacher: Because they're all immigrants and even though we've translated our report card into their languages, they don't understand the concepts.

Coach: What might be some other reasons they don't come to conferences?

Teacher: The kids loose the flyers we send home informing them of the day and time.

Coach: Why does that happen?

Teacher: Because their backpacks are messy and disorganized, and they just shove them in.

Coach: Why do you think that's happening?

Teacher: They don't take the time to organize them. Maybe I don't give them enough time at the end of the day to put away their stuff.

Coach: OK, I hear you naming something you might be able to do differently. Let's look at some of the other reasons that surfaced: parents don't understand aspects of the grading approach and parents may not know when the conferences are going on. What patterns do you see here?

Teacher: I guess those are communications issues.

Coach: That's what stood out to me — perhaps communications systems that could be developed. Do you think it's possible that if parents get more information about your grading systems and assessment, and if they definitely know when and where conferences take place, there might be a greater likelihood that they'd show up?

Teacher: Definitely. I know they care about their kids and want to know how they're doing.

Coach: Great! Let's talk about what needs to happen next then ...

When we use The Five Whys strategy (which can extend beyond five *whys*) we try to move clients form focusing blame on events and individuals to look for the underlying systemic explanations for the dilemmas they're facing. Often what emerges is that a number of different problems trace back to a few systemic issues. These systemic issues often affect the entire organization—the above mentioned teacher with undeveloped communication systems might also experience other frustrations that have the same systemic breakdown at their core.

Tips for Using a Catalytic Approach

- Nudge gently through questions.
- Notice metaphor and symbolic language; explore.

The Supportive Approach

 Administrators: principals often need to play a supportive role with staff. These tips will be helpful.

I had a hard time with this stance as a new coach. It felt dangerous to venture into the realm of judgment. Being supportive felt like casting positive judgment on someone and I worried that perhaps the flip side of being supportive was being critical, which was a door I never wanted to open.

Then one day, a principal I was coaching broke down. She'd been subtly asking me to be supportive and I hadn't responded. "Everyone around me is telling me what a bad principal I am," she said. "My teachers, my boss, my staff are all telling me what a weak leader I am, what a bad job I've done. Can't you just tell me something I'm doing well?"

I saw how much this principal worked, how hard she tried; my heart softened. "Of course," I said. "I can help you identify the things you are doing which are leading toward your goals. I see a lot of things you're doing well. I can share my observations with you." I am grateful that this principal called my attention to this; I became much more effective with her when I coached from a supportive stance. Furthermore, once she felt supported I was able to use other approaches that deepened our coaching work.

Coaches often witness clients go through painful realizations, take huge risks and sometimes fail, and make difficult changes to their behaviors. From the supportive stance we provide confirmation, offer encouragement, and help our client maintain focus and motivation. We intend to build the client's self-esteem and self-confidence, help clients notice and experience their moments of success, and encourage risk-taking to promote further learning.

This is a critical role for a coach to play. It's not just about making another person feel good about himself (which is valid in its own right) but also about helping the client see all the micromovements toward meeting the goals he laid out in the work plan. Most likely, they are happening regularly but it is very hard to see daily growth because it's often so small. Our job as coaches is to identify all the little positive behavioral changes and draw attention to them. By acknowledging the behaviors that will lead to large-scale success, there is more of a likelihood that the client will repeat those behaviors.

The coach's main role deals with expanding the ability to see contexts, rather than supplying content. The person being coached then sees new ways to utilize existing skills.

JULIO OLALLA (BLOOM, CASTAGNA, WARREN, AND MOIR, 2005, P. 4)

For this reason, when we make supportive comments, we must be very specific. For example, rather than saying, "You did great leading that meeting!" a coach might say, "The opening activity you led got everyone involved and grounded. They were all talking to each other as you'd asked. You closed that activity and reviewed the agenda for the afternoon and everyone was looking at you; many were nodding their heads … These are all indicators that you're on the path toward meeting your goals. How did it feel to you?"

Supportive questions or statements sound like the following:

I noticed how when you … the students really … (To identify something that worked and why)

It sounds like you have a number of ideas to try out! It'll be exciting to see which works best for you!

What did you do to make the lesson so successful?

I'm interested in learning (or hearing) more about …

Your commitment is really inspiring to me.

It sounds like you handled that in a very confident way.

You did a great job at that meeting when you …

I'm confident that you'll be successful.

COMMON CHALLENGES AND HELPFUL RESPONSES

Challenge: My client is always emotionally distraught and wants me to be a therapist. We can't get to the work.

The Lens of Emotional Intelligence. There's a fine line that a coach needs to explore—that between supporting the client to release emotions and moving into the work of creating the future, which is the point of coaching. The tricky thing is that no teacher can analyze student work immediately after emerging from an emotionally draining day. It's not unusual for coaches to think, "Wait. I'm not a therapist!" as a client talks and talks.

You might start by considering whether the issues raised by the client are ones that should be addressed by a therapist. Sometimes when we're asking confronting or cathartic questions, painful life experiences might come up. It is important that if they do, or if we think that our client could benefit from mental health attention we address it.

We also need to consider whether the conversation is actually releasing emotions. What is being said? Is it complaining and venting? Is the client trying to sort through her feelings? Is she looking for your sympathy? A coach can say that releasing emotions is useful and guide the client to notice and name the feelings and find a way for them to sit on the side while we get into the work that will help the client meet her goals.

It can be useful to set up some agreements with a client who tends to need time for processing emotions. You can get to this by sharing your observation that a lot of time seems to be spent on the emotional experiences and you're wondering about how the client will meet her goals. Does she want to agree, for example, to spend a set amount of time, say fifteen minutes, each week "releasing emotions" and then getting into the work?

While we can try to make agreements with our client, and we can try to structure our conversation so that we're supporting our client to release emotions, we may have clients who seem to use us as a therapist. As long as they aren't experiencing serious mental health issues, we also need to be OK with this. If this is where our client is at, then we need to accept her.

I'm surprised by how many times I've told myself: You need to just be OK with wherever she's at, accept her and don't make her wrong—and with time, my client has moved into a reflective, open, and transformational learning place. However, I've later recognized that had I not allowed her to move on her timeframe, she might not have moved at all.

Challenge: The teacher I'm coaching just wants me to give her positive feedback. She whines about how everyone is so critical of her teaching and just wants me to tell her things she's done well. Am I really just supposed to stroke her ego?

The Lens of Emotional Intelligence and the Lens of Adult Learning. Maybe you'll need to just give her positive feedback for a while. What's wrong with that anyway? If your client is in a place where she feels under attack, unappreciated, and insecure, then that's where she's at. You're not going to get any traction if you start sounding like her critics. So give her authentic positive feedback and help her expand the areas where she's effective. These are the kinds of supportive interventions that she is asking for and needs—trust her.

At some point, once she's developed some trust in you, she'll be ready to expand her reflective capacities. All people want to get better at whatever they're doing—if you don't see this, or it takes a long time to see this, it's because there's a really hurt, scared person in front of you. Be patient and kind. Keep your eye open for entry points and indicators that she might be ready to reflect on areas for growth, but don't push.

The challenge for coaches in schools is that we're always straddling two realities: our clients have their own histories, experiences, needs, challenges and issues. We have to meet them where they're at and the going can be slow. On the other side is the daily reality that our students experience: the children in our education system need reflective educators who are ready and willing to grow and meet their needs. As painful as it can be for coaches to recognize this discrepancy between current realities, it is what it is. We will only make it worse by forcing our adults to move where they're not yet ready or able to move. We really have no choice but to meet people where they are and trudge onwards, keeping the faith that we can move.

CHAPTER 10

Facilitative Coaching Activities

Read this when:

- You've had many conversations with your client and you feel like you should do something with him

- Your client responds well to facilitative coaching conversations and you want to engage her in activities that will continue to help her learn

- You want to engage your client in activities that might release emotions

ENGAGING CLIENTS IN LEARNING ACTIVITIES

If you asked a hundred educators who have never worked with a coach what they think a coach does, the majority will say something along the lines of: "A coach observes a teacher delivering instruction and gives her feedback." Some might add that a coach helps a teacher plan lessons or lends a sympathetic ear when times are rough. This image of a coach is not wrong, it's just limited. There are many things that a coach working in schools can do with a client. This chapter begins to explore some of these learning activities (Chapter Twelve also suggests coaching activities).

How might a coach determine which activity to engage a client in? So much of coaching is done in our heads: it is an invisible process by which we consider a pile of information through a number of frameworks, stay focused on the end goal, and take into account our current reality. When we suspect that by engaging our client in a learning activity she might move closer to her goals, then we can suggest an activity and discuss what the client might gain from it. Other times a client might put forth an idea: "I really want to observe another teacher," or "It would help if you could model the lesson." In these moments, we welcome the initiative and discuss what she might gain; we want to make sure that the activity will align with the goals, and furthermore, that the client has the skills, abilities, and capacities necessary to engage in it. Everything done in coaching needs to be intentional.

SCAFFOLDING THE LEARNING

Early in my experience coaching school leaders, I felt frustrated with Isabel, a principal I was assigned to coach. I debriefed these challenges with Kristina, my manager and a master coach. "She has set some realistic goals that could impact her school deeply," I said, "but she can't seem to do anything to get there. She says she wants to do data conferences, but then she does them and they're a disaster. She wanted to do a professional development (PD) session with teachers on formative assessment, but she was unprepared and didn't seem to know what she was talking about. I don't know what to do with her!"

Kristina listened carefully and then started doodling all over her notepad. "You have to create a scaffold," she said as she drew a building under construction and a scaffold along the side. "Huh?" I said. "She's building a new skill set," Kristina explained. "It's your job to build the scaffold, take apart the skill set into manageable pieces and help her acquire each one. Then you need to gradually release the responsibility. When the building is done, the scaffold comes down."

This notion, I realized, had been the missing element in my coaching. I had neglected to break down the learning that my clients needed to do, to build a scaffold alongside their emerging skills, or to intentionally design a plan for the gradual release of responsibility. Seeing Kristina's scribbled sketch prompted an epiphany that transformed my coaching.

In Chapter Seven, I described the stage of the work plan where a coach needs to think through the scaffold she'll construct for her client. The coach applies her knowledge of the skill set that her client wants to build and needs to identify the chunks of learning that the client needs to do. With each chunk, the coach needs to consider where the client's skills are at the time — she needs to know where the client lies in relation to where she wants to go and what her zone of proximal development is. What I realized was that with Isabel, I was often coaching outside of her ZPD and I hadn't articulated the continuum of learning and skill development that would lead her to reach her goals.

When we're engaging clients in learning activities such as those described in this chapter and Chapter Twelve, we need to apply this framework: we need to have articulated the sequence of skills—to "chunk" the learning, we need to have a strong understanding of her ZPD, and we need to have a plan for the gradual release of responsibility. It is within this framework that we identify the coaching activities that will move our client's learning.

FACILITATIVE COACHING ACTIVITIES

I've divided up coaching activities by whether they are facilitative in nature—they pull the client toward learning, or directive—the coach pushes the client toward learning. To some extent, this is a false distinction because all coaching activities can be experienced as facilitative and/or directive, but many activities fall more on one or another side of this divide. It's useful for a coach to think about activities in this way in order to be aware of whether she's falling into a comfort zone of activities. For example, I love doing role-plays with clients but need to be mindful that I'm also engaging clients in activities that allow them to get more direct and concrete feedback. The following activities are not listed in any particular order.

Visualization and Guided Imagery

 Administrators: visualization is a powerful exercise to engage a staff in at the start of a school year.

Visualization and guided imagery are powerful tools to engage adults and children in learning. There is growing research on the way that visualization actually changes brain chemistry to make us happier and even healthier. Guided imagery can help people gain insight into an issue, shift their thinking and perspective, deepen and anchor their learning, feel more empowered, increase their motivation, and change their target behavior (Schwarz and Davidson, 2008, p. 133). What we imagine, we can bring to fruition, and imagining is inspiring and motivating.

In Chapter Eleven, I describe Daniela, a principal who wanted her staff's respect, but was afraid to stand in front of them during meetings. When she shared this with me, I suggested we try a guided imagery exercise. She agreed and after leading her through a short relaxation exercise, I guided her in imagining a different scenario than the one that was her current reality. "Imagine yourself walking into a staff meeting," I said, "and standing in front of your teachers. They are looking at you, several are smiling slightly. You are feeling calm, confident, and self-assured. You know exactly what you'll say, you look around the room and make eye contact with each one. They are listening to you, their complete attention is on you. As you explain the day's agenda, you see heads nodding. You are standing tall and you feel powerful." I continued guiding this imagery, and then, while she still experienced the image with her eyes closed, I asked her to describe how she felt—physically and emotionally.

When she opened her eyes, she burst into tears. "That's what I want it to be like," she said. "I want to feel like that every week, not small and scared like now." Reflecting on the guided imagery exercise, the principal noted that it had been like watching a movie in her mind, but that now that she'd seen this possibility somewhere—even just in her mind—she felt one step closer to the reality. "But it'll probably be years before I can actually do that," she said. However, only three weeks later, after a couple of role-plays and other coaching activities, this principal walked into a staff meeting and spoke to her teachers from the front and center. The result was as she'd envisioned—the staff gave her their complete attention, she spoke clearly and concisely, she smiled and looked at everyone.

Visualization exercises can also be used with an entire staff. They are particularly helpful to envision a change that a group of people want to make. Visualizations are distinct from guided imagery as they are more facilitative in nature. The prompt might be: "Imagine yourself walking into your classroom next year. What does it look like? What do you see? Where are you when the students arrive? How do you interact with them? What do they say to you?" Whereas guided imagery is directed by the coach, for example: "I want you to imagine that your students are arriving and you greet each one by name and smile at each one." Both approaches can be very useful. Deciding which will most help a client learn is another moment when the coach uses her judgment.

Visualization draws on the imagination and the senses, which is where the deepest learning takes place. Naparstek, a noted researcher in this field informs us that, "Imagery works because the body doesn't altogether distinguish between images and real events" (Naparstek, 1994, p. 209). When we guide someone through a mental experience, when they can see themselves in their mind's eye accomplishing a goal, parts of their body feel that they've already done it. When they move into the physical reality and need to accomplish the same task, it's already been done once before—even only in the imagination.

Guided imagery exercises can be found online and on my website.

Role-Playing

 Administrators: role-playing can be done by teachers when exploring how to address issues that arise with students or parents.

Role-playing is similar to what many of us do when we call a friend and talk something over—we practice, play with the words and build our confidence. We encourage our clients to have scary, honest, and courageous conversations, but we want to make sure they can have them successfully. Role-playing gives clients an opportunity to test their skills in a safe environment before attempting them elsewhere.

I often suggest a role-play when a client speaks about an interaction that didn't reach the outcomes he had hoped. Perhaps it went poorly, or he lost his nerve, or he felt that the recipient didn't hear what he'd really wanted to say. "Let's role-play!" I say, enthusiastically. I love role-plays.

First, we identify the situation to address, as well as the skills the client would like to practice. I always ask the client what role he would like me to play: "Do you want to be the teacher and I can be the parent, or the other way around? What would help you most?" Usually I play the "other person" so that the client can practice the skills he's developing but sometimes it can help for the client to see a coach model the skills. We can also enact the same role-play a few times, alternating roles, and revising and refining what we've said.

Before role-playing, we make agreements about when and how often the client will get feedback. "We can go for eight minutes and then stop and reflect, or we can stop after each time you say something, or we can go until you feel stuck and then discuss the role-play. What would you like to try?" Generally, don't role-play for more than ten minutes—it's too long.

Although we want to enact the scenario as realistically as possible, we also don't want to make it too hard or too easy. The coach needs to keep in mind the skills the client is practicing and stay within his ZPD. Furthermore, while a coach is in a role, it's also critical to keenly observe our client's verbal and nonverbal cues for indicators of how he is feeling. Role-playing can be mildly anxiety producing—clients can feel on the spot and exposed. As long the anxiety is low, it's OK. A coach can also diffuse anxiety by incorporating laughter, lightness, and a sense of play (it's called a role-*play* after all). Sometimes, if I'm asked to play my client's role, I share my own insecurity that I might not be able to model the skills. I laugh at myself and when I'm honestly stumped, I'll stop and even ask for the client's feedback. Role-play is practice, not performance.

At the end of a role-play, the coach leads a reflection. Our goal is to support the client to articulate a couple of learnings and then we explore whether the client feels ready to use the skills we've been practicing. It's critical that when we reflect on the role-play we draw attention to what the client successfully did. We need to share concrete, positive feedback, for example: "When you asked me that question, I really felt that you genuinely wanted to know what I thought because of your facial expression, the way you leaned forward, and the way you framed the question. It was open and inviting."

Clients who are working on improving their communication skills often report that role-play is the most effective activity that I engage them in. I frequently hear: "When I had the real conversation with that teacher (or student or parent) it was easy!" Although apprehensive at first, I have converted many teachers and principals into regular role-playing because it is a transformative experience.

Videotaping

Using video is an extremely effective tool in facilitative coaching. In recent years, researchers have compared changes in teacher practice based on feedback from principal observations to what happens when teachers reflected on videos of their instruction. It probably won't be a surprise that the changes that result after teachers watch videos of themselves far outweigh those that result from principal observations.

Although everyone's first response is usually, "I hate seeing myself on video!" I strongly encourage my clients to record themselves several times a year: teachers in classes, principals leading meetings or having one on one conversations with teachers, and teams of educators who want to examine group dynamics. It's essential to have a focus question or issue to explore, ideally that's connected to the goals in the work plan. For example, a teacher might look at patterns of participation in her class, how she gives directions, or her interactions with students. A principal might want to consider whether or not he is able to say everything he wants to say in a difficult conversation with a staff member or how another receives his communication.

After the video has been shot the client can watch the video alone or with a coach. We look for data related to the question or issue that we identified but other reflections also surface. It's not unusual that the client observes herself in a way that she's never noticed before, saying, for example, "I can't believe how much I talked!" or "I never knew I did that . . . " Clients can feel embarrassed or frustrated by what they see; a coach might use a cathartic approach to help the client process and learn from the video.

A confrontational approach may also be appropriate when debriefing a video. A client might avoid information, such as a preference for calling on boys or a tendency to speak louder and slower to English language learners (ELLs). With the data in front of us, a coach could confront the client to examine the data: "What did you notice about your voice when you called on your ELLs?" "I counted that out of twelve times you called on students, ten of those were male students. Were you aware of this?" Particularly when we notice inequities we need to raise these with our clients. When we do this, videotaping becomes an activity that crosses the boundaries between a facilitative and an authoritative activity.

A few technical notes on videotaping:

- Sometimes I've held the camera, other times we've tucked it discretely on a shelf so that everyone forgets it's there.

- Make agreements about who will see the video and what will happen to it after. For example, "Only you will see this" or "We can save this for your portfolio" or "We'll erase it right after."

- Also offer the option of deleting a video if, for example, the lesson went horribly wrong, or the principal completely lost her composure during a meeting. The client reserves the right to trash it. It is essential that the client have a sense of control over this learning.

Surveys

Surveys can be administered to all stakeholders. A teacher can survey her students or a principal might survey teachers and staff members. They can be a useful tool when a client's goals include areas of culture and climate, emotional intelligence, and building collaborative cultures. They can be a way for stakeholders to give input on decisions and general feedback. Surveys can be administered on an as-needed basis, or every quarter, semester, or year if a client wants to track changes over time.

The survey should be co-constructed with the client and tailored to his specific concerns. The role of the coach is to help the client figure out what he wants and needs to know and then how to phrase questions that will elicit that information. It can help to have examples of surveys (Exhibits 10.2 and 10.3 at the end of this chapter offer sample surveys), but the client should also be invited to generate questions. A coach might help with wording—survey questions shouldn't be leading or limiting—but the client needs to feel that he's driving the inquiry.

Surveys are usually most effective when responses can be anonymous. There are a number of online sites where this can be done. A coach can also administer a survey and transcribe the results. If a coach plays this role, it is extremely important that she protects the identity of the survey takers.

If the coach will transcribe the data, then before the survey is administered, the coach and client need to agree on what the data report will look like. For example, if a group of stakeholders—students, for example—will respond to a set of short-answer questions, the coach can summarize those statements or quantify them in some way, such as, "25 percent of students mentioned that the project was too difficult." The coach could also transcribe each comment and provide the raw data. What is important, again, is that the client makes this decision and that it is communicated in advance to the survey takers. They need to know how their feedback will be shared.

Debriefing the survey is the most critical step. Clients usually need time to read and silently process the data, and then discuss it with the coach. After a number of experiences with surveys, I've concluded that a client should never be given the data to process alone—for example, do not e-mail the client the transcripts and agree to "talk about it tomorrow." The experience for the client is often difficult and raises many emotions. It's the coach's responsibility to guide the client through this. In the debrief, a coach might use a number of approaches—she might empathize with the client and be supportive, provide cathartic ways to move through the emotions, and incorporate catalytic approaches so that the data leads to learning and growth. Surveys can be a catalyst for tremendous change in beliefs, behaviors, and being, but they must be facilitated well and the client must want to do them.

Positive Self-Talk

Lisa was a skilled novice principal who took on an exceptionally difficult school. The task was overwhelming and she worked eighty to ninety hours a week. In March of her first year, in a moment of exhaustion and self-doubt, Lisa confessed that she didn't know if she was going to make it through the year. "I want to be performing at this level," she said, her hand held at shoulder height, "But I'm performing at this level," her hand plummeted to the ground. "I feel inept," she said. At that moment, her office door opened and the secretary reminded Lisa that she hadn't yet made an important call. Lisa looked at me, her eyes welling with tears. This was after an extremely challenging day. "See what I mean?" she said. "I promised I'd call by 4:00." It was now 4:30.

I decided to get tough. "Lisa, you're going to have to squash those kinds of thoughts. You recognize how hard everyone here is working and show your appreciation all the time, but you don't do that with yourself. You have to start, right now. You are going to forget things, you're going to make mistakes. You can repair this mistake and I know you will. But if you beat yourself up all the time, you're going to drown. Everyone is doing the best they can, yourself included. Say that to yourself, now," I ordered. She did.

Lisa was sabotaging herself with her negative self-talk and she wasn't seeing the things she was doing well—of which there were many. I suggested one of my favorite assignments. At the end of each day, for one week, I asked her to write down three things that went well and identify her role in them. I asked her if she'd be willing to share these with me. She agreed. The following week Lisa reported that she'd had a much better week. "So many things went well," she shared. "I don't even know if good things have been happening all along and I just didn't notice them, or if it was just a good week. I don't care. I feel much better." Her list ranged from small things like, "The bathrooms were cleaned on time because I asked the custodians to check in with me at noon," to "Everyone who came to the parent meeting participated and left feeling inspired because I used different speaking structures to ensure equitable participation." Lisa continued this daily practice for the rest of the year, sharing that it made a pivotal difference in her self-perception, mood, and energy levels.

This cathartic strategy can be used with clients who are struggling to see their successes. Another way to reach a similar outcome is to ask a client to set his watch or cell phone to ring every two hours. When the timer goes off, he identifies what he's doing well or what's going well at that moment. This is just another way to take note of the positive moments in our day and those moments when we're doing good work which we often miss.

Our brains are programmed to notice what's *not* working. They are "like Teflon" to positive experiences and "like Velcro" to negative experiences (Hansen, 2009). As coaches, we support clients to shift their awareness. It is a key strategy for building resiliency.

Writing

Michelle was an experienced teacher who was transitioning into a number of leadership roles in her school when I coached her. We met for ninety minutes every Friday after the kids left; Michelle often arrived late and frazzled. "I have a hard time focusing on our reflective conversations," she confessed soon after we'd started working together. "My mind is going a million miles an hour." I appreciated her candor and asked if she knew of any strategies that helped her mind settle. "Writing!" she told me, "I love to write and it really helps me sort my thoughts out, but I never have time for it." I proposed that we start each session with fifteen minutes of reflective writing—I could supply prompts or she could journal. As with all other activities, I always say something like, "Let's just try it. Who knows? It might help, maybe not. Let's try!"

Michelle was eager to write and we quickly saw the impact of using a focusing strategy at the beginning of our meetings. Journaling also allowed Michelle to identify the specific issues she wanted my support on. After a while, Michelle began to add ten minutes of writing immediately after our meetings—she'd journal on our conversation or record ideas that had arisen. Michelle attributed a great deal of the growth she made in the year I coached her to the reflections and learning that came from her writing, coupled with the space to engage in a conversation about those ideas.

For clients who are receptive, writing can be a powerful way to record thoughts and events, process feelings, and clarify issues. Using writing as a way to visualize can also help concretize a person's goals. A teacher can be prompted to write about how she'd like to feel at the end of the school year, or what she'd like to see during tomorrow's science lab. A principal might write about how he wants to see teachers collaborating or engaging with parents. These exercises help bring out unconscious beliefs, creative ideas, and stumbling blocks. They give the coach more "data" to engage a client on, more information about how our client thinks and feels, and more information is always good.

Exploring Metaphors

I had coached Tina for a year and planned on working with her for another. One morning she casually told me about a documentary she'd watched the previous night.

The show explored the process of returning an injured, orphaned baby river otter to the wild. The naturalist slowly taught the otter to survive on its own, allowed it a larger and larger terrain to swim in, and finally, one day, released it into the Amazon. At this point in the telling, Tina's voice filled with emotion. "I'm that baby otter, but I'm not ready to be released yet."

We spent quite a while exploring the symbolism in this story and how it applied to Tina. "Tell me more about what the naturalist did," I said.

"He was so gentle with the otter. He encouraged and it and waited for signs that it wanted to go. He didn't make it do things it didn't want to do, he just kept expanding the space it could swim in," she said.

"How do you think the otter felt when it was released?" I asked.

"Good, I imagine. I think it felt ready. It just swam off and wasn't concerned about how far away the scientist was," she said.

"How did it know it was ready?" I asked.

"It didn't have to think about what it was doing. It could swim and fend for itself without having to plan every step."

"What could that mean for you, as a principal? What could that feel like?"

Tina spoke about what she'd want to be able to do in order to feel ready. She was very clear about what she wanted me to do and about the kind of encouragement she needed. For one thing, she couldn't identify the gradual release model that I was using in my coaching and she wanted me to make this explicit for her, which was very useful feedback to get. For the rest of that year, we both used the metaphor of the river otter to contextualize our work. This reference allowed Tina to hold a big picture understanding of coaching, to access her own confidence and agency, and to be clear with me about what she needed. I affectionately called her my "baby otter."

Exploring the symbols and representations that clients bring up in coaching is a powerful way to help someone gain deeper self-understanding. Metaphors, images, and allegories can be used to describe feelings or experiences. We want to grab onto these offerings if they are put forward and dig into them, for they offer a glimpse into someone's subconscious, a different perspective on how someone sees herself, and a high-leverage point from which to work.

Metaphors, analogies, and similes "seem to sit at a subtle boundary between the verbal and the visual aspects of our minds," write Schwarz and Davidson (2008, p. 129). This is an area rich with creativity, where we can see solutions to a problem and where we can access different skills and abilities. Metaphors also reveal how we're defining a problem, and how we make sense of and represent our experiences at a given moment in time. When we hear our clients use metaphors, it is important to pause, listen carefully, and explore. We want to understand their thinking as best as we can, but also, in the act of asking for explanation, we create a catalytic space for our clients to explore their feelings. Exploring metaphors can help us discover solutions we hadn't considered.

Asking clients to think metaphorically can help them access their knowledge and capacities. Carla was a successful principal reassigned to a struggling school in our district. Although she felt confident she'd be able to manage it, before school started she experienced a wave of intense anxiety. "Respond to this question really fast, Carla," I said one morning as we walked through the halls. "If you could transform into any animal right now, what would you be?"

She laughed. "I'd be my cat," she said. "My cat is calm, sweet and caring, and playful at times. But she also notices everything and if necessary, she'll pounce." As we talked about cats and the feline attributes that Carla could emulate, Carla became more energetic and her confidence resurfaced. Using a metaphor was a way to bypass some thoughts and feelings that were blocking Carla. Imagining her cat became a way that she was able to quickly access her skills when she felt nervous, and referencing the cat was a way that I could remind Carla of this shift.

Exhibit 10.1 offers question stems to explore metaphors and symbolic thinking.

Exhibit 10.1. Question Stems to Explore Symbolic Thinking

The following questions attempt to access the right side of the brain, the creative side that thinks in symbols and metaphors. Information from this side can be very revealing and helpful in coaching. You don't need to ask all of them—be selective.

1. If you could be any animal right now, what would it be?
2. What animal is like your problem?
3. When you're at work, what kind of animal do you feel like you are?
4. When you're in a nonwork environment, what kind of animal do you feel like you are?
5. If you could transform into another person—past or present, famous or not—who would that be? Why?
6. What famous historical person would be able to tackle your problem? What would he/she do?

7. If you could have any kind of superpower, what would it be?
8. Imagine your school is a kind of water-traveling vessel such as a boat or a ship. What kind do you envision and where are you on this vessel? What are you doing?
9. Think of all the different forms of water that you can: glaciers, lakes, ponds, rivers, streams, the ocean. Which one of these most resembles what change feels like to you?
10. Complete the statement: In my next life I want to ...

Storytelling

Storytelling is one of the most powerful tools we can use when working with individuals and groups. Stories can bring people together, create deep wells of empathy, facilitate the release of emotions, and help us create narratives in which we are powerful, resilient, and transformed. When clients tell a story to a coach, they also communicate raw data about feelings and beliefs. We can use this information to determine our next move: to predict what kind of coaching approach might help our client, or what kind of activity might be useful to engage in.

I love stories, I love creating, reading and telling them. But stories are not real—they are simply an interpretation of some things that happened. Perhaps that's why I love stories—because facts can be interpreted in so many different ways and because we can become our stories. Therefore, we storytellers have tremendous power over how we see our lives and the course of action we take given the interpretation we make. Stories can liberate or they can limit us. A coach can help people surface, question and, redefine their stories.

I frequently feel that people walk into a coaching session clutching one story and leave embracing a completely different one. When offered a choice, they gladly create something that connects to their core values and to their ultimate goals. My role is to help them see the impact of holding the story they came in with (which is often comforting but limited) and to consider alternatives.

I frequently use the following prompt: "Tell me a story about ..." Clients come to recognize this refrain as an invitation to share experiences and feelings. I'll use this prompt when I hear that a client feels stuck. For example, a principal might express that he feels that he's "tried everything" to get a certain teacher to change her behavior. "Can you tell me a story about a time when you changed one of your own entrenched behaviors? What happened? What helped you change?" My first intention is to help the client get grounded in his or her own previous success. Then I will help the client bridge his experience and learnings to his current challenge.

Recalling previous positive or successful experiences always makes for powerful story prompts. "Tell me about a time when you were successful with a child," "Tell me what you love most about your work," "Tell me a story about a lesson that went better than expected," "Tell me a story about someone who inspires you." All of these questions help clients shift their energy and reconnect with their own sources of power. This reconnection can serve as a catalyst toward being able to manage a challenging current reality.

Another effective approach is to invite a client to tell a story from another person's perspective. This usually follows their own rendition of an event. Daniela (a principal who I'll tell you more about in Chapter Eleven) was very upset by her teachers' behavior at a staff meeting. She had noted that all her teachers, except for Lucinda and Michael, were disrespectful. "So, let's play for a minute—let's create a narrative," I said. "Imagine that Lucinda goes home tonight and tells her partner about her day. What would she say?"

Daniela thought for a moment. "She'd probably say, 'The principal let everyone grade papers, talk amongst themselves and do whatever they wanted. She didn't even tell them to stop. And she doesn't recognize that Michael and I are onboard and supportive." I followed this by asking Daniela what she'd like Lucinda to go home and say to her partner. Asking clients to tell a story from another person's perspective can be catalytic.

A third approach in storytelling is to ask a client to create alternate stories to what actually happened. We can ask, over and over, "What if?" and ask the client to change the storyline at our prompt. "Daniela, what could you have done differently in that meeting when you noticed several teachers engaged in conversation while you were sharing information," I asked. "I could have ...," she responded.

"And what if they ... ?" I pushed on. Daniela brainstormed other alternatives. This kind of imaginative storytelling helps clients envision other actions they could take. It is particularly effective when a client seems to frequently confront similar situations.

When we inquire about clients' work outside of life, they sometimes tell stories and reveal aspects of their character and personality that can be very useful to reference in coaching. One principal I worked with was a marathon runner: I used running analogies to support her reflection: "At what mile do you often feel like you can't go on? That your legs are giving out? How do you manage those feelings? What do you say to yourself? How do you feel at the end?" Another client had done some acting in college, yet he struggled with performance anxiety in front of his staff. "How did you deal with that kind of anxiety when you were acting?" I asked. He reported that he'd practiced a great deal and then just "flicked an internal switch" and was able to detach from the audience. "Could you try that when you have to speak to your staff?" He agreed and I often used a shorthand code to remind him of this skill, "flick the switch," I'd say as he'd go into a staff meeting. The more we know about our clients the more we can help them; stories sometimes encourage people to share information that they wouldn't otherwise share. An artful coach finds many ways to prompt storytelling.

Storytelling can also reveal painful past or present experiences. We invite stories to explore emotions, but sometimes we need to remember that there are limits to the kind of support we can provide. It is not unusual, or even inappropriate, that there are moments when a coach might need to gently suggest that a client consider the support of a mental health provider. On a number of occasions, I have said, "I think that the kind of support you might need with this issue is the kind that a therapist might offer. I'm afraid that I'm not qualified to help you in this way and I want to be sure you can get your needs met. Is that something you think might be helpful for you to pursue?"

It is to be expected that unresolved issues from our childhoods might show up when we're working with children or other adults. While we want to validate a client's courage in sharing the information they share with us (I have heard stories of child abuse and other trauma) we want to make sure they don't confuse a coach with a therapist, and we want to make sure they get the help that they need. Often, by the time they share this kind of information with a coach they deeply trust us and are receptive to our suggestion. We may be uniquely positioned to guide a client toward the healing that he or she really needs.

Visual and Artistic Activities

Using artistic processes can be deeply cathartic and catalytic. Art can help some people quickly get to the heart of an issue and communicate it to others. When we are invited to think in pictures, colors, lines or shapes, we access the part of our brains that "knows" visually (Schwarz and Davidson, 2008, p. 197). This is an untapped source of information and inspiration.

Collage is one of my favorite activities to do with groups or individuals. For those who feel intimidated by art (those who say, "I can't draw!") collage is a way to combine images that speak to the nonlinguistic part of our brains. Teachers and principals can create collages with images from magazines that reflect their visions, hopes and dreams. Playing music while creating art can also help people access other ways of thinking.

 Administrators: collaging is a powerful activity to do with a staff at the beginning of the year.

"How is this coaching?" teachers have asked as I arrive carrying bags of magazines and glue. "My role as a coach is to help you learn more about yourself," I explain, "to access all the parts of yourself that you can draw on as you work toward transformation. Our creative sides are powerful sources that we often don't tap. I hope to help you connect with those sources."

The authors of *Facilitative Coaching* suggest an activity called "shaping your reality" which can help clients become present, stimulate self-reflection and access their deepest thoughts. Clients are offered a piece of plasticine clay. "Hold the clay in your hand," I say. "Feel the texture and weight and pay attention to the temperature of the clay. Smell it. Notice what happens when you put pressure against it in your hand. Attend to how you feel holding the clay. Now let your hands begin to form the clay in any way that your hands choose. Let your hands play with and form the clay." After a few minutes, ask participants to place the form on the table. "Ask your clay creation to speak to you. Write down what it says to you. Begin by using 'I' and let the clay speak in the first person" (Schwarz and Davidson, 2008, p. 215).

I have used this activity with individuals and groups to help them learn about each other and reflect on issues that surface. In a team of eighth-grade teachers, one teacher who had enthusiastically engaged with this exercise revealed that her clay creation had told her something that no one else had ever had the courage to tell her: "It said I was too hard on the kids, that I'm strict with them and they don't know I care about them. I know this is the truth; I've had a really hard time accepting this." During the debrief, a coach might use other coaching approaches—a confrontational or cathartic approach to help a client make sense of the experience.

Incidentally, once they know you have clay, many clients ask for it during a coaching session—it can help them stay focused or relieve anxiety that surfaces. And sometimes, if a client is holding a piece of clay, I'll play with one too—it helps me stay focused.

CONCLUSION

As with any coaching activity that we engage clients in, afterwards we want to elicit their reflections and feedback. We need to know how they experienced the activity, what they learned, and what worked or didn't work. In order to best support clients, and to continue building trust, we need immediate feedback on the activity we engage them in. Furthermore, we need to look for indicators in the following weeks or months that the activities resulted in some changes in behaviors, beliefs, or being. If we lead a client through a series of guided imageries intended to help him develop positive interactions with students, then we need to look for indicators that this is resulting in changed practice. We need to look for these indicators and we also want to invite our clients to be on the lookout for them too.

Exhibit 10.2. Sample Survey for Principals: Staff Relationship

1. How long have you been at this school?

Less than 1 year   1–2 years   2–4 years   More than 4 years

2. Rate your overall level of satisfaction at this school:

Very unsatisfied   Unsatisfied   Neutral   Satisfied   Very satisfied

3. Rate your overall level of satisfaction with your principal:

Very unsatisfied   Unsatisfied   Neutral   Satisfied   Very satisfied

Check the box which most accurately reflects your feelings in response to the statement:

	Strongly Disagree	Disagree	Neutral	Agree	Strongly agree
I trust my principal.					
I feel appreciated by my principal.					
I feel like I can have open conversations with my principal.					
I feel that my principal respects me.					
I feel that I can talk to my principal about challenges I'm facing.					

(continued)

Exhibit 10.2. (*Continued*)

	Strongly Disagree	Disagree	Neutral	Agree	Strongly agree
I feel that my principal listens to me.					
I feel that when I'm speaking to my principal his words and tone of voice convey respect.					
I feel that when I'm speaking to my principal his body language conveys respect.					
I feel that my principal listens and takes teacher ideas into consideration before making schoolwide decisions.					
I feel that the principal has a vision for the school that I share and support.					
I always know what the principal expects from me.					
I feel that the principal communicates information in a clear and timely manner.					

4. Please explain any of the above ratings or comment on any of these questions.

Exhibit 10.3. Sample Teacher Survey: End-of-the-Year Survey for Students

Dear Students:

I need to know what you think about this class and my teaching this year. Your ideas and feelings are very important to me. I'll use this information to make my class better next year. It's important that you are as honest as possible.

Thank you!

In the following chart, check the box that most accurately reflects your feelings in response to the statement.

	Strongly Disagree	Disagree	Neutral	Agree	Strongly agree
I learned a lot in this class.					
I felt challenged by this class.					
I was clear about the goals for this class.					
The content of this class connected to my life and was meaningful to me.					
My teacher cares about me.					
My teacher respects me.					
My teacher gave me timely and useful feedback on my work.					
My teacher is fair.					
My teacher had high expectations for me.					

Please explain any of the above ratings.

Then please answer the following questions.

1. Which project did you enjoy the most this year?

2. Tell me about a time in my class when you felt respected.

3. Tell me about a time in my class when you felt frustrated.

4. What advice can you give me about how to be a better teacher?

5. What advice can you give me about changing my class next year?

CHAPTER 11

Directive Coaching
Conversations

Read this when:

- You want strategies to push your client's thinking; you sense that he might need a stronger nudge than the ones you've been trying

- You feel stuck in your coaching and want different ways of engaging in conversation with a client

WHEN IS DIRECTIVE COACHING USEFUL?

Have you ever heard yourself say something like, "I'm so unlucky!" or "I'll never be able to lose weight (or find a partner or buy a house); I just need to accept that I'll always be fat (or single or a renter)"? When you've heard those thoughts filter through your mind or come out of your mouth, have you also heard a little voice say, "Um . . . maybe part of the problem is the way you're thinking?" These beliefs, or mental models, prevent us from real change. However, if a coach can address these beliefs and help a client shift the behaviors that emerge from them, then transformation is within reach. One of the highest leverage ways that a coach can work is by interrupting mental models which if left untouched create impenetrable fortresses around transformation. Using the directive strategies (those that John Heron calls "authoritative" approaches) can be a very effective way to interrupt these mental models.

A coach must hone her ability to recognize when a directive or authoritative approach is called for. This chapter starts with a closer look at mental models and the kinds of storytelling that hold us back. Once we learn to recognize and understand those "symptoms" we'll look at Heron's approaches and consider how and when to use each one.

A STORY ABOUT A PRINCIPAL WHO NEEDED A DIRECTIVE COACHING STANCE

Daniela was in her third year as principal when I started working with her. The first time I observed her was at a beginning of the year planning day that she led for her staff. The desks were arranged haphazardly in the classroom where the twenty-five teachers met. Daniela sat in a chair amongst her teachers, barely visible from where I sat, and facilitated the morning session. Her volume was low, her voice wavered occasionally, the directions she gave were unclear. At least half the teachers paid no attention: they texted on their phones, scanned through curriculum guides, or carried on low conversations about their summers with their colleagues. Afterwards, Daniela and I met to debrief. She had noticed that the teachers weren't engaged, and said, "See? What did I tell you? They don't respect me."

Daniela continued to detail the ways in which her teachers demonstrated their disrespect; her mental model was solid and getting in the way of literal action—she wouldn't stand in front of them or make eye contact with her teachers. And yet, I knew that she was deeply committed to the community of students that she served and wanted to be a powerful leader.

"Can we explore this, Daniela?" I asked. "Would it be OK if we took a look at your beliefs about your teachers?" She agreed. "Tell me more about why you think that they don't respect you," I asked.

"I'm a young principal and there are many veteran teachers. They think I don't know anything. Also, they seem so stuck in their ways. I want to really change things at this school and they don't seem interested." Within her statements, I heard many assumptions and conclusions. I wanted to bring Daniela to the level of data—at least the data set that she had selected.

"So when you started here," I asked, "can you give me some examples of what the teachers said or did that made you feel like they weren't interested in changing?"

Daniela gave me a number of examples. She seemed to have mentally catalogued her teachers' transgressions, which she acknowledged when she said, "You probably think I'm a little crazy remembering every comment and thing they did."

"That must have been hard," I said.

"The frustrating thing is," Daniela replied, "this always seems to happen to me. I just feel like whatever school I've worked at, people don't respect me."

This—as you might suspect—is where flood lights saturated my mind. This was a coaching moment when the truth is so bright you feel stunned and can only respond by nodding your head. Whenever you hear "this has happened elsewhere," you've struck a golden mental model.

Daniela had a warehouse of data that validated that teachers didn't like her. There were many ways to go with this inquiry. "I'm just curious, Daniela. What would respect look like from one of your teachers?"

"They wouldn't fight me on everything. They'd do what I ask—I mean, not blindly, but they wouldn't push back on every little thing. They'd also listen to me in meetings, they'd put away their books and engage in what I ask."

"OK," I said, "So what about this morning? Were any teachers doing any of these?" Around half were.

"I know what you're saying," Daniela said. "I know they don't all disrespect me. Lucinda is totally on board, so is Michael. They're model teachers . . ."

"OK, but you started off telling me that your teachers don't respect you and that they're rude."

"They are."

"Well, not all of them."

"No, but most of them."

"OK. I'm just wondering, is it possible that there could be other ways to understand their behavior? And that perhaps there are behaviors that you're not noticing—like Lucinda's, Michael's, and others' who are engaged?"

She nodded.

"Could we explore this some more? We could go on a data quest to notice their actions." She agreed.

Over the following months, I helped Daniela gather a range of data including survey responses, observations, and video recordings so that we could see what her teachers were doing during meetings. The first thing that Daniela needed to do was apply a wide-angle lens to her observations of her staff.

We also explored the notion of respect—what it meant to different people, how we demonstrate it, and the role it plays within a staff. As Daniela's thoughts began to shift what she noticed was that her teachers seemed more respectful. She stood up in front of her staff at meetings. She clarified expectations for behavior ("no texting, no side conversations"), which was appreciated by teachers like Lucinda and Michael.

The conclusion she came to was that her teachers, given where they were at in their careers and in the context of their school, needed her to show up differently as a leader. When she was clear and direct about how she wanted them to engage in meetings, they responded. However, had Daniela's mental model remained intact, she wouldn't have been able to institute the instructional reforms she envisioned.

MENTAL MODELS

Like a pane of glass framing and subtly distorting our vision, mental models determine what we see.

PETER SENGE (1994, P. 235)

Mental models, or mind-sets, are our values, beliefs and a series of assumptions about how the world works. Unconsciously, we create a story about other people, institutions, and the world which drives our behavior. While everyone has them, in fact, we need them to make sense of the complex world in which we live, all mental models are flawed to some extent. Usually our mental models are invisible to us. A coach attempts to bring them to the surface, explore them, see the effects of the mental model on the client's life, and find ways to create new mental models that serve us better. Some aspects of our mental models may hold us back, or hold others back. Many of us could benefit from reframing negative thinking into empowering thoughts, or from modifying our picture of who we think we are.

This is a useful juncture to distinguish between coaching and therapy: a therapist will explore the origins of those mental models while a coach is less interested in where they came from (although we acknowledge their origins) and more interested in considering the effect of operating from within them and then in changing them. We help a client make these mental models visible, we look to see if there's anything problematic in how they're working, and we explore how to change, replace, or demolish them.

River and Rut Stories

Robert Hargrove offers another way to think about mental models: We all tell stories about our lives, he explains; stories are our interpretations of what happens. Some are very helpful—he calls these "river stories," but others limit and define our way of being as well as how we think about and interact with others—he calls those "rut stories" (Hargrove, 2003, p. 87).

A river story reflects a commitment to learn and grow. For example, "My first year of teaching was brutal but I was so ready for the second year." A river story doesn't limit us. A rut story, however, uses defensive reasoning to protect one's self. Daniela's rut story, "my teachers don't respect me" was a classic example. A rut story is constricting, cuts us off from other people and usually leaves us feeling somewhat powerless.

This is an extremely useful framework for a coach. It is our role to listen for and then surface, test, and revise rut stories: they usually reflect a mental model that is getting in the way of our success. Intervening in a rut story is a confrontational coaching act; we work to bring awareness to the story and its unintended consequences. And then we help our client transform it into a river story.

So what can we do when we hear a rut story? This is a confrontational approach:

First, interrupt the story: "Wait a minute. I hear you telling a rut story." Or "I hear you making some assumptions about this situation. Could we explore that?" We don't make the client wrong for his rut story; we just name it.

Then we invite the client to look at the effect on himself and others of holding this story. We ask questions exploring the possibilities and limitations of working from such stories. "I hear your story that your teachers don't trust you. If those are their feelings, what can you do? What actions are available to you? What might happen if you do those? What might be the effect on students if you took those actions?"

Next we ask the client to step back and observe the facts; we guide them down the Ladder of Inference to data sets. We ask, "What are other ways to view what happened? Did you notice anything else? Is there any data you might not be considering?"

Finally, we propose creating a river story: "How you see yourself or what happened is one possible interpretation. What are other possible interpretations that might be more inspiring, empowering, or accurate?" We help our clients generate alterative interpretations, but we don't provide them with a better belief system. That's not our job. They need to own the river story they create.

Daniela changed her story from, "My teachers don't respect me," to "Some of my teachers need me to show up in a different way as a leader." This allowed her to feel confident and hopeful, and she realized there was a wider array of actions that she could take in order to reach her goals.

Classic Rut Stories

Many of the classic rut stories identified by Hargrove are prevalent in schools. Hargrove identifies a number of classic rut stories (Hargrove, 2003, pp. 98–99). It's useful to name and discuss them with teachers and principals. Read these three rut stories and see if they sound familiar:

The "victim story": When someone is stuck in this story, she gives away all her power to others or the situation and is unable to create what she wants. (This was Daniela's classic story.)

The "tranquilizing story": When someone doesn't achieve a result he wants, or does something to get himself in trouble, he comes up with a set of reasons and excuses. This makes him feel better about himself. "I did my best, but we didn't have a copy machine for the first half of the year; I had a cold for almost the entire winter; and I got a tough group of kids." While a client might achieve a superficial numbing, the coach can support the person to process the feelings of guilt, shame, and sadness.

The "why bother?" story sounds like, "I don't have the time;" "There's no money;" "I don't have the authority." It is what we hear when someone is feeling that she's unable to create what she wants because her possibilities and choices are limited. This is often a cover-up for wanting to stay in a comfort zone or not wanting to take responsibility. Below the surface is an attitude of resignation.

A coach's job is to help clients see their situations and actions in ways that allow them to make other choices if they want. As long as they are willing, we help clients see that they are the authors of their stories and they can create new ones — the way they interpret something that happens can be energizing and empowering, or it can be self-destructive. We look for ways to help people get unstuck from their stories and develop a new perspective of themselves, others, and their circumstances.

This kind of change takes time. As we build our awareness of the stories we've told for decades, and as we reframe our stories over and over, our brain literally changes: neurons and synapses find new ways to wire together. We coaches have our rut stories too. One that I had to transform was, "Adults resist change"; which was not useful if I wanted to help adults learn. I worked to replace that with, "Adults seek change; they want to be supported and guided through change; they are eager to learn." I'm a much more effective coach when this is my driving narrative.

Another essential tool for deconstructing mental models and rut stories is Chris Argyris's Ladder of Inference, which I introduced in Chapter Three. The *Ladder of Inference* is the term for the cognitive pathway that people travel up when they form beliefs that can lead to fixed mental models. It is invaluable in deconstructing mental models.

Webs of Belief

Our mental models are sometimes invisible to us. We might notice that we feel "stuck" in an area of our life, but not quite sure how to get out of bad habits or negative trains of thoughts. Drath and Van Veslor (2006) use the term *webs of belief* to describe the interconnected threads of beliefs that are mutually reinforcing and that guide our actions. These threads form a mind-set—an overall habitual way of understanding and approaching the world around us—and they become our river or rut stories. After a while, we don't even notice them—they are so deeply embedded in the way that we think. I appreciate this metaphor and sometimes, when I hear a client sharing a rut story, I visualize her stuck in this web like a trapped insect that's been paralyzed by a spider's venom. She's lying there, comfortable perhaps, unaware of the danger.

A confrontational approach can take apart these webs. However, coaches need to prepare to deal with the emotions that surface. As clients become aware of their mental models (which often affect their personal lives as well) they can experience a range of feelings: anger, shame, sadness, embarrassment. A coach may need to take a cathartic approach for the client to process and release these feelings before the client can move onto building a new mental model.

Furthermore, when the threads of belief collapse, clients can experience major anxiety—it can feel as if the ground beneath their feet is giving way. After an intense confrontational conversation with a veteran principal, she said, "I feel like I'm tumbling down the rabbit hole like Alice. Nothing makes any sense anymore." As coaches, it is our responsibility to help our client build another web so that the client has somewhere to go. We can't just destroy their web. The Ladder of Inference can help guide a client into new mental models as we expand their data set. We also need to encourage clients to try new ways of thinking, to don them like a new outfit and see how they feel. Creating new mental models is a process and a practice. The webs can quickly crumble, but the rebuilding can be slow.

Tips for Shifting Mental Models

1. Listen for stories.

2. Interrupt rut stories. Ask the client, "What are the unintended consequences of this story?"

3. Step back and observe facts. Ask the client, "What are other ways to view what happened?"

4. Create a river story.

Directive (Authoritative) Coaching

When a coach recognizes a fixed mental model, a rut story, or a paralyzing web of belief, a directive (or authoritative) coaching stance can be very effective. From this stance, a coach pushes a client in her learning. In order for us to be successful, however, we need to be artful and skilled—pushing is delicate business. Within masterful coaches, Robert Hargrove identifies a "potent combination of toughness and compassion" (Hargrove, 2003, p. 18). This is what we'll need to access when we take an authoritative stance in coaching.

Heron's framework names three directive approaches: confrontational, instructive, and prescriptive. Each is distinct in how it's delivered, and can have different effects on shifting a client's behavior, beliefs, and being. As with the facilitative coaching stances, we often move back and forth between approaches in response to how a client engages. Let's start by taking a close look at confrontational coaching.

THE CONFRONTATIONAL APPROACH

 Administrators: this is a highly effective strategy for principals to explore with teachers.

A confrontational approach can raise awareness, challenge the client's assumptions, or stimulate awareness of behavior, beliefs, or being. It can also help a client see the consequences of an action or boost the client's confidence by affirming success.

This term—*confrontation*—makes many of us uncomfortable. Confrontation is often seen as a negative thing and it seems very uncoachlike. I think of it as an *interrupting* stance to use when I need to mediate a behavior, mind frame, belief, or way of being; it's a way to generate a little cognitive dissonance. Coaches are often positioned ideally to use this strategy. We get to know a client very well, we see him in many different contexts, we've heard his stories, we care about him and he trusts us. It is our responsibility to our client, as well as to the larger change efforts to interrupt behavior, beliefs, or being which are not leading to transformation.

Most of the examples given about interrupting rut stories, deconstructing mental models, or moving down the Ladder of Inference are confrontational strategies.

Confrontational coaching questions sound like the following:

Would you be willing to explore your reasoning about this?

Would you be open to examining the assumptions behind your reasoning?

I'd like to ask you about ___. Is that OK?

What's another way you might . . . ?

What would it look like if . . . ?

What do you think would happen if . . . ?

How was . . . different from (or similar to) . . . ?

What sort of an effect do you think . . . ?

I'm noticing (some aspect of your behavior) . . . what do you think is going on?

What criteria do you use to . . . ?

When have you done something like . . . before?

How did you decide . . . (or come to that conclusion)?

What might you see happening in your classroom if . . . ?

Tips for Using a Confrontational Approach

- Listen for rut stories and interrupt them.
- Guide clients down the Ladder of Inference; present data that they're not noticing.
- Identify mental models that are fixed and constricting.
- Rebuild models and mind-sets, and create river stories.

THE INFORMATIVE APPROACH

I once coached a new area superintendent who had a long series of decisions to make. We'd just started working together and I was standing firmly on my facilitative coaching stone, asking open-ended, probing questions to elicit reflection. She brushed these off for a few minutes and then, with blatant exasperation, she put down her pen, looked me in the eyes and said, "Just tell me what to do." I was grateful that she was able to let me know what she needed.

I shifted my feet onto the directive stone, and although I didn't tell her what to do (that's a very risky stance for a coach to take), I did get far more concrete in my questioning. I invited her into decision-making by proposing a solution and then asking what she thought would be the implications of taking those actions. "OK," I said, "what if you told your principals that they had to complete a professional portfolio this year. How about that?" She shook her head. "That's too far out of their comfort zone. But that raises a good question—how do I know what they learned this year?" This leader needed to come to her own conclusions and she had plenty of ideas to tap on; however, I needed to be more instructive in order to get her there.

The informative stance (and the prescriptive, which follows this one) is the approach that new teachers often want a coach to take. "Just tell me what to do!" they ask, with justified need as they recognize the limitations to their knowledge bank about teaching. In this approach, a coach imparts knowledge and information. We provide curriculum, lesson plans, templates for agendas, books, and so on. We supply missing facts, ("Report cards are due a week before the date on the calendar"); tell clients where they can get extra help ("Ms. Sanchez is a fantastic math teacher; try to observe her"); and explain events that the client might not understand ("Last year the union negotiated . . . and so now . . . "). In an informative approach, a coach can be a "thinking partner."

Most coaches play this role at some point with most clients. Hopefully, coaches are experts in their fields and have deep resource banks to draw from. We should know about best practices and should share them. However, there are dangers lurking in this stance and we must proceed with caution. Because our clients—especially new teachers and leaders—have such great need, and because a coach is usually a kind, caring person who wants to help, it is easy for this role to be the only one that a coach plays and for our clients to become dependent on us playing this role. The problem is that when we use an informative and prescriptive approach exclusively we may not build someone else's capacity. If we find our clients wanting us to engage in this way, it can be helpful to use a gradual release model to support the development of their autonomy.

Informative coaching stems sound like these:

There's a useful book on that topic by . . .

An effective strategy to teach ____ is . . .

You can contact ____ in ____ department for that resource . . .

Your principal will be in touch about that.

Tips for Using an Informative Approach

- Be sure to coach within the client's ZPD.

- Release responsibility gradually, but as soon as possible.

- Offer a selection of resources and guide the client to make decisions.

THE PRESCRIPTIVE APPROACH

Once, on a classroom walkthrough with a struggling principal, I observed a teacher punishing students in a way that was unethical and offensive and possibly illegal. The principal was upset by what she'd seen, but she was reluctant to confront the teacher. At this point, standing outside the teacher's door, I did not ask probing or reflective questions. I said, "You have to meet with her immediately, insist that she stop doing that, and document her actions with a formal letter of concern." There are times like this when a coach hears or sees something that merits a response which is very directive.

From a prescriptive stance, a coach gives directions, recommendations, or advice; we direct behavior — not beliefs or being. This is another stance to take very rarely and with caution, but it is appropriate when the client lacks confidence, is unable to direct her own learning yet, or if there are legal, safety, or ethical guidelines which are not being followed.

Sometimes from this stance we might need to give advice. Robert Hargrove offers some useful tips for giving advice, suggesting that it must be caring, candid, practical, wise, and well-timed — given only when a client is open to hearing it. Hargrove reminds us to ask for permission to give advice and recommends that if we hear a lot of "yes, but" comments or if a client debates everything we say, we need to stop giving advice. Our client can no longer hear us (Hargrove, 2003, p. 75). Chapter 12 expands on how to give feedback.

Prescriptive coaching sounds like the following:

I would like you to discuss this issue with your supervisor.

You need to know that the school's policy is _____.

Have you talked to ____ about that yet? Last week you said you planned on doing so.

Would it be OK if I shared some advice that I think might help you? You're welcome to take it or leave it, of course.

I'd like to suggest . . .

Tips for Using a Prescriptive Approach

- Use the prescriptive approach to direct behavior around legal, safety, or ethical issues.
- Use when client lacks confidence or can't direct her own learning.
- Use with caution.

COACHING FOR SYSTEMS CHANGE: INSTITUTIONAL MIND-SETS

I have worked in dozens of schools and I've noticed that just as individuals develop mind-sets and rut stories about what has happened to them, organizations (large and small) also develop narratives about their experiences. These stories become shared by a community, told in many ways year after year, and reinforced. They are often reflected in the school's policies, personality, and climate. Such schools seem to attract staff who are inclined to take up these stories, for whom they resonate, where they can fit right in. The stories (which can be empowering or destructive) affect the way decisions are made and the way people treat each other. For coaches who are working with leaders or who are engaged in whole school transformation, helping the staff in a school to identify these mind-sets can be transformational. When confronted with the story they are telling and when supported to create a new one, the majority of educators are willing to make a change.

I coached a principal and teachers at one school that had adopted a victim story. They spoke about their school as being under siege ("The district is just trying to close us down. They never wanted us here in the first place.") Whenever a central office administrator came to visit the school, the principal would warn the staff, mandate that they dress up, fix their bulletin boards, and bribe the kids to behave well. "They're looking for any reason to ding us," he said. This story permeated the site: there was little joy in classrooms, just a feeling of impending doom. Teachers would say, "I'm just waiting for the axe to fall," and "Nothing we do is good enough; I'm not even going to try to do anything ambitious this year." Regardless of this story, five hundred children showed up day after day ready to learn.

The observations I'd made in my first months at the school crystallized on a fall afternoon when I was leading an exercise with the staff. I'd given them a prompt asking them to think in metaphors. I asked, "If your school was something in the natural world, what would it be?" Their responses—which they wrote on sentence strips—included the following: "A tree stump," "a rabbit caught in a snare," "a decaying leaf," "a blue whale," and "a lone wolf." While there were a couple of exceptions, the overall depiction was of the victim story.

I taped the sentence strips onto a whiteboard. "What's the story here?" I asked. "What is possible for this school if the story you tell is one of powerlessness? And what are you all getting from holding onto this story?" I pushed on, hoping to create some cognitive dissonance. "What do you think is the effect on your students? Who do they need you to be?" Finally, I said, "You are the authors of this narrative. You created it. Are you willing to give it up? Could we create a new one?"

Two years later, the staff had cultivated such a different institutional mind-set that they had even amended the name of their school to include a word reflecting this empowered new story and they adopted the bristlecone pine, a tree that can live for a thousand years, as their mascot. A few teachers had left, unwilling or unable to take apart that web of beliefs. But most had slowly, cautiously taken up a mind-set that allowed them to learn and grow. According to every indicator of the health of a school (culture and climate, suspension data, test scores, instructional practices, and so on) the school was a transformed place—a much happier, more successful place. And with that, the rumors leaking from "the district" that the school might be closed stopped.

Site-based coaches or those who work with several teachers and leaders at a school are well-positioned to hear dominant stories, consider how those affect the functioning of the school and learning for children, and to interrupt them if necessary. As coaches engaged in transformation of systems, a high-leverage area to work in is the way an institution thinks about itself. If we find an entry point, if we can take up this work, we can make profound changes.

COMMON CHALLENGES AND HELPFUL RESPONSES

Challenge: I'm coaching at a high school where I often hear teachers make all kinds of negative generalizations about African American kids, many of which have offensive racial overtones. They say the kids are like animals and that they need cages, that they are untamable beasts, that some of them should be "put down." I'm tired of hearing this—can I just confront them?

Lens of Inquiry. You could use a confrontational approach to guide them down the Ladder of Inference. I once coached at a school where a number of staff held attitudes such as these, but also where many were concerned about the achievement of African American boys. I suggested to the leadership team that I help them gather some qualitative data on this population. We identified a black male "focal student" and I followed him through a day of eighth grade to see what his experience was like. "Marcus," who was neither a "big discipline problem" nor a stellar student, didn't notice me trailing him. I had informed the leadership team that I'd just jot down everything that was said to Marcus by adults at the school.

The following week I brought the transcript to the leadership team. "What do you think this data will look like?" I asked before sharing it. Their predictions were a stark contrast to the data. Here's a sample of the transcript, of what Marcus heard during part of his day in school:

"Take your hoodie off . . . Hurry up and sit down . . . Where's the other paper? . . . You need to raise your hand . . . Quiet now . . . That's a warning . . . I don't want to ask you again . . . I asked you for that already . . . We covered that last week—don't you remember? . . . Wrong . . . Keep your hands to yourself. Don't run. Take your hoodie off . . . Pay attention . . . Sit up straight . . . You have thirty seconds to sit down and be quiet . . . Wrong. Check your work . . . You're mumbling—speak clearly . . . "

The leadership team was shocked by the number of negative interactions that Marcus had experienced. Of the total number of adult-student interactions that day, 97 percent were corrective or negative. "This kid isn't even a problem," said one of the teachers. I named a white student whom everyone knew—one who also wasn't a problem, but wasn't an exceptional student. "What do you think the data might read like if I was to follow him?" I asked. Very different, everyone agreed. This data set was an entry into examining issues of race at this site.

Challenge: I'm using lots of coaching stances with my client and our conversations are powerful. We have such an easy rapport and there's so much to talk about, I don't feel we need to get into the goals. Do I need to look at the goals?

Lens of Inquiry. You might want to reflect on the effect of the conversation on the client's professional growth and student learning. Is growth happening in areas that weren't articulated in the work plan? Are specific topics consistently addressed in conversations, and are you working toward an outcome? Sometimes the work that was determined for the work plan wasn't the right work to do at that time—the goal was too ambitious, or the learning wasn't broken down enough.

However, if learning isn't happening, there might be a problem with this conversational style. Do you feel that you can use confrontational approaches when necessary? Do you feel you can push your client to the edge of her comfort zone? Has the client bought into being pushed and challenged? What do each of you expect and want from a coaching relationship?

And what exactly is discussed? Are conversations all over the place? What are the results of the conversations? What action is the client prepared to take after a coaching session? How does the client feel about the conversations? Would she agree that rapport is easy and goals are unnecessary? What are her hopes and expectations for coaching?

Sometimes when rapport is too easy, and conversations are all over the place, there might be some avoidance going on—on the part of the coach or the client. A starting place would be to use an inquiry lens in a conversation with the client about how the coaching has been going, where the client is feeling successful and seeing her own changes in practice, and what the client might need or want from coaching. Finally, perhaps there's nothing wrong with feeling comfort and having good rapport when we're learning.

CHAPTER 12

Directive Coaching Activities

Read this when:

- You are not sure what to "do" as a coach
- You are coaching someone in a new role — a new teacher or new principal
- Your client is a "doer" and likes to engage in coaching activities rather than just sit around talking

FURTHER ENGAGING IN LEARNING ACTIVITIES

As a new coach I sometimes sat in my office, twiddling my thumbs, wondering what I should *do* as a coach. I knew I should probably observe teachers, but observe for what? And then what would I do with that observation? And what else could I do? This chapter presents some activities that a coach can engage a client in that are directive in nature — that is, the coach will push, nudge, and direct the teacher or principal into a learning experience.

Directive or instructive activities are sometimes the most appropriate way for a coach to work — when coaching new teachers, for example, or teachers who are implementing a new curriculum. However, while new teachers need modeling, feedback, and elbow support on lesson planning, they also need to engage in facilitative learning activities to release emotions, develop their own visions, and become thoughtful, reflective practitioners who can direct their own learning. As I mentioned in Chapter Eleven, to some extent the way I've divided up learning activities is a false dichotomy: reflective questioning should always be incorporated into each of these activities, the data that is gathered in the following strategies must always be put forth for the client to interpret as he wishes. Transformational coaching always honors the autonomy of the learner.

How does a coach decide which activities to engage a client in? She first uses the analytical frameworks presented in this book to understand a client's situation.

The activities listed in this chapter are not presented in sequential order. A coach needs to suggest an activity after considering where the client currently is in his learning, where he's going (his goals), and the data we gather by applying a set of analytical frameworks. We engage clients in activities that we hope will deepen their learning and propel them toward their goals, therefore we are very intentional when we make decisions.

OBSERVATIONS

 Administrators: many of these tips on observations and giving feedback could be relevant to your observations with teachers.

It's common for a teacher to invite a coach to observe her, or for a coach to suggest this activity, but observations can be very tricky things. Although many teachers and principals say they welcome observations and feedback, without clear agreement observations can be problematic. There are several keys to making an observation be a learning experience for the client.

1. *Focus.* It is critical that a clear, narrow focus is agreed on before the observation. Whereas a teacher might say something like, "I'd love to have you observe my class," a coach needs to help the teacher identify a specific area of practice or focus for the observation. What exactly does the teacher want the coach to look at or look for? Ideally, the focus is connected to the client's goals and usually, the narrower the focus the better. It is essential that this conversation happens before the observation (not on the side of the classroom as the students are entering). In this planning conversation, the coach needs to use clarifying questions and paraphrasing to ensure that she's accurately understanding the client's needs and requests, and that there's a clear agreement on what will happen during the observation.

2. *Data Collection Tools.* Once the focus of the observation is clear, then the coach engages the client in a discussion of how the data will be collected. A principal, for example, might want a coach to pay attention to his communication with a variety of stakeholders. This data could be collected through a script of the principal's exchanges with others, or on a quantitative record that tabulates the number of questions he asks, the groups he has exchanges with, the nature of interactions with students, and so on.

   Many schools and districts have created tools that they use to gather data on teaching effectiveness, leadership and instructional practices, and classroom observations. Some of these can be very useful; some schools may even mandate that coaches use these tools. What's essential is that there is agreement about what will be used. You don't want to surprise a teacher by showing up in her class and using a checklist that she's never seen before.

   The Two-Column Note Taker. If no data tracker exists, then a coach can use a two-column note taker to script what teachers and students say. This is a raw form of data that can be used to begin a reflective conversation. Sometimes it can also be useful for a coach to jot down her own questions, "wow and wonders" or noticings. These should be shared with a client with caution—our questions and "wows and wonders" are often laden with our values and judgments. We can gather wows and wonders for our own purposes—so that we can reflect, see patterns, and come to conclusions, but we have to be careful about sharing this raw data. I like to keep a separate document where I record the questions I have. My preference, when there's no specific data-gathering tool, is to gather just the kinds of data presented in Exhibit 12.1 (a basic data collection tool for observations) and use this as a conversation entry point. I might direct the client to a piece of data, but I'll also leave some space for the client to direct his learning.

3. *Debrief.* The third essential agreement to make with a client *before* doing an observation is about the debrief—when will it happen? Where? Whenever possible, the debrief should happen on the same day as the observation. The client will be anxious to hear your feedback and the details will be fresh on everyone's minds. But a coach should always use her best judgment—if she observed a particularly difficult encounter, the client might want to postpone the debrief until he's had some time to process it alone, or he might be anxious to debrief immediately in order to get the coach's support in processing what happened.

Frequently, a coach will observe a client and notice interesting data that falls outside of the agreed-on focus. For example, the teacher may ask a coach to observe how students engage in a cooperative learning structure but our attention might be drawn to the teacher's interactions with students. We may notice, perhaps, that when interacting with male students the teacher is notably more impatient, brusque and demanding. However, in the debrief on this observation, we need to be careful about how we bring up these observations. If the teacher didn't feel like she gave the coach permission to observe those interactions, she can feel defensive and distrusting. We might try to lay the groundwork for us to be able get the teacher's permission to gather data about this dynamic. Or, sometimes, we might try raising the data point and seeing what happens. The next section elaborates on how to give feedback.

Exhibit 12.1. Classroom Observation Tool

Teacher: Debbie Cohn   **Date: 4/11/11**   **Time: 10:15–11:00**

Time Recorded every 5 minutes	Teacher words and actions	Student words and actions
10:35	We're going to start with reading, we'll do choral reading with the same groups that we had this morning. So this group is 1; can you start choral reading the first paragraph? One, two, three.	4 students asked to choral read; I can hear 3 students' voices.
	Stop. We did read this before but we're going to use it to pick out these elements. OK, second group next paragraph, one two three.	3 students asked to choral read; I can't hear them from where I'm sitting.
	OK, when we are reading chorally, as a reminder, group 1, when another group is reading what should you be doing? Do you have pencils in your hands? I believe I said pencils down, Dawanna.	Dawanna: "I'm going to write my name."
	I believe I said pencils down, Dawanna.	
	We're not writing anything, we're reading. If your group isn't reading, you're following along. I want you to be reading in ready position. OK, group 3, one two three.	Group 3 choral reading.

Time Recorded every 5 minutes	Teacher words and actions	Student words and actions
10:40	All right, group 1 next paragraph. One two three. I would like everybody to read the last paragraph together. One two three. You know, this particular passage I believe the setting is pretty explicitly stated. Where does this story take place? Turn to your neighbor and tell them where you think the story takes place. *Teacher at front of room, talks to a student sitting alone*	Dawanna looking around, opens notebook. 19 of 24 students reading. 2 students are looking out window. 1 is leaning under table scratching foot. All students turn to neighbor and talk. The two pairs in front of me are talking about the setting. S1: It's in the forest. S2: In the trees. S1: That's the forest. S2: Do you ever go there? To the forest? I do. S1: Sometimes we go.

Giving Feedback

Feedback is very tricky. We all need it, many of us know we need it and say we want it. But it's also very hard for a coach to effectively deliver feedback, and it's often very hard for us to hear feedback.

Part of the reason that feedback is so tricky is that the big picture in education right now is a cruel, unforgiving, and frightening place. Teachers have been blamed for far more than their share of the failure of schools; in general, those who work in schools are suspect until they show the test scores. Appreciation for educators is token and infrequent. We are all very sensitive when it comes to feedback on our work, particularly if it comes from people who haven't been in our shoes.

And yet, effective feedback can propel a person forward toward reaching his goals. In the world of sports, we see how coaches provide players with precise, on-the-spot feedback that can immediately improve their performance. Likewise, there are certain actions that a teacher can take that can immediately result in a change in what happens in the classroom; as a coach, we might see these possibilities jumping out at us and yet be unsure of how to communicate our observations in a way that the client will hear us. Delivering feedback is an art that takes coaches many years of practice.

The following are suggestions for giving feedback:

1. *Assess for trust.* First, don't give direct feedback until you are certain that your client trusts you. You also need to have a deep understanding of who your client is and how he might receive feedback. Some people respond well to direct feedback and appreciate it; others may feel defensive and may shut down.

2. *Always ask for permission.* This could sound like, "Can I share a couple things I observed that might help you address those issues you're raising?" Or "Would it be OK if I gave you some feedback on the interaction you just had with that student? My intention is to help you feel more empowered." Always declare that your intention in giving feedback is coming from a place of caring and concern, and a desire to help the client move toward her goals.

3. *Ground feedback in observational data.* It can sound like, "I noticed that when Michael walked in the room, you said, 'Take that hat off. I don't want to tell you this every day.' Then your next interaction with him was when he asked to sharpen his pencil. You said 'You need to come prepared.' The next time you addressed him, you said, 'Michael, what's the correct verb form here? Are you paying attention?' Then he exploded and said, 'You're always picking on me!' At that point, you sent him to the office for being defiant. Can you see his perspective, given these were the only interactions you had with him in ten minutes? What might you have done differently?"

4. *Restrict critical feedback to one or two key points.* It's common to observe a teacher, for example, and note a long list of instructional or management practices that could be improved. We might have noted that the classroom was a mess, there was no system for students to turn in homework, there was no agenda or objective on the board, the teacher's verbal directions were confusing, the teacher gave students far too much time during the opening activity, students were off-task and messing around, the opening activity wasn't connected to a learning objective and seemed to be a time-filler, and so on. The first step is to look at the data we collected and determine which pieces are connected to the school or client's goals. For example, this teacher might be working on her organizational skills, therefore, those are the areas we will address when giving feedback.

It always helps if the coach has some time between the observation and the debrief to be able to digest the observation and think through the debrief.

5. *Find the phrasing.* The language that you use with clients differs with each one based on what you know about how they will hear your feedback. Before a debrief, I think through and sometimes write out or role-play what I'll say. There are clients who respond well if I say something like, "You have got to clean up your room and post an agenda every day. You said you wanted to do that weeks ago and I still don't see it." Others need to hear something like, "A few weeks ago you talked about wanting to clean up your room. You've said several times that your disorganization gets in the way of being able to be the teacher you envision. I noticed that along the back wall there were a dozen stacks of papers, books, and files. What do you think could be getting in the way of addressing this goal area?"

In order to give effective feedback we must know how others will hear us.

6. *Invite reflection.* After we've shared one or two pieces of feedback with a client, we invite reflection on how the feedback was received and plan for next steps. We listen carefully to how someone responds to our feedback, noticing if the client becomes defensive, embarrassed, curious, relieved — there are a whole range of emotions that people can experience. It's our job as a coach to notice them and address them if necessary — if it feels like the client can't proceed to the next steps without processing them.

Once it seems like the client can move on to the "what's next?" phase, we can support him in determining how he'd like to act on the feedback. For example, perhaps a coach observed a teacher trying to use small group structures and perhaps the students didn't engage with each other in the way the teacher had hoped. The coach has just shared that she noticed that out of five groups, only one followed the directions the teacher gave. The teacher might feel frustrated and disappointed. The coach might ask the teacher what she'd like to try next and what kind of support she'd like from the coach, or the coach can offer ideas. What's essential is that there are next steps. Especially when the feedback is critical, the client must finish the conversation feeling that she will be supported in some way to develop those skills and capacities that aren't where she wants them to be yet.

Specific Observation Tools: The Teacher-Student Interactions Tracking Tool

In order for kids to learn, they have to feel emotionally safe with their peers and their teacher; their affective filter has to be low. This shows up in many ways in a classroom and is evident in how a teacher interacts with individual students and the whole class on a moment to moment basis. There's a "magic ratio" that psychologists believe is essential in relationships — 5:1 — five positive interactions for every negative interaction (neutral interactions are fine). It can be very useful for a coach to pay attention to this relational dynamic in a classroom and school. Exhibit 12.2 offers a data collection tool for this purpose.

A coach should only enter this terrain with permission from the client. "Positive" and "negative" are subjective categories. As a coach, if we're gathering this data we'll be heaping our own judgments onto it in order to sort it into positive or negative. The conundrum, however, is that if you tell your teacher-client that you're going to look specifically at the quality of interactions — at whether they are negative or positive, then the data will be skewed. She will be so conscious of you sitting in the corner, judging her actions that she won't behave as she usually does. However, you also need to make sure you aren't violating the teacher's trust. You need to make sure your relationship is strong enough and that she trusts you enough to allow you to gather data on her relationships with students.

You might say something like this: "Thank you for being open to having me observe your classroom. I have a variety of tools that I use to understand the different dynamics in your room and it'll take me three to five observations to use them all. Afterwards, I'd like to share what I've learned with you and show you the tools and data. Would that be okay?" Then use the tracking tool in Exhibit 12.2 for three to five times, for 15–20 minutes each time. This tool is available on my website.

Exhibit 12.2. Teacher-Student Interactions: Tracking Tool

Teacher	Subject and Period	Date and Time
P. Cruz	Science, fifth period	May 11, 2011 12:37–1:00
Total Number of Students: 24	**Number of Male Students: 8** **Racial Breakdown**: African American: 3 Latino: 4 Other: 1	**Number of Female Students: 16** **Racial Breakdown**: African American: 3 Latina: 12 Other: 1

Interaction	Time	Positive*	Negative*	Neutral	Male or Female	Ethnicity	Notes
1	12:37			X	F	AA	Whatever's in your mouth, just get rid of it
2	12:38			X	F	L	B, you're going home
3	12:39	X			F	L	Bye. Have a great weekend
4	12:39	X			M	AA	Thank you, have a seat
5	12:40			X	M	AA	Pass the papers
6	12:41			X	F	L	Put pencil down, J
7	12:42			X	F	AA	5, 4, 3, 2, 1 (redirect)
8	12:45	X			F	AA	G, go ahead
9	12:46			X	F	AA	Yes, OK
10	12:47	X			M	O	Please read, D
11	12:48			X	M	AA	Come in quickly, please
12	12:48	X			F	AA	Go ahead, S. Excellent
13	12:48	X			F	AA	D, thank you
14	12:49			X	M	AA	Into back table, please
15	12:49			X	M	O	D, yes?
16	12:50			X	M	AA	Please, keep going
17	12:50		X?		F	AA	D – (redirect—"if that happens again you're going to go in the book")
18	12:51			X	M	AA	L, do you have a question?
19	12:52	X			F	AA	Yes, please, G
20	12:52	X			F	AA	Good suggestion
21	12:52	X			F	L	Please, ask your question
22	12:53	X			M	O	Yes, D, yes

(continued)

Exhibit 12.2. (*Continued*)

Interaction	Time	Positive*	Negative*	Neutral	Male or Female	Ethnicity	Notes
23	12:53			X	F	AA	Yes, S
24	12:54			X	F	AA	Yes, D
25	12:55			X	M	AA	L?
26	12:55		X?		F	AA	G (redirect)
28	12:57			X	F	AA	G, attention here
29	12:59	X			F	AA	Excellent, D
TOTAL		11	2	16	F: 18 M: 11	L: 4 AA: 21 O: 4	

*Interactions are classified as "positive" or "negative" according to the specific words that are said, the tone that is used, and any nonverbal communication that accompanies the interaction.

Another way to use this tool is in analyzing a video of a teacher. The teacher herself can do the analysis and discuss the results with you. After either watching a video, or your observation of the teacher, share the data results with her. Then ask some or all of these questions:

1. What do you notice in these data?
2. What surprised you?
3. What feels good to see? What's affirming?
4. Is there anything that raises questions for you?
5. What do you want to know more about? Is there anything you want me to collect more data on?
6. Is there anything you might want to work on now that you've reviewed these data?

Modeling

Coaches can model lessons, record keeping, routines and procedures, facilitation of a meeting, or creation of an agenda. Hopefully, coaches were exemplary teachers—whenever appropriate, we should take the opportunity to demonstrate our skills and capacities as instructors and facilitators.

There are a few caveats to consider when modeling.

1. Before proposing this strategy, we need to consider how our client might experience observing us. If by modeling we intend to demonstrate a standard to which our client might aspire, we need to consider our client's zone of proximal development. Some elements of what we model need to be within that zone. If what we demonstrate is far out of the client's zone, observing a coach modeling a behavior or activity can be overwhelming, intimidating, and daunting. It's not that we don't model—but we need to be selective about what and how we model.

2. What we model is determined in agreement with the client. Perhaps a teacher wants to see a coach model questioning in whole group discussions or a classroom management strategy—it's essential that the specific behaviors a coach will model are identified and agreed on beforehand. If a coach offers to "model a reading comprehension lesson" this may be too broad for a teacher to identify any replicable behaviors. The coach and client need to be very clear about what will be modeled and what the client will observe. The goal is for the coach to demonstrate a few actions that the client can do by herself fairly soon.

3. Also agreed on ahead of time is what the client will do while the coach is modeling in order to anchor her learning. For example, a coach might model the use of questioning to deepen reading comprehension. During the lesson, the teacher agrees to script the questions that are asked as well as the student responses. Clients may need support in narrowing a focus when observing a coach model a strategy, and may need guidance on what to do during the observation. Ideally, we want to elicit this from the client in our questioning: "What might help you see the effects of the strategies I use on the students?" Or "What kinds of data would you like to gather when I facilitate this meeting? What might you notice or look at that would help you see whether my facilitation is effective?" But we need to be ready with suggestions as well. We need to set up the client so that what she observes is the action we're taking (the comprehension strategies, meeting facilitation, and the like) and the effect it's having on others—the students, staff members, and so on.

4. As a coach is modeling, she needs to mentally notice what the client might or might not notice. While we're skillfully delivering instruction, for example, we note the data that the client has agreed she'll gather—for example, on how students respond to questions. Afterwards, when we debrief with the client, we want to make sure that the client noticed anything we might have observed that was key.

5. When a coach models, a structured debrief should occur ideally within twenty-four hours. If the modeling has been set up with a clear focus and agreement about how data will be gathered, then the debrief can flow out of those points. During the debrief, we want to hear what the client noticed and engage in a conversation about the actions that we modeled and we want to explore how prepared he feels to implement the actions (provided, of course, that they were exemplary). A coach needs to make sure to break down the strategy modeled into a series of actions—because actions are replicable.

6. We want to avoid modeling our own personality or charisma—our clients can't be who we are. It's not uncommon for a client to say something like, "I could never do that. You did it so well; I can't be you." If we hear this, we must deconstruct these perceptions and what's perceived as "style." We need to help a teacher or administrator see that we implemented a series of actions, and we also need to affirm our client's personality. We don't want our clients to be us (sometimes coaches need to remember this); they can't be us.

7. Finally, in the debrief ask for the client's feedback on the practice we modeled: "Did you notice anything that I didn't notice? That I could have done better? That wasn't clear?" Although hopefully our modeling is exemplary, we can always learn more and clients can be insightful in their observations. It's also critical that coaches model being reflective, life-long learners who elicit feedback from everyone.

Modeling specific instructional or leadership practices can be very valuable for clients. Whether we're working with new educators or veterans, it's not uncommon to hear people confess that they haven't seen a lot of stellar practices in their career. However, we also don't want to overuse modeling. What's essential when using modeling is to keep in mind a gradual release of responsibility—modeling is a form of "direct instruction." We need to intentionally plan what comes next—the guided practice—so that we are always working toward developing autonomous, self-directed educators.

Elbow Teaching

 Administrators: don't forget that teachers often love seeing their administrators model lessons or elbow teach with them.

"Elbow teaching" can be a guided practice to release responsibility. In this approach, the coach can teach side by side with the regular classroom teacher and can model use of a strategy and then turn the lead over to the teacher. For example, a coach could model a think aloud strategy for solving an algebra problem while students listen and take notes. Then the teacher could model the subsequent problem, having just heard how the coach explains his thinking. This can be a useful strategy when content or curriculum is new to the teacher. Its impact also lies in the immediacy of the practice for the client.

Lesson and Unit Planning

Lesson or unit planning with a coach can also be a guided practice. While supporting the teacher to think through the steps of planning, a coach can model when necessary or explain his process. As with other guided practices, the coach needs to be sharply attuned to the client's needs — releasing when necessary, when she sees that the client can move forward successfully, or instructing and directing when the client needs support.

While engaging in any of these activities, it is critical that the coach keep two things in mind: how is the client emotionally experiencing this learning activity? And what is the client's ZPD? We need to be acutely aware of any anxiety that might arise for our client and we need to constantly gather evidence that the learning activity is within the client's ZPD.

When the client doesn't seem to make the kind of growth we hope for, when the learning falls flat and doesn't result in any real changes in practice, it is most often because one of these two considerations wasn't accounted for — either emotions surfaced that shut down the learning or we were operating outside of the client's ZPD.

On-the-Spot Coaching

Coaching on-the-spot is feedback in the moment. It can be very useful, but is also tricky. A strong trust between the coach and client needs to exist in order for this to be effective, otherwise the client can feel embarrassed. A coach should either have explicit permission or should have a very, very strong reason to believe that the client will be receptive.

Once permission has been established and the parameters for on-the-spot coaching are clear, the coach can offer the client feedback while he is teaching. As with all feedback, the content needs to be selective and narrow. For example, if a teacher is working on increasing student talk in the classroom, and the coach is observing a lesson in which the teacher seems to be calling on the most verbally proficient students, the coach might communicate this observation to the teacher. The coach might scribble a note saying, "You're only calling on English proficient students. Call on an English learner." This is very direct, but it can be appreciated if the trust is strong and the feedback is something the teacher wants to hear.

There are a number of technical skills which teachers struggle with that on-the-spot coaching can help reinforce. These include things such as wait time after a teacher asks a question or checking for procedural understanding before releasing students into an activity. These are skills that a teacher can quickly acquire if she gets immediate feedback. Likewise, there are similar leadership actions that administrators need help to practice and internalize. It's important that the coach can distinguish between which behaviors are useful to name in the moment and redirect, and which are not technical adjustments. The coach needs to be sure that the suggested feedback is definitely within the client's ZPD — "call on English learners," or "wait for five seconds," as opposed to a suggestion like, "Ask a higher-order question" that requires more thinking.

Coaching on-the-spot can be shared on sticky notes, through quick verbal exchanges, or by using technologies that allow for the coach to communicate directly into the client's ear. Devices for direct translation can be used for this purpose and are barely noticeable to others.

What is essential is that the coach offers a discrete piece of feedback which is clearly within the client's ZPD. If the client receives a suggestion and acts on it, and immediately sees the effect on students, his trust for the coach will increase and he'll be more receptive to immediate feedback.

Field Trips

One way of determining which learning activity might be most helpful to a client is to ask him how he learns best. Frequently people say that they learn best by watching someone else perform the tasks they aspire to master. Although the client can observe the coach teaching a lesson, leading a meeting, or holding a data conference, for example, it can also be very helpful to observe others who are in the same role. It is critical that the coach accompany the client on the observation, the reasons for which will be clear as we consider the necessary steps for a field trip to be meaningful.

1. *Identify the specific behaviors.* Before the observation agree on a couple specific skills to observe. These skills should align with the goals the client is pursuing.

For example, a principal working on developing his emotional intelligence might shadow another principal for an afternoon and observe how he communicates with staff. The first step is identifying the specific behaviors that the client would like to see someone else model.

2. *Ensure quality.* It is essential that the practitioner who will be observed is indeed exemplary in the specific areas that your client wants to see. Sometimes we might be told, "Mrs. W at XYZ school is a brilliant kindergarten teacher! You've got to see her." Although we can ask about what makes her brilliant, a coach must visit and affirm this recommendation before taking a client on a field trip. While a case can be made that the "nonexample" is valuable to observe, I would suggest that given that it's usually tricky to get release time to observe other teachers, and that you really want developing practitioners to see exemplary practice, it's better to make sure that the quality is what you want it to be.

3. Once the focus of the observation is clear, the coach engages the client in a conversation about how the data will be gathered. It's not uncommon for a new teacher, for example, to observe a master teacher and be overwhelmed by what she sees: her attention flutters all over—to the filing system by the door, the extensive routines and procedures that students have internalized, and the teacher's comfy shoes. It's the coach's responsibility to make sure that before entering another classroom, the client has some ways that she has agreed to document what is related to her goal area. For example, if the client wants to observe routines and procedures, she might write down as many as she sees—pencil sharpening, entering the room, turning in homework, and so on. While she might not understand how they are used, and this can be discussed during a debrief conversation with the observed teacher, her attention can focus. Or perhaps the client wants to observe how a sixth-grade teacher redirects challenging student behavior—she can script what the teacher says or take notes on her nonverbal communication. It's the coach's role to help the client determine what she'll notice and how she'll document it. You can encourage a client to jot down other topics she'd like to bring up with the educator who is being observed, but it's essential to have a focus.

4. On the field trip the coach should engage in the same kind of data-gathering protocol as the client—scripting teacher talk or documenting patterns of participation or whatever was agreed on. The coach can also note other effective practices that can be discussed with the client if he brings them up. Finally, the coach needs to model good field-trip etiquette.

5. After the visit we debrief with reflective questioning strategies to prompt the client's learning. We want to hear what the client saw, learned, and can take back and act on. Close the debrief by asking the client to commit to taking certain actions based on what he learned. For example, if a teacher is really excited about the way another teacher had his classroom set up, then we might ask, "Tell me two things you'd like to try implementing in your class? When do you want to have that done by? What support do you need in order to meet that goal?" Our role is to elicit reflection, encourage experimentation and risk taking, and then push for our client to do it. Sometimes coaches are the only ones who can add the push—because we're not the boss, and often clients appreciate this.

Taking a client to observe a colleague also serves to build connections between educators. Whenever possible, we want to bring people together, foster relationships, and help our client find other resources to draw from.

Shared Reading

Most coaches read a lot about best practices and current research and acquire extensive libraries on topics related to the areas they coach. If a client identifies reading as a way that he likes to learn, then a coach can suggest a shared reading. A coach can also anticipate this and can come to a meeting prepared with articles. For example, if a coach knows that at her next session with a principal they will discuss distributed leadership, she might show up with an article in her bag on this topic. As their conversation develops, the coach can offer the reading if the client says he needs more information. The coach and client can then read the article together and discuss it immediately, or the coach can leave the article.

Whenever possible, I encourage the client to read the article during our meeting. My role is to carve out learning time and hold that space. Many of us have stacks and stacks of books and articles we intend to read, someday. It can be a real gift to a client to sit and read and engage in a discussion together. We can also help the client focus on a specific area or two, and then consider what he can use, apply, or attempt. We are always nudging our client toward his goals.

Looking at Data

Data analysis is another activity that coaches frequently engage in with clients. Data includes student work, survey results, test scores, suspension data, graduation rates and so on. There is no shortage of data analysis protocols, but Exhibit 12.3 offers a basic template.

Exhibit 12.3. Learning from Student Data: A Discussion Protocol for Three-Phase Dialogue

Phase I: Prediction

Before looking at the data set, respond to these questions:

- What might we *expect to see?*
- What might we *expect to learn?*

Phase II: Observation

Look at the data and make observational comments:

- What do students *actually present?*
- What *facts or patterns* do we notice in the data?

  Sentence stems could include:

- One fact I notice is ...
- I am surprised by ...
- A trend I think I see is ...
- I can quantify that by saying ...

Phase III: Inference and Conclusion

After all observational comments are made, discuss inferences and conclusions:

- What *hunches* do we have about causes for what we observe?
- *Why* are we getting the results we are?

  Sentence stems could include:

- This pattern or trend might be because ...
- Maybe we're not seeing ____ because ...
- A reason for this result could be ...

  Then ask:

- So what? And, now what?

A set of guidelines for coaches can make this a learning experience:

Refrain from all judgment about the data: Coaches do not blame but we insist on thinking about what can be done and what is within our sphere of influence.

Employ an asset approach: What's working here? Where do we see growth, learning, or affirmation?

Support the client in disaggregating the data: we need to examine the experience of students who have been historically underserved—including African American and Latino boys, girls in math and science, English language learners, and so on. We apply the lens of systemic oppression to looking at data and consider whether all children's needs are being met.

Use a confrontational questioning strategy to raise inequities that surface in the data: A coach prepares by thoroughly analyzing the data beforehand and preparing the questions she will pose if the client doesn't identify the inequities in the data. The questions need to be very mindful to avoid blame, but they also need to surface uncomfortable data. For example, a coach might ask a client, "What do you notice about how your English learners did on the exam?" We can explore the root causes for what's being observed in the data and offer probing questions to deepen the client's thinking.

Guide the client to determine one or two areas where growth can be made: A coach encourages the client to make specific plans to interrupt inequities. We direct the client to think about what she could do within her sphere of influence. We always ask, "Now what?" "What would you like to try?" and "What can you do that will result in increased student learning?"

Debrief the learning experience: As with all of the activities we engage clients in, after we've done any kind of data analysis work we need to check in about how our client experienced the work. Coaches need to be very mindful of how teachers and principals feel about data: the larger context in which we work is highly charged and rather scary when it comes to data.

Coaching on Time Management

Many teachers and administrators request support with time management. Steven Covey, the author of *Seven Habits of Highly Effective People* (1989), provides an indispensable framework for thinking about how we use our time. He offers a simple graphic of four squares and suggests that all time is spent divided between four kinds of activities:

1. *Urgent and Important (Quadrant 1)*: putting out fires and dealing with crises and last minute tasks
2. *Not Urgent and Important (Quadrant 2)*: planning, preparing, relationship building, reflection
3. *Urgent and Not Important (Quadrant 3)*: low value but required tasks, some e-mails, calls, and meetings
4. *Not Urgent and Not Important (Quadrant 4)*: busy work and some e-mails and calls

The graphic Covey offers to represent this is easily found online and is very useful to share with clients and to reference.

One activity to do with clients is to ask them to sort their daily activities into these quadrants. Just helping them reflect on how they spend time can be helpful. The domain of not urgent and important is the highest leverage area to work in: this is where relationship building takes place, as well as long-term instructional planning, positive phone calls home to parents, systematic analysis of student data, and so forth. This is also the domain in which efforts toward systems change take place and the one where most educators spend the least time — given the amount of urgency we encounter on a daily basis, it's really hard. This is where a coach plays a critical role — we carve out that space and time, we nudge toward exploring root causes, we help our clients recognize that much of their daily responses to the urgency could be mitigated by spending time working in the not urgent and important zone.

Once clients are familiar with this framework for thinking about time, you can often just ask clients, "What quadrant are you working in?" to provoke reflection about their decisions.

CONCLUSION

Sometime our clients are "doers"; the thought of "just sitting and talking" with a coach can make them very anxious. Directive coaching activities can feel satisfying to such adult learners. At the same time, a coach can integrate reflective conversations into the activities and help the client deepen her learning.

A coach needs to try using all kinds of approaches with clients. We don't want a client to get stuck in one way of learning—they might be settling into their comfort zones and apprehensive about taking a risk. And we need to remember that the purpose of engaging in activities is to help a client make progress toward meeting her goals. We are always working from and toward goals.

CHAPTER 13

Technical Tips and Habits of Mind

Read this when:

- You are a brand-new coach and want to address issues of scheduling and time management

- You suspect that your coaching conversations don't flow or don't get where you want them to get or feel awkward

TRICKS OF THE TRADE

The coaching tips and habits of mind in this chapter are shared as they arise sequentially in coaching. I'll begin with the logistics of setting up a coaching schedule, planning a coaching conversation, and preparing for a coaching meeting. Then I'll describe the arc of a coaching conversation, how to manage some of the technical elements during a conversation, and which habits of mind a coach may need to hold during a conversation. Finally, I'll suggest some routines for closing a coaching conversation.

SCHEDULING

If a coach can construct his own schedule, (as opposed to being handed one) then he can consider how to use his time. This gives him the opportunity to manage his time well and also develop a valuable communication tool so that his supervisor and teachers know what he is doing and how he spends his days.

A coach may be most effective when his time is distributed amongst five task areas:

1. Coaching observations and conversations.

2. Preparation: gathering materials for clients, reading research and best practice, analyzing student data, planning meetings and coaching conversations, and so on.

3. Collaboration: the meetings that a coach might have with a principal, another administrator, or a district partner, or participation in site walkthroughs or instructional rounds.

4. Team participation or facilitation: Coaches may support teams at the sites they work at — maybe an English department, or a fourth grade circuit of teachers. If they are site-based, then coaches may also participate in leadership and decision-making teams.

5. Coach reflection and professional development: It can be very useful for a coach to dedicate some time each day to reflection. Coaches should also be engaged in their own systematic professional development, ideally guided by a more experienced coach. Chapter Fifteen will expand on this.

Figure 13.1 offers a sample weekly schedule for a site-based coach. On my website there's an example of a centrally-based coach schedule. All coaches should develop a weekly schedule for their own focus and direction and for external accountability and communication purposes.

PLANNING FOR A COACHING CONVERSATION

Planning for a coaching conversation is similar in some ways to planning a lesson — we construct a couple clear goals, design a route to meet those goals, anticipate the challenges that might arise, and review material that might be helpful. As when you design a lesson, when you plan a coaching conversation keep in mind that you may need to change course, modify plans, or even abandon the directions and activities

	Monday	Tuesday	Wednesday	Thursday	Friday
8:00		Analyze student data	Read literature on assessment practices		Review lesson plans from teachers; give feedback
9:00	Observe Teacher A			Weekly meeting with principal	
10:00	Plan Wednesday's PLC meeting	Model lesson for Teacher B	Prepare materials for PLC meeting	Observe Teacher D	
11:00		Observe Teacher C	Model lesson for Teacher A	Observe Teacher E	Facilitate eighth-grade team meeting
12:00	Debrief with Teacher A	Gather materials for ILT to use next week	Debrief with Teacher A	Facilitate cross-department meeting on integrating writing	Review work plans for teachers; document growth and collect evidence. Determine next steps.
1:00	Reflective writing time: Reflect on Teacher A and plan next conversation	Facilitate walkthrough observations with ILT	Reflective writing time: Reflect on Teacher A and plan next conversation	Participate in walkthrough observations with principal	
2:00	Read literature on teacher leadership		Facilitate ELA department PLC Meeting	Read literature on English Language Development practices	My PD: Coach's PLC meeting
3:00	Instructional Leadership Team (ILT) meeting	Debrief with Teacher B		Meet with Teacher D	
4:00		Meet with Teacher C	Write up notes and documentation from PLC meeting	Meet with Teacher E	
5:00		Reflective writing time: Reflect on Teachers B and C and plan next conversations		Reflective writing time: Reflect on Teachers D and E and plan next conversations	

White: coaching observations and conversations; light gray: reflection and professional development (PD); medium gray: preparation; dark gray: team participation and facilitation; black: collaboration

Figure 13.1. Sample Weekly Schedule for Site-Based Coach

you planned because some other skill gap becomes apparent or a more pressing need presents itself.

Planning for a coaching session is essential. After some experience, we might be able to walk into a meeting with a client and wing it but we will be much more effective if we have a plan tucked into our coach-minds. As we move through the conversation the client won't notice when we subtly guide the conversation, the thoughtful questions we seem to pose on the spur of the moment, or the way we calmly react to whatever comes up. If we have planned, then we might have anticipated that the client could need a particular resource and we'll have a copy of that resource copied and ready to hand over. If we have planned, then we walk into the coaching meeting with the big picture fresh in our minds — the needs of the client and his goals, as well as the needs of the students and community he serves.

So how do we plan this meeting?

Step 1: Where Does My Client Need to Go?

The first step to plan a coaching conversation is to identify where my client needs to go in a particular session. To do this, I read over the notes and reflections I made after our last meeting. This helps me remember where my client was in her learning the last time we met. Then I consider where the conversation might need to go to move the client toward her goals. In order to do this, I review the work plan and my notes from recent sessions. I consider the evidence that my client is making progress and speculate on remaining gaps in skill, will, knowledge, or capacity. I look through my notes to see if there are any patterns in the holes — are there topics or issues that the client seems reluctant to address?

Based on the client's goals and recent sessions, I plan for the upcoming meeting. What might be a meaningful outcome for this meeting? What might be helpful for my client to think about or do? Which coaching approach might be the most effective? Might it help to engage in some action together? Or have we been doing a lot of activities but not spending enough time reflecting on them? Exhibit 13.1 offers a template for a planning coaching conversation.

Step 2: Who Do I Need to Be?

Once I have determined where the client needs the conversation to go, and I have some ideas about how we can get there, then I figure out who I need to be as a coach. This is the second step in planning a coaching conversation.

Exhibit 13.1. Coaching Session Planning Tool

These reflection prompts can be used to prepare for a coaching session or conversation. It can be very helpful to write out responses and to look back at them after the meeting and over time.

1. Where did our last coaching conversation end and what do I need to come back to with my client? Was there anything I said I'd check in on next time?
2. What are the goals for this coaching conversation? Are there goals related to the work plan that need to be addressed?
3. What are my intentions for this meeting? What do I want my client to think and feel by the end of it?
4. What might my client's disposition be? What do I know about where he or she is going to be?
5. What do I anticipate might be happening with my client or might be challenging? How can I prepare for this and manage these challenges?
6. Do I anticipate my client will need to release emotions? If so, how can I do this? What works for him or her to process emotions?
7. How can I enroll my client in this conversation? How can I make it matter to him or her?
8. Of the six coaching stances, which might be most effective? Is there a coaching stance that I haven't used much that might be worth trying?
9. Can I anticipate that my client might want to engage in any coaching activities? Which ones might I suggest? Which might help my client reach his or her goals?
10. Are there any materials (articles or tools) that I might gather and bring with me in case my client requests them?
11. Who do I need to be in this conversation? Who does my client need me to be? How do I need to show up?
12. How do I want to feel at the end of this coaching session?

I know my clients need me to be grounded and present when I walk into their rooms. Simply by conveying a sense of calm a reflective space is opened that invites others to slow down and learn. I consciously, regularly cultivate a grounded state of being. There are many ways to do this. Some are daily habits such as getting exercise, prioritizing eight hours of sleep, and eating nutritious food. I encourage coaches to consider how they attend to their own emotional, physical, social, and spiritual needs—doing so will definitely improve a coach's skills.

I also have a set of practices which I engage in right before a coaching session. First I take stock of my own mood—am I feeling tired? Agitated? Worried? And what kind of disposition might my client need me to be in? And then I work to make any shifts that might help. I often listen to music while driving to a meeting—music always transforms my mood. I rarely go into a coaching session without spending at least five minutes, almost always in my car, quietly breathing. I schedule this in my day—I arrive early, turn off the music, close my eyes, and breathe. Those five minutes are critical to the effectiveness of my work.

Some of the other strategies I use to become calm and grounded are the following:

- A quick, fast walk
- Yoga stretches
- A journal write where I get out all the thoughts that might distract me
- Saying mantras or affirmations such as, "I am focused and calm," "I can hold a space for learning," "Everything is OK."
- Talking with a trusted coach-colleague to clear my mind if anything work-related is clogging it.

I've discovered that even if it means I'll be late, I can't go in to a meeting without taking time to get grounded—five minutes is usually enough and makes all the difference in the subsequent hour. When my client greets me and asks, "How are you?" I need to be able to smile and honestly respond, "I'm good."

Getting grounded is essential, but it's not the only preparation a coach can do. I know that for a client to be receptive to coaching, I need to be nonjudgmental—and I am not always in that frame of mind; before a meeting, I often activate my compassion for a client. Sometimes I visualize that I am the teacher or principal I'm about to meet with; I imagine what his day has been like—what he's seen, done, heard, felt, wondered, feared, and needed. I recall his core values, vision, and commitment to students—all things that inspire me and make me believe in his potential. I remind myself of how grateful I am to have this client's trust and how privileged I am to be a witness to his growth and development. I can't take this for granted. This visualization often helps me transition into a more compassionate stance as I enter a meeting.

Sometimes if I'm particularly plagued by judgmental thoughts about a client, I visualize taking all my feelings and putting them into a big box. I put the lid on, and tell myself that after the meeting, if I want, I can open the box and reclaim them. Of course, sometimes they sneak out of the box during a coaching session, or sometimes a judgment surfaces that I forgot to stuff away. But before I go into a coaching meeting, I scan my mind for any thoughts that might not help us reach our goals for that day and then I clear them out of the way. Most of the time, I am more committed to being a good coach and transforming schools than to letting my judgments run wild.

When I knock on a client's classroom or office, I know that a large part of what will make the meeting successful is my disposition: If I'm confident, compassionate, grounded, and present, I know I can create a learning space for someone to explore his beliefs, behavior, and being.

THE ARC OF A COACHING CONVERSATION

Effective coaching conversations have a structure. A coach needs to be aware of these and of the arc and flow of a conversation. Sometimes it can also help to make these elements explicit to a client.

A coaching conversation usually starts with a general check-in—the informal chatting or settling into a meeting. Although this dialogue should be limited so that we can get to our coaching work, we also look for opportunities to make personal connections with our clients. Asking a question such as, "How was your weekend?" is an invitation to raise topics outside of the work sphere. These brief conversations can help build and establish trust; they can also help us get a pulse on what's going on with our client outside of work (which, of course, can affect their work).

However, I am very cautious about revealing personal information. I do share, otherwise this chatty conversation would feel strange and one-sided, and, of course, sometimes clients ask questions. But I am very selective—I never want a client to be concerned with my emotional state. I also don't want to offer information that might raise any emotions or conflicts of interest for my client. Before I share anything personal, I think through how my client might hear, experience or interpret my story. How could it affect the way she thinks about me? About herself? If I have any question or doubt about how a client would hear a piece of personal information, I don't share.

Sometimes it's useful to make an agreement about how long you'll spend on a check-in, especially if working with a client who enjoys, or gets stuck in, the informal chatting phase of a coaching conversation. In addition, if the points raised in the check-in were weighty, we might ask for permission to set them aside for the duration of the conversation. We can also ask if there's anything the client needs to release so that he can engage in coaching. This can sound like, "Is there anything you'd like to put aside so that you can be present for our conversation?" Or, "Is there anything you need to do or share in order to be present without distraction?"

Once it feels like there's been enough warming up and checking in, it's the coach's responsibility to shift the conversation. We might say, "So, what's on your mind today? What would you like to talk about?" and jot down the topics that come up.

Another routine to begin a coaching conversation is to return to what was discussed at the last meeting. At the end of each coaching session, the client will usually have some follow-up actions to take. It is important that the coach return to these to gently hold the client accountable for what she says she is going to do. If we miss this step, we can undermine our credibility. We can open this conversation by saying, "Last week you decided you wanted to try ... How did those things go?" or "Last week you committed to ... What happened?" Depending on what the client says, this may constitute the entire coaching conversation—either because we continue to reflect on what happened or we move into next steps.

After checking in, creating a plan for the conversation, and returning to the previous week's commitments, the coach moves the discussion into the agreed-on topics for the meeting. Now the coach engages in the various approaches and strategies discussed in Chapters Eight through Twelve and moves through listening, questioning, and learning activities.

Let's take a look at a couple more elements from the coaching conversation before exploring how a session can wrap up.

Arc of a Coaching Conversation

1. Check in and chat.
2. Create a plan for the conversation: "What's on your mind?"
3. Check in on previous commitments: "How'd that go?"
4. Engage in coaching stances and approaches.
5. Determine next steps.
6. Reflect on conversation and ask for feedback.

LOGISTICS DURING A CONVERSATION

When we engage our client in creating a plan for the conversation, we want to be clear about how much time we have together and make agreements about how to use it. Often, I've found that clients name a list of topics to discuss that will exceed the time we have. I help prioritize the list and create time frames for how long to spend on each item. Usually, when we're prioritizing the list, I'm conscious of the plan I made for the meeting and what I suspect could help the client move forward on her goals. If so, I suggest we start with a particular item or I add a topic or an activity to the list.

During the conversation, I agree to keep track of time. I set the timer on my phone and tuck it out of sight so that we're not distracted by it. I also make sure that we'll have a few moments to reflect on today's work and determine next steps. Frequently, conversations become so engrossing that the end is cut short. It's the coach's responsibility to calmly wrap up a meeting so that the client can feel a sense of closure and be clear on next steps.

The other responsibility a coach has during a meeting is to document the conversation. I take notes for several reasons: first, so that I'll remember things. Sometimes I also jot down words or phrases a client says that I might want to return to. Second, I feel it is my responsibility to notice and document the client's changes in practice, developing beliefs, and shifts in ways of being. I'm always listening for indicators of growth in those areas and at different times I'll share what I've recorded. I often compile what I've heard and e-mail a summary to clients after our meetings. I also need this kind of documentation for the progress reports I write for supervisors and for my own reflection. Finally, I need notes so that I can plan our subsequent coaching session. Exhibit 13.2 offers a basic template to take notes on. There's an example of this kind of documentation on my website at www.elenaaguilar.com.

Technical Tips on Note Taking

I prefer taking notes by hand, in a notebook. I like a different colored spiral-bound notebook for each client. When I'm meeting with someone, I'm acutely aware of my body language; having a computer between us feels intrusive and blocks my line of view. Since I want to minimize every possible distraction, pen and paper are my preferred tools.

Another technical note: When I first started coaching, and hadn't yet internalized the kinds of questions that I wanted to ask in a coaching session, I kept a list of questions that I'd printed on cardstock tucked into my notebook. When I got stuck and couldn't remember how to phrase a confrontational question, for example, I subtly flipped the pages of my notebook and glanced at my list.

Exhibit 13.2. Record of Coaching Conversation

School _____ Client _____ Date _____

Client's Changes in Practice	Client's Next Steps	Areas for Follow Up

Coach's Next Steps/Follow-Up Agreements:	Goal Areas:

I staple my work plan to the inside cover of my notebook. I don't always remember the entire plan and sometimes I reference it. I also paperclip my plan for a coaching conversation to my notebook—usually on the page preceding the blank one I intend to write on during a meeting. I'll review it if I need during a conversation. Don't worry about clients noticing when you use your resources—there's nothing wrong with being transparent about our practice. Letting clients know that you planned and thought carefully about how to support their learning can build trust and confidence in your competence.

COACH RESPONSIBILITY DURING CONVERSATION

During a coaching session, the coach is responsible for guiding the conversation, keeping the client's history and goals in mind, listening deeply, using various questioning strategies to advance the client's thinking, looking through a set of lenses in order to have multiple perspectives on the situation, offering activities that can deepen learning, managing the time and taking notes, and finally, the coach is responsible for monitoring her own mental and emotional processes in order to be able to do all of this. This is the art of transformational coaching.

When we come into contact with the other person, our thoughts and actions should express our mind of compassion, even if that person says and does things that are not easy to accept.

THICH NHAT HANH (2012)

In order to ensure that our client is fully engaged in the learning space we're holding, we need to pay close attention to our client's verbal and nonverbal cues. We want to be particularly attuned to any indicators that our client is experiencing distress. If for example, a client gets restless and finds several excuses to get up and move about, something might be going on. When we notice behaviors that might indicate the client is upset, it can be useful to ask about what's going on. For example, you can simply say, "What's coming up for you right now?" Invite the client to notice and reflect on her emotions—and then adjust your coaching approach. Sometimes we may also notice physical cues such as smiles, unfurrowing brows, dropping shoulders, or deep exhales that let us know that we're on the right track—these changes in body language are good data points that our coaching is effective.

We also want to notice when a client uses language that may reflect emotional distress. If a client engages in "Yes, but …" dialogue with us or debates everything we say, he may be shutting down to the conversation. If we're not sure what's going on—we might observe cues that indicate distress or disconnect—it's always useful to ask. We can simply say, "Is this helping?" or "Can I check in on what's going on for you—I want to be helpful but I'm having a hard time reading how you're receiving this?" A client may take up this offer, and may have the emotional intelligence skills to name what he's experiencing, but he may not. It can be helpful to support the client by asking questions such as, "Can we explore some of the emotions that might be coming up? What part of your body are you feeling distress in? Can you describe it?" We also want to be cautious that we don't make our client feel more uncomfortable by naming the emotional discomfort that we observe. This is tricky, but necessary, terrain to negotiate on the journey to transforming behaviors, beliefs, and being.

Maybe you're reading this thinking, "I'm a math coach. I am assigned to help eighth-grade teachers improve their algebra instruction and conduct accurate assessments. Do I really have to deal with all of this emotional stuff? Can't we just talk about instruction?"

The answer, unfortunately, is no. Adults, just like children, cannot learn when their anxiety levels are high. Coaches must develop skills to address emotions and support our clients in managing them. Although some coaches are effective at supporting teachers in implementing a new curriculum or improving classroom management skills, coaches can be exponentially more powerful and effective when they also respond to the emotions that arise in teaching. Education is a deeply emotional arena for just about everyone who enters it—the beauty of coaching is that we are uniquely positioned to help these be positive emotional experiences where healing and transformation are possible.

CLOSING THE CONVERSATION

The way a coaching conversation wraps up is critical. We hope our sessions facilitate learning, push a client's thinking, open up emotional spaces, and provoke reflection and growth. We need to know, at the end of a meeting, if the client felt inspired, empowered, clear about his next steps, and confident that he can take them.

Sometimes a client offers unsolicited feedback by saying something like, "This was helpful," or "I feel better." If a client makes comments like these, a coach can ask for clarity or more details—both for herself as feedback and to push the client's reflection. You can say, "Would you mind sharing what exactly was helpful in today's session? I want to make sure I can do that again." If a client doesn't volunteer feedback, then you can pose questions such as the following:

- How do you feel about our meeting today?
- What has been valuable in this session?
- What else might be helpful for me to do?
- What would you like more of or less of in our coaching work?

If the client's response is vague, that's OK. Ask follow-up questions if it feels like the client is receptive to giving you feedback, otherwise, let it go. You also don't want your client to feel pressured to praise you or say the time was helpful if it wasn't.

The second essential element to close a coaching conversation is to identify next steps. It's critical that our clients come out of a coaching session ready to take some actions. The end of a coaching session should always include a review of what the client is going to do next, when it will be done by, and anything the coach is going to do to support these next steps. For example, the coach might say, "I'm going to send you the notes I took by 8 a.m. tomorrow. I'm also going to find another sixth-grade math teacher you can observe. I'll do that by Monday. Let's go over your next steps, OK?" You might also close the meeting by agreeing on how you will check in with your client and see that he's doing what he said he'd do. For example, "So, you've determined that by Wednesday you're going to convene your leadership team for a meeting. I'm going to e-mail you on Monday to check in on how this is going." Many clients want and appreciate this kind of gentle accountability.

COMMON CHALLENGES AND HELPFUL RESPONSES

Challenge: I'm always asked to do all kinds of jobs that have nothing to do with coaching. I'm supposed to be a literacy coach but I'm doing lunch supervision, translation and testing coordination!

Lens of Inquiry and Lens of Systems Thinking. Many site-based coaches end up doing a range of tasks outside of coaching. Applying an inquiry lens and a systems thinking lens can help identify root causes and solutions.

Consider these questions:

- Are your roles and responsibilities clearly articulated? Who defined them? Have they been shared with the whole staff? Who is directing your work? What are you accountable for?

- What other tasks need to be done at the site (such as yard supervision) that could be done by someone else? What is the effect of using your time to do these jobs? What are you then unable to do? If you do these other jobs, will you reach your coaching goals?

Next, the questions are, Who do you need to talk to about this dilemma? Who makes decisions about your work? For a site-based coach, this is usually the principal or another administrator. Prepare for a conversation with this person, gather your ideas and proposals for solutions, and discuss your dilemma.

Challenge: It's impossible to find time to meet with teachers. I observe their lessons, but we never have time to debrief.

Lens of Inquiry. This is another very common challenge that coaches face, which again often stems from the fact that coaching is an evolving field. We can begin exploring this issue by understanding how coaching has been framed and set up at this school. In order for coaching to be effective, we must consider and analyze the conditions for it to be taken up. Who has defined the coaching work? How do teachers and administrators understand what coaching is and what it is supposed to do? How have these understandings been developed and communicated? What are the expectations for teachers to engage with coaching? How have expectations been communicated? How much of a priority is coaching and to whom? What can be done so that time is allocated and held sacred for this work?

Because coaching is sometimes perceived as a "soft and fluffy" thing, and not as rigorous professional development, it's sometimes seen by administrators and teachers as optional. If a genuine commitment exists at a site or in a district for teachers to participate in coaching, then this commitment needs to be communicated and prioritized.

If this is the case, and you still struggle to find time to debrief, then you might benefit by considering the state of your relationships with teachers—how do they view you? How much do they trust you? What do they feel about the debriefs they've engaged in? How have those been helpful or not? A coach might consider that there are other activities that teachers would find more useful. It's worth having a direct conversation about this and making some explicit agreements about time spent in coaching.

The underlying area to explore is decision making: Who decides how time is spent doing what and based on what criteria? There will never be enough time and time is never the culprit. Whenever we hear complaints of "not enough time," we need to dig fast and deep or we're caught in a trap from which there is no way out. The lens of inquiry can be instrumental in these situations.

Challenge: At the end of each coaching session, the principal I'm working with agrees to do a number of things before our next meeting. But then she never does them, and I get so frustrated!

Lens of Adult Learning. First, you'll need to start by addressing your own emotions. You need to work through them so you don't get frustrated, because that's not going to help anything. Release some attachment to outcome.

Why do you think your client isn't following through? Have you asked? There could be a number of reasons: perhaps the tasks you agreed on are too challenging for this principal to do alone. Perhaps she agreed to do them, in order to please you, but isn't able to do so. Exploring the client's zone of proximal development could be a good place to start. How were the tasks determined? How did you know that she could do them independently? Use the lens of adult learning to make sure that the tasks are the right ones.

If you feel like you have data indicating that your client is capable of engaging in the assignments independently, and if you suspect that it's a matter of will (why isn't she *willing* to do this?) then new questions open up to consider. What does this principal believe is the purpose and benefit to doing these things? How does she see them as connected to her goals? What does she hope to get from doing them? Who decided these were the things to do anyway? Was it the coach—or did they emerge from the client?

Once you have thought through some of these questions, raise them directly with the client. You can frame this as, "I've noticed that you haven't done the things you agreed to do. This is a pattern. Can we talk about what's going on?" Explore what she thinks, feels, and wants. Find a way to be curious about what's going on rather than frustrated. It's a much easier stance to take.

CONCLUSION

Peter Block's suggestion has become almost my singular aspiration in a coaching conversation— it's my main indicator of whether I did a good job. After a coaching meeting, the first thing I ask myself is whether I think my client is feeling more optimistic about what he can do. Does he feel more empowered? Did he reconnect with his vision, values, and abilities? This is sometimes a

Start measuring your work by the optimism and self-sufficiency you leave behind.

PETER BLOCK (2011)

hard road to chart—optimism and self-sufficiency are challenging outcomes in our schools—and sometimes the journey is rough and painful. I don't always reach this end but I'm always aiming for it—and when I hit it, and I know I've reached it, it's been a good day of coaching.

CHAPTER 14

Reflection and Assessment: What's Next?

Read this when:

- You want some strategies to lead your client through a midyear or end-of-year reflection
- Your client feels like she hasn't made much progress and you need to help her see her growth

A MIDYEAR CRISIS

Only three weeks had passed since the winter break and Ana was telling me that she couldn't go on. "I'm not going to make it through the second semester," she said, "They'll have to find a substitute principal for the rest of the year. I just wrote my letter of resignation." Her neck was covered in hives, her eyes were puffy, and her desk was piled with papers, books, files, empty coffee cups and shriveled apple cores. "I'm a terrible principal, I haven't done any of the things I wanted to do for these kids; it was a mistake to take this position. I wasn't ready for it. Tell them you tried coaching me but I couldn't do it." Someone knocked at the door. "Tell them to go away," she said to me. "I can't do this." She burst into tears.

Follow effective action with quiet reflection. From the quiet reflection will come even more effective action.

PETER DRUCKER (2008)

Ana's administrative assistant stood outside the door, her eyes wandering behind me toward the slumped figure of her principal. "I think we're going to need a few uninterrupted hours," I said to the older woman who had seen dozen of principals cycle through this high school.

I tossed out the trash, stacked up the books, and sat down opposite Ana. "I've let them down," she sobbed. "Do you know how that feels? They know I'm from this community, they thought I could do something about all the problems, and now they see that I'm a failure."

I let Ana talk for a while. I gave her space to cry and vent. Then I made a proposal: "I'm wondering if we could spend some time reviewing the work we've done together this year—going over the goals you established?"

"I haven't met those goals," she said. "I'm miles away from them."

"OK," I said. "But I think we might be able to find some evidence that you're moving toward them. Let's just try it, OK? And then you can quit." Ana smiled and nodded her head. Although I had been preparing for a midyear reflection, I was nervous that I wasn't quite ready. Oh well, I thought, sometimes you just have to trust that you're ready enough and it'll be OK. I knew this conversation needed to happen at that very moment if Ana was going to stop spiraling down.

Start out by celebrating the best in the situation because it allows us to fall in love with it, which connects us to our passion and emancipates the energy.

DEWITT JONES (2012)

Over three years have passed since this day. Ana has led her school through a transformation that no one believed could have been possible given her experience and the reality at the site when she took over. She often points to that January reflection in her first year as a principal as a pivotal moment in her career. This chapter describes what happened in that reflection and how a coach can use reflections to move coaching work forward. This chapter also explores how applying a systems lens approach can shift coaching from an individual professional development strategy to a transformational endeavor.

THE MIDYEAR AND END-OF-YEAR REFLECTION

There are times when a reflective process can be used as an intervention—as a cathartic, catalytic, and confrontational coaching strategy. This is how I used it with Ana on the day she was poised to turn in her resignation papers. But a midyear and end-of-year reflection can also serve many additional purposes: it can provide critical feedback for a coach on where a client is in her learning and how a coach needs to adjust her approach, it can help to redefine goals and actions plans for the subsequent period of work, and it can help to surface systemic questions that need to be addressed. This kind of a reflection is just good practice in the work of learning. By engaging our clients in it, we are modeling a practice that principals can do with their teachers and that teachers can do with students.

 Administrators: You can also do midyear and end-of-year reflections with those you supervise. These steps can serve as a guide.

Following are the five basic steps to reaching a healthy and satisfying midyear or end-of-year reflection:

1. *Review the work plan and coaching notes.* The work plan (Chapter Three) is the starting point for these big reflections. A coach can prepare for this conversation by reviewing the client's SMARTE goals, the strategic activities that were intended to lead to meeting these goals, and the evidence and data that were identified as indicators of progress toward the goals.

   Throughout the months of coaching since this plan was created, the coach may have documented the journey in weekly or monthly reflections or reports. Ideally, the coach has a pile of notes that she can review to remember the details of what's happened and to look for indicators of growth. Exhibit 14.1 offers an example of a monthly report.

2. *Reflect.* As the coach reviews the work plan and coaching notes, the following questions can support reflection:

   - Which of the strategic activities did the coach and client do together? Which did the client and principal do alone?

   - What were the results of engaging in the strategic activities? How did they change the client's practice?

   - What evidence do we have of a change in practice?

   - Can we anticipate that the client will see evidence of these changes in practice? Is there evidence beyond what might be the client's self-reported belief that she's changed her practice?

Exhibit 14.1. Transformational Coaching: Monthly Progress Report

Coach: Elena Aguilar   **Client: Teresa Phillips**   **Date: March 31, 2011**

Total Number of Hours Engaged with Client this Month *(include explanation if necessary)*:

Six hours; Teresa was out sick one week during our scheduled time.

SMARTE Goal 1: *[Complete a separate reflection for each coaching goal.]*

To provide verbal and written feedback to all students on their writing assignments every other week within two days of submission of the assignment for the entire school year.

1. **Strategic Activities Engaged in This Month to Meet Goal** *[Include those from the work plan, as well as any others that were used.]*

   - Analyze student writing.
   - Analyze writing rubric and identify lessons that could demonstrate the elements that students are struggling with.
   - Coach models writing lessons on rubric elements that students struggle with. Teacher observes. Debrief together.
   - Coach observes teacher giving student feedback; debrief and reflect.

2. **Progress toward Goal**

   Teresa has made significant progress toward her goal. She has consistently given students feedback on their writing this year and she's starting to see how this feedback is resulting in their writing improving. This month we continued to analyze student writing together in order to identify which elements on the rubric were still hard for the kids. We categorized the students into groups depending on their results and Teresa created a plan to support those who are still struggling. I modeled one lesson on the rubric element "voice," because Teresa had tried teaching some lessons on it but wasn't seeing the results she wanted to see in student papers. After I modeled the lesson, then the next day Teresa did a follow-up lesson and we looked at the work that students did.

   I also observed Teresa giving students feedback as she regularly does during silent reading time. One thing I noticed, which I discussed with Teresa afterwards, was that she made some assumptions about her students' ability to use idioms. Given that all of her students are English language learners, we discussed that she may need to do some more direct instruction on idioms. In this conversation, Teresa became very emotional because she said she felt overwhelmed by how much she needed to teach her students to prepare them for high school. I used a cathartic approach to help her process these feelings. When reflecting on her goals, Teresa felt very satisfied with what she has accomplished.

3. **Evidence of Changes in Practice**
   - The number of students who needed reteaching on three elements from the rubric decreased from last month. This month there were only four who needed reteaching. Last month there were nine.
   - Student writing from after Teresa did voice lessons—after she observed me model a lesson—showed that student were internalizing the learning. We found a number of specific pieces of evidence.
   - Teresa's one-on-one feedback sessions with students are precise and quickly get to the points that she wants to share with students. I have transcriptions of these conversations from the whole year that show how her instructions get more precise and also that students demonstrate an understanding of what she's saying.
   - Teresa was really hard on herself in the beginning of the year. It is getting much easier for her to recognize her own accomplishments and growth and to share those without feeling like she's bragging. My notes from our coaching sessions provide this evidence.

4. **Next Steps and Coaching Moves**

   Teresa is feeling very confident about meeting her year-long goal. Next month she will teach a new writing genre and she's nervous about whether her students will be able to apply their newly acquired skills. She wants me to observe her a few times as she teaches mini-lessons. I suggested that we use video and that we debrief it together, but she's apprehensive. I think she's getting a little too dependent on my opinion, even though I try not to give it, so I'd like to push her to try the video. I want to make sure that she feels she is the owner of her learning and that she doesn't think it's all my coaching. In these last months, I want to make sure that I'm playing a facilitative role and releasing the responsibility of learning even more to her. I think I'll need to make this explicit so that she understands my coaching moves, and I think this will be OK with her.

- When has coaching felt most successful? When have we noticed the client experience a big "aha"? What does the coach think is the biggest "bright spot?"

- What's gotten in the way of coaching? What might need to be addressed, confronted, or dealt with in order for coaching to be more effective?

- What have we learned about how our client learns? About what changes her practice and which strategies are most effective? Do we tend to coach mostly through a cathartic or supportive approach? Do we engage mostly in activities — and if so, which kinds?

- In order for the client to meet her goal, does it seem like the same strategic activities need to be repeated? Do new activities need to be added? Are we spending enough time reflecting on the activities?

- Does the coach need to further scaffold the activities so that the client can engage in them alone? Are we ready to release more responsibility so that the client can be more autonomous in her learning?

- Which coaching strategies do we want to be sure to use regularly? Which ones do we want to try using more often?

It's important that as the coach reviews these questions and the data she's gathered, she is careful not to tumble into judgment or self-critical blame. It doesn't help if we start to beat ourselves up over what didn't happen, or if we get judgmental about what our client did or didn't do.

3. *Plan the coaching conversation.* Once the coach has reviewed the plans and considered these questions, then she can design the conversation she'll have with her client. Although we spend time planning it, it's critical that this conversation is driven by the client. We might prepare some questions to pose and keep our reflections in mind, but then we'll let the client direct the conversation.

We'll come to the meeting with the work plan in hand and lay it out on the desk. We'll ask the client many of the same questions that we reflected on, but phrased slightly differently. These can include the following:

- Which of these strategic activities felt useful to you?

- What evidence would you cite that indicates a change in your practice? How do you know you're making progress toward your goals?

- What do you feel good about in terms of your growth this semester (or this year)? What learning do you feel has been most powerful? When have you felt a big "aha"?

- Which changes in practice or learnings do you feel have positively affected students? What do you think has made a big difference to them? How do you know that your learnings positively affected them?

- What's gotten in the way of doing some of these activities that we'd planned on doing? Are they activities that you'd still like to try? That you think would be helpful? Or are they activities we need to let go of? Are there other things you think we should do that would be helpful?

- What's been hard about engaging in coaching?

- What could I do that would make it more effective for you?

- Is there any feedback you'd like to give me about how I'm working with you?

As I plan this reflective conversation, I engage in the same kind of thinking and writing as I described in Chapter Thirteen: I consider where my client needs this conversation to go and who I need to be in it. I try to anticipate how she'll respond, what might come up for her, and how I'll react.

4. *Determine the when and where of the conversation.* Ideally, it's best if the coach can make an agreement ahead of time with the client about when the midyear and end-of-year reflections will take place. This allows the client to ensure that the logistical factors are in place so that they won't be interrupted. Sometimes this conversation is nice to have outside of the regular meeting place—in a café, an outdoor setting, or just in another part of the school, but it's important that this conversation be private and not interrupted. Furthermore, if the client gets advance notice about the conversation, she'll often start to reflect on the work you've done together. Anticipating it will prime the client's mind.

Sometimes it's hard to find time for this conversation: everything else feels so urgent and there's so much to talk about. The coach or the client can subtly resist this stage in the coaching cycle—but the coach must insist. I've framed it this way: "Next week when we meet I'd like to discuss our work together so far this year. I want to look back at the goals we set and consider where we are in meeting them. This is a really important part of coaching and I think it will feel really satisfying to you—you'll recognize how much you've learned and grown this year. We're going to need a couple hours of uninterrupted time." I want my clients to look forward to this conversation.

5. *Engage the client in the reflective conversation.* Hopefully, most of the time we'll be prepared and we'll settle into a conversation which will yield insights, positive feelings, and ideas about where to go next. To illustrate how this conversation can flow, I'll go back to Ana, the principal who was quitting in late January when on the spur of the moment I decided to engage her in reflecting on our work. Fortunately, just the week before, I'd been reviewing our coaching in a conversation with my supervisor and I had a copy of the work plan in my bag.

Learning from experience is not inevitable. It must be intentional.

ROLAND BARTH (2001, P. 65)

Ideally, a coach will have ample time to prepare for this conversation. A template for a midyear or end-of-year reflection can be found in Exhibit 14.2.

Exhibit 14.2. Transformational Coaching: Midyear Progress Report or End-of-Year Report

Please note: this document is for the coach to use in reflecting on her work and to share with her manager—*only if* the manager is not also the client's supervisor. This is not to be shared with an evaluator or with the client.

Coach _____   Client _____   Date _____

SMARTE Goal 1 *[Complete a separate reflection for each coaching goal.]*
  Description of change: *[a narrative description]*
  Specific indicators of progress: *[bulleted list of specific indicators]*
  Sources of evidence: *[lesson plans, meeting agendas, videos, e-mails, coaching notes, survey data, and the like]*
  Contributing factors: *[Which factors got in the way? Which factors helped coaching efforts?]*
  Lessons learned and next steps: *[a narrative]*

Midyear Reflection with Ana

I pulled out the work plan we'd developed in September and spread its five pages across Ana's desk. "Let's start with looking at the goals," I said. I quickly drew circles with a yellow highlighter pen around the boxes with the goals. Ana had set goals in three areas; each goal had several components.

She was quiet for a few minutes. I stayed in the silence, refraining from asking questions. "Wow," she said, shaking her head. "I sure set a lot of goals. What was I thinking?"

"Tell me more about that," I said, hoping to invite Ana into a deeper reflection on where she was in the first month of her first year as a principal.

"Well, these were totally unrealistic. I was so naïve about what I was getting into. When I interviewed here, the superintendent told me this place had a toxic staff culture, I knew what the test scores were, and I was aware of the problems in the community. How did I imagine I could do all of this?"

"So what were you thinking?" I asked.

"I guess I wanted to set ambitious goals. I felt confident, I felt clear about what needed to happen, and I wanted to model that I wasn't going to be timid about taking on a major challenge."

"Who needed to see or hear that from you? Who did you do that for?"

Ana's posture straightened, her shoulders dropped. "For me," she said. "That's how I have always taken on big challenges. I tell myself I can do it, I set audacious goals, and then I communicate these intentions to others. So for me first. And then for my staff."

I remembered that Ana had shared her leadership goals with her teachers in their first month of school. She'd wanted to model being a reflective practitioner who was engaged in her own learning. "What effect do you think that had on your staff when you shared those goals?" I asked.

Ana chuckled. "They had never seen anything like it. I think they thought I'd never make it. Maybe they were right." She paused. We sat in silence for a minute. "But maybe not—I think it gave me a way to push when I met with each teacher for their goal-setting conference."

"Ana, do you remember when we set these goals and I expressed some concern about how many you had and whether they were realistic?" She nodded. "Remember how we also prioritized them?" Again, she nodded. "Let's start with a close look at the one that was your top priority and consider which of the strategic actions we've engaged in."

Ana's top priority was to address the staff's approach to discipline which resulted in the school having the highest suspension rates in the district. African American males were disproportionately suspended at rates of twice their counterparts. When Ana had visited the school the previous spring and spoken to the outgoing principal, she'd been told that teachers threw kids out of class for any minor reason. Ana knew that it would be impossible to improve student achievement if she didn't start with this issue.

"When you look at this goal and these activities that we determined might help you reach it, what do you think?" I asked.

"The first thing that comes to mind is that this was the right goal to prioritize. If there's one hill I am ready to die on, it's this one — you can't throw your kids out of class. I got a lot of push-back from staff on this, they have complained that I don't understand how hard the kids are, but I know I'm on the right track with this."

"That's great," I affirmed. "To recognize that you still feel your priority was the right one."

"But I haven't been able to do all of these things," Ana said as she marked checks and Xs next to the strategic actions.

As we reviewed what had and hadn't been done yet, Ana recognized that many of the barriers to getting the work done were beyond her control. The data was surprisingly hard to come by — the tracking systems were ineffective, incomplete, and hard to access. She'd only been able to convince two teachers to join the culture and climate team, and these two were anxious about playing a leadership role and possibly alienating their colleagues. There were fewer hours for professional development with teachers than Ana had anticipated — there were so many operational issues to address that time was always cut short.

Several of the strategic activities had been accomplished — a new referral form was in use in every classroom, we'd been able to share some data analysis with staff and they had been concerned about what they'd seen, and we'd visited some neighboring schools where restorative justice practices were in use and effective.

As we reflected on why some of the activities hadn't been done, Ana named a number of other leadership actions that she felt she'd been taking that we hadn't identified when we'd created her plan. "It's the conversations I have all the time with teachers and staff members that are so important," she said. "I'm constantly listening to them and then pushing them to think about what they are doing and what they believe about students. I don't think that they were ever challenged in this way before, and I think that many of them are actually receptive to me."

I agreed. I'd noticed Ana talking to her teachers on several occasions about how they could manage student disruptions in a way that deescalated the behavior and that ultimately kept kids in class. I shared my observations with Ana and she smiled, thanking me.

I wanted to keep pointing out what Ana had done well, how much she had done and the data that indicated that her leadership was resulting in teachers changing their practices and in changes for students. I knew that referral numbers had plummeted since the new system had gone into effect, that student attendance was improving and that other indicators showed that the school was moving in a positive direction. But I also knew that in this conversation Ana had to identify her actions and the positive indicators by herself. I knew that that was the only way she'd authentically feel ownership over her accomplishments.

Slowly we continued reflecting on the previous months of work—what had happened, what was the impact, what hadn't happened, why hadn't it happened. And then, what might need to happen next. I recognized that Ana was ready to engage in this part of the conversation when she started talking about wanting to share her midyear reflection with her staff. "I shared my goals with them in the beginning of the year, and I'm going to have midyear reflections with each teacher on their goal soon, so I guess I could move toward that by sharing my own midyear progress toward goals."

I smiled and nodded my head.

"Well," Ana said, as if anticipating my question, "I guess I'm not going to quit." She stood and opened the blinds behind her desk. I hadn't seen them open in weeks and the low January sun streamed through the window. Her office looked out onto the corner of an intersection where three weeks before there had been a drive-by shooting. The sidewalk was still covered in melted wax from the dozens of candles that had burned in memory of the twenty-two-year-old who was killed. "I'm not going to be another person to give up on this community," she said.

"So what do you want to do next?" I asked. "Where are we in this plan?"

"I still don't think these are too many goals," she said. "But I think these goals are going to take me two or three years, realistically."

"Ok, so what do you want to be absolutely sure you've done by June? What has to happen?" We spent a while determining what that should be—refining one goal, narrowing it, and identifying the indicators we could look for in the next few months that would reflect progress toward meeting the goal.

Throughout our conversation I'd been taking notes. "Before we finish, Ana, I want to go review what you have done this semester—what you've done well and which leadership actions you successfully took. Is that OK?"

"Sure," she said, shrugging her shoulders. Ana was ambitious and energetic, and she also was uncomfortable with public appreciation or receiving praise.

I'd been compiling a list of actions that she'd named as effective and I read back my notes. "You began to share data that hadn't ever been explicitly shared with staff and you shared it in a way that made many curious and concerned. You engaged in daily conversations about how to help students to manage their behavior, stay in class and learn—and teachers are now coming to you for advice, recognizing you as a support. You inspired two teachers to take leadership and share your commitment to reversing this data trend ..." I continued reflecting back what I'd heard. Ana nodded her head, looking at a distant point over my shoulder. When I finished the list, I added my own commentary, "And you are a first year principal! I know you've worked almost seven days a week, ninety hours a week, for six months! Can you own what you've done? Can you feel good about it?"

"There's so much more to do," Ana said.

"I know. There will be so much more for a long time. But can you own your accomplishments?"

"Yes," she said. "I can see how much I've done, how much has started to change." Ana leaned back in her chair and closed her eyes.

"Great." I said. "Let's wrap up for today and then next week we'll take a few more steps forward in the direction you want to go."

Even the smallest victory is never to be taken for granted. Each victory must be applauded.

AUDRE LORDE (1984)

As I left the school that day, the administrative assistant caught me in the hallway. "Is she quitting?," she asked.

"No," I responded. "She's just tired."

"Oh, thank God," said the elderly woman. "She's the best we've had in a long time. I don't want to see her go. I'll bring her lunch tomorrow; I know she never eats."

"I'm sure she'd love that," I said.

The Midyear Reflection

I've always found that the midyear reflection feels like it couldn't have happened any sooner, but also couldn't wait another week. It's a pivotal moment in a year—reflecting on what's gone well and adjusting our course of action. Even when the work hasn't gone where we want it to go or the reflective conversation is challenging, by the end the client and I are usually much clearer on what needs to happen next.

It's not uncommon to discover that one or more of the goals we'd set hasn't been addressed at all or that another area of work has surfaced as a necessary focus. In such cases, we can cross out a goal and create a new one. Sometimes we discover that we'd articulated too many goals—which I usually frame as good news: the client had high expectations of herself. I want to make sure the client recognizes all the factors that detracted from focusing on the goals—there are always plenty of reasons why we had less time to do what we'd hoped.

> *What gets measured gets done. What gets measured and fed back gets done well. What gets rewarded gets repeated.*
>
> JOHN E. JONES (1996, P. 155)

The End-of-Year Reflection

At the end of the year, we engage our client in a similar reflective process. At this time we might be planning for the next year or wrapping up coaching work. You can follow the same process and use the same prompts as you did with the midyear. This can be another opportunity for reflection, and acknowledging growth and success.

At this point, a challenge that a coach might encounter is a client who has accomplished little of what he'd set out to accomplish and who somehow blames the coach. This is more common if the client did not willingly engage with the coach—perhaps he'd been mandated to work with a coach. He might try to turn some of the lack of success onto the coach, saying things like, "Oh, remember when you were going to come and do a model lesson for me and then it didn't happen? I couldn't teach that writing unit because you didn't do it for me." A coach needs to be prepared for such a scenario and make sure she manages her own emotions. In this case, it's useful for the coach to have solid records on what happened in this coaching relationship—did the client cancel many appointments? Or cut them short? Did the client fail to undertake the actions he agreed to, which prevented the coach from taking others? The coach needs to be prepared to share this data in a way that shifts responsibility back to the client.

"According to my records," the coach can say, "we were only able to meet twice in January, once in February, once in March, and not at all in April. In May we met twice but you wanted to talk about test-taking strategies. Our original agreement was that we'd meet weekly. I also noted that in April, when I was scheduled to model a lesson, you were absent. I think the reason we haven't met these coaching goals is because we haven't met enough. Do you see this another way?"

The coach can then continue using a confrontational approach to ask the client to respond to this data. "Coaching requires time. And I'm wondering if you'd rather not engage with coaching any more. If you do, you will need to make time for it."

Data from the midyear and end-of-year reflections are sometimes shared with a client's supervisor—with permission, of course. What can be shared is the *progress toward goals* and the *changes in practice*. Principals want and need to know this information about those they supervise and it's important for them to receive reports when coaching *is* resulting in change. However, this can be tricky if the client has avoided coaching or is not making growth. In these cases, the coach needs to negotiate what is shared and how it is communicated; we also want to share the intervening factors that prevented coaching from progressing.

COACHING FOR SYSTEMS CHANGE

The midyear and end-of-year reflections are key points at which to apply the lens of systems thinking. During these reflective periods, we'll be surfacing and examining a large amount of "data"—we're taking stock of where everything and everyone is. We want to intentionally look for indicators of systemic change. When we look through a systems thinking lens, we'll clearly see how interconnected everything is at a school. The complexity can be overwhelming, but when we analyze it we can see how the situation we're in and the results we're getting are exactly what the system is set up to produce. In order to intervene in this system and produce different outcomes, we need to first understand all the elements at play and how they interact with each other.

The lens of systems thinking offers a way to understand the complexity. It presumes that whatever is happening in the moment is exactly what is supposed to happen in the system as it is—there is a logical, rational explanation for what we see. Although we may experience the system as chaotic or disorderly, this framework suggests there is an order and a sense that can be made. It suggests that everything we observe is the result of a complex set of interactions, and that we must understand them in order to intervene and change those interactions. This lens compels us to look at the pieces, the whole, and the interactions in order to understand how the system works and to change it.

The lens of systems thinking also makes some assumptions that can alleviate our anxiety when facing a seemingly disorderly system. It contends that change is a given, which is always a useful reminder. It also proposes that conflict and tension are necessary and natural, and that complexity and diversity are good, healthy things. Finally, it reminds us that all energy moves in cycles—the energy in a classroom, in a school, and in our education system is in some phase of a cycle. If we can identify the point, and understand conditions for change, we might be able to move it into a different phase of the cycle. This is what we return to reflect on in the midyear reflection. It is essential at this phase to pull out the lens of systems thinking and reflect alone and possibly with our client about our work on system change.

A masterful coach's inspiration . . . comes from being genuinely excited about the possibilities in front of you, from knowing that there is some part of yourself that is bigger than your circumstance. And it comes from being a monster of effectiveness, leaving behind a track record of successes.

ROBERT HARGROVE (2003, P. 51)

COMMON CHALLENGES AND HELPFUL RESPONSES

Challenge: I've been working with a new principal for six months, and I can't see any growth.

Lens of Adult Learning. Although it can often feel to a coach like a client is stuck or isn't making the kind of growth we want to see, if a client isn't making progress, we need to start by carefully examining our own coaching. First, go back to the goals. Do they still seem realistic? How often do you return to the goals and plan coaching sessions around them? How often do you engage the client in reflecting on the goals? Do the goals need to be broken down into sizable chunks?

Let's take a step even farther back. How did this coaching relationship come to be? What was the client's willingness to engage in coaching? What did he understand that it would be and hope to get from it? What have you noticed about how he's engaged with it? Have you engaged the client in a reflective conversation about what he's learning or how he feels he's growing? What is at stake for him in this professional development—what does he hope to get from it? What tools could you use to help the client reflect on his learning and what might be getting in the way of even greater growth?

I have sometimes felt impatient to see change in a client—I want to see growth on *my* timeline! Sometimes I just haven't been looking in the right place, or for the right things. Sometimes I've seen few indicators of change, and then all of sudden the client experiences a growth spurt and I'm amazed. Change is hard to predict and sometimes tricky to spot.

And sometimes people don't change—they may not want to, the conditions for learning might not be present, they may feel as if the coaching is being imposed on them, and as a coach, we have to be OK with that. Our job is not to change people; it's to offer a safe learning space.

Challenge: I've been working with a new principal and it's been going really well. Our midyear conversation was deep and intense, but I'm getting uncomfortable: I think my client might be developing romantic feelings for me.

Lens of Emotional Intelligence. Transformational coaching goes deep. We explore the depths of a person's beliefs, values, way of being, and feelings. Particularly when our clients are in vulnerable stages of their lives—taking on a new challenge, for example, and if they are in situations in which they feel isolated and in need of support, as principals often do, it's not unusual that they can develop feelings for a coach.

The feelings themselves are fine—feeling drawn to someone who has shown you kindness and compassion, who has listened to you without judgment, and who is supporting you to make big changes in how you work is understandable. But this is the coach's *job*, not a personal relationship. We do this because we are committed to supporting a principal or teacher to be able to better serve children. Clients can misinterpret our work with other feelings that they project onto a coach. There is nothing wrong about the client having this experience, but it is crucial that professional boundaries are clear and respected.

It is also our job to use the Lens of Emotional Intelligence to notice, name, and address these feelings which are inappropriately projected onto a coach. What is underneath is an emotional experience which the client needs to address: he may be feeling lonely in his personal life or going through a difficult time with a significant other. He needs to acknowledge his feelings and figure out how he can meet these needs, but a coach should not engage in a romantic relationship just as psychologists should not do so with their clients, or teachers with their students.

Challenge: I'm almost through my first year coaching and I feel like I'm suffering from coaching fatigue—I'm tired of being in "coach mode" all the time. I feel I always need to model coaching behaviors—the communication skills, attitudes, and beliefs. I feel like I can't ever just say what I think or feel directly. When can I just be myself?

Lens of Adult Learning. This dilemma points to where the coach is in her own learning and development. Part of the reason I became a coach is because my inclination was always to be direct and upfront, but when I told other teachers what I thought, or what they should do, I didn't see the results I wanted. They generally didn't listen and my words didn't yield the impact I wanted. I knew that being directive and instructive wasn't the most effective way to change adult practice.

When I became a full-time site-based coach, I felt I needed to be someone I wasn't. I didn't want to phrase every statement as a question, as in," I wonder, what would happen if you didn't shout at your students every day?" I just wanted to say, "Stop shouting!" But it didn't work when I did that. I didn't earn anyone's trust.

Coaching is a set of skills and knowledge that can be acquired. They take practice, intentionality, and time to master. In the initial stages, we can get tired. It is important to recognize our own learning trajectories and be patient with ourselves.

A coach *does* need to show up 100 percent of the time as a coach. That means that she never engages in unproductive conversations such as gossiping or complaining; that she consistently speaks about children in a respectful, kind way; that she honors her word; that she keeps her commitments, and that she always behaves ethically. When a coach breaks her coaching stance, even momentarily, she risks losing credibility. Clients may begin to have doubts and unconscious concerns. This stance is hard for a coach to hold; we need to be mindful and notice when we're getting tired and need a break. For all these reasons, coaches need to be connected with other coaches (ideally in a team) and we need space outside of our primary work place to off-load emotions, say whatever needs to be said, and get support.

Reflection and Assessment   **263**

Challenges: I'm coaching a principal who is making huge progress. We have intense conversations and she's made many changes in her practice. However, none of the central office administrators think I'm doing anything of value. They are talking about cutting funding for coaching. I want them to see how valuable coaching is!

Lens of Systems Thinking. This is a common dilemma for coaches. Our "work" often happens in private conversations behind closed doors. It can be hard for others to "see" what we're doing, but it's critical to share our practice—especially with those who make resource and funding decisions.

This dilemma raises a systems issue. The question involves how different parts of an organization share work, what outcomes are expected from different members in the organization and what kinds of data sets are considered valid. What did central office administrators believe would be the outcomes from coaching? How were these articulated? What knowledge and understanding do they have about coaching? What access do you as a coach have to these administrators? What systems are in place for you to share your work?

Another paradox in this situation is that the central office administrators might be evaluating your principal, and your work with your client is, for the most part, confidential. So how can you share your coaching work and honor the confidentiality agreements you've set with your client?

This is a dilemma, meaning it's something to manage rather than solve. Coaches need to be proactive about getting central office administrators enrolled in coaching as professional development. We need to be explicit about how we work, what we do, how we plan our work, how we measure our work, and how we gather feedback and data on it; we need to ask for time and audience with decision-makers so that we can help them understand what coaching is. With our client's permission, we can share work plans and progress reports. We also need to ask clients to share what they're learning through coaching and how they see their practice changing. It's very useful for coaches to gather anonymous survey data every year from clients which can be shared with administrators.

Whenever there's an opportunity, a coach can also informally engage a central office administrator in a coaching conversation. Often when they get a taste of the way we listen and ask questions, they start to "get it." They get curious and sense the possibility that coaching offers. As the field of coaching develops, coaches in schools will benefit by exploring ways to make our work public.

PART FOUR

Professional Development for Coaches

CHAPTER 15

What Is Professional Development for Coaches?

Read this when:

- You are a coach seeking to develop your practice and looking for some exercises and activities you can do on your own

- You are in a team of coaches engaging in professional learning

- You supervise coaches and want to design support structures and a course of professional development

THE IMPORTANCE OF A TEAM

For a couple years, I belonged to a team of transformational leadership coaches in the school district in which I worked. Our manager was a brilliant master coach and every week we gathered for reflection and professional development. We used structures and protocols (many of which I'll share in this chapter) to learn, to push each other's thinking, and to refine our coaching practices. We delved into book studies, conducted action-research, engaged in inquiry cycles and developed curriculum for administrators. Our team space also provided the kind of relief and rejuvenation that we needed in order to do our work—the emotional support was invaluable and impossible to garner elsewhere. I became a transformational coach through this team, with the partnership of my coach-colleagues.

My hope is that all coaches have an opportunity similar to what I had. Coaches are by nature reflective, we relish interpersonal exchanges, and most seem to have an incessant yearning to learn. But the majority of coaches I have come across work in isolation—either at a site or deployed around a district. Coaches clamor for our own PD, supervisors nod their heads in agreement, but very few opportunities or structures exist for coaches in schools to develop their practices. In order for coaching to be maximized and to deliver on its potential, coaches will need formalized, systematized structures in which to learn together. As the field of coaching develops and as the education community recognizes the impact that coaches can have on student learning and school transformation, I hope to see robust, ongoing professional development for coaches. This chapter attempts to contribute to this end.

 Administrators: if you have coaches at your site, this chapter might identify ways to support them.

Who Leads a Team of Coaches?

Perhaps it is an obvious fact, but the manager of a team of coaches should be a highly experienced coach with extensive knowledge of adult learning and team development. For example, a team of math coaches must be managed by someone with deep knowledge and understanding of math and math instruction, *and also* of coaching—someone at the modeling level on the transformational coaching rubric (see Appendix C).

The manager of a team of coaches ideally has a vision for coaching and works from a theoretically based coaching model. A coaching program composed of a hodgepodge of activities will not be as effective as one that has a clear foundation in adult learning and theories of change, and that aligns the elements of its program to this base. A coaching model should also be driven by an explicit theory of action. Coaching programs that struggle seem to be those in which these key elements are undeveloped or missing. Finally, a robust and effective coaching program *must* attend to the learning needs of its coaches.

Focusing Professional Development for Coaches

Professional development for coaches must focus on refining coaching skills. Deepening a content coach's knowledge of specific instructional practices and curriculum is important for content area coaches but they also need to learn coaching skills. If a coach is an expert on early literacy practices but knows nothing about how to get a reluctant teacher to try them out, this knowledge is useless. A content coach must also learn how to engage teachers in conversations about the equity issues that surface in their classroom and about how to interrupt those inequities. These are not skills that most of us inherently have and as soon as we begin coaching, we recognize the need for a vast skill and knowledge set.

Ideally, coaches would work together in teams under the guidance of a master coach. However, if these conditions don't exist, coaches can partner with and support each other. Coaches can establish structures such as peer coaching to learn from and support each other. This chapter offers many ways for coaches to reflect on our practice and improve our skills.

Often the question comes up about what makes a great coach. The answer is a coach engaged in ongoing work on him- or herself. The answer is not someone who asks great questions ... All our "doing" is affected profoundly by the way in which we "be."

FRANK BALL (2008, P. 33)

PROFESSIONAL DEVELOPMENT FOR COACHES

To plan PD for coaches we follow the same steps as when planning PD for any other adult learner. First, we need to know what kind of coach we're developing—which coaching model will be used and how the coach's work will be defined. We also need a way to assess a coach's skill set and knowledge base. Finally, we need to identify which learning activities could best help a coach develop her practice.

Start with the End in Mind

In order to design a professional development program for coaches we need a comprehensive definition of a school-based coach. While we have standards that describe the skills and knowledge components for students, teachers, administrators, and teacher leaders—there is no general equivalent for coaches. (However, a set of standards for middle and high school literacy coaches has been created—see the recommended resources in Appendix E.) Therefore, first we need to articulate the requisite skills, knowledge, capacities, and perhaps dispositions for coaches working in schools.

The International Coach Federation (ICF), the world's largest nonprofit coaching organization, offers a useful starting point. Although not grounded in an education context, this organization's professional coaching core competencies identifies a lengthy set of foundational coaching skills and dispositions that all coaches could work toward refining. However, school-based coaches need an additional set of competencies that reflect the context in which we work and a commitment toward a transformed education system.

In Appendix C I offer a transformational coaching rubric for self-assessment and reflection and as a framework for professional development. This rubric proposes a set of essential competencies and establishes a starting point for a discussion on what an education coach should know and be able to do. A coach could use this in a variety of ways: to reflect on her own capacities and identify areas of growth, to support a peer coaching arrangement, or as an evaluation tool with a supervisor.

With a rubric or set of coaching competencies, a coach can identify her strengths and areas for growth. The following section describes activities that can help refine a coaching practice. These incorporate various aspects of coaching including the practical and technical, activities, questioning skills, and techniques to develop a grounded and calm presence.

Learning Activities

The activities suggested in this chapter are aligned with the six domains of coaching in the transformational coaching rubric. The first two learning activities—role-plays and consultancies—are highly effective and can support development of all competencies on the rubric. However, they require a team. These two exercises are extremely high leverage in developing coaching capacities.

Role-plays. A role-play creates a real or fictional coaching scenario to act out with a colleague. Exhibit 15.1 offers an example of this process. On my website there are scenarios that could be used and tool to assess role-plays. The best role-plays are usually those in which a coach poses her own authentic challenging situations.

Exhibit 15.1. Role-Playing

Three people are ideal for a role-play—one person is the coach, another is the client, and the third is the observer who scripts the conversation and takes notes.

To prepare:

1. Select roles—coach, client, and observer.
2. Determine the scenario for a role-play. This could be a past coaching conversation where you felt stuck or a future coaching conversation that you'd like to practice.

3. Coach explains the scenario and provides necessary background information. Coach might ask the "client" to be a specific way ("be resistant to my suggestions"). Coach might also ask the observer to pay attention to specific areas on which he or she wants feedback (on questioning strategies, nonverbal communication, and the like).
4. Role-play for ten minutes.
5. Observer shares observations with the coach in response to the feedback he or she requested. Share specific quotes whenever possible.
6. Coach and client reflect on role-play and observations.
7. If desired, coach can practice again on the same issue trying different strategies, or participants can change roles and practice the same scenario again.

The Consultancy Protocol

Another extremely useful structure is the consultancy protocol shown in Exhibit 15.2. This is a structured process to help someone think through a dilemma or problem. The purpose of using this structure is for the presenter to share her dilemma and get multiple perspectives that can help deepen her understanding and uncover ways to work through the issue.

Coaching teams can take up consultancies as they are described in Exhibit 15.2. During the fishbowl discussion participants can also apply the coaching lenses from the Coach's Optical Refractor as a way to deepen the conversation. The presenter might ask the participants to apply a specific lens or two, or each member can agree to listen through a different lens and contribute to the discussion from that perspective. The resulting conversation is often rich and enlightening. As a coach, I always learned the most through consultancies — whether the issue was my own or a colleague's.

 Administrators: this protocol can be used with any team of educators.

Exhibit 15.2. Consultancy Protocol

Time: 50 min.*		
2	Facilitator welcomes group and reviews protocol	*Facilitator reviews process and adjusts time if needed.*
5	Presenter preparation	*Presenter can do a quick write or think about what s/he'd like to ask the group for support on. If presenters know ahead of time that they'll be engaging in a consultancy, this stage may not be needed.*
10	Presenter shares	*Presenter shares the dilemma he/she is struggling with. He/she might also share data and might ask for feedback or input in one area or around one question. If the coaching lenses are being used, presenter can ask group to focus on specific lenses.*
8	Clarifying questions	*Group asks presenter clarifying questions. Clarifying questions are yes/no or require very short answers—"who, what, when, where, and how" questions. The facilitator needs to intervene if probing questions are asked.*
5	Group reflection on question and think/planning time	*Group reflects on the presenter's question and prepares for discussion. If the group is familiar with the coaching lenses, this can be a time to apply them.*

15	Group discussion—fishbowl	*Presenter sits outside of circle while group discusses dilemma presented. This is an appropriate time to raise "probing questions"—although the presenter doesn't respond, he/she can consider them. The group might use any of the following questions in discussion: What did we hear? What didn't we hear that might be relevant? What assumptions seem to be operating? What questions does the dilemma raise for us? What have we done in similar situations? The group can also share insights from applying the coaching lenses.*
		Presenter can take notes if desired.
5	Presenter reflection	*Presenter shares any reactions, insights, feelings about protocol or what was said; presenter doesn't need to respond to questions that were raised in the group discussion.*

*A consultancy can last from twenty to fifty minutes. These times can all be adjusted but usually a minimum of ten minutes is needed for the fishbowl discussion.

Rubric Domain 1: Knowledge Base

Expanding core content knowledge. An instructional or leadership coach needs a level of mastery and expertise in the area he coaches. As what is known about learning and school transformation is constantly expanding, a coach needs to be on top of the latest research. Furthermore, as a coach moves through his work, or as his assignment or context changes, he may realize that he needs to strengthen his knowledge in specific areas. As schools in the United States transition to the Common Core State Standards, all coaches will want to devote time to understanding this framework and its implications for teaching. The opportunity to grow professionally in a content area appeals to many coaches and can be done by reading, attending conferences, participating in workshops and so on; however, learning must extend beyond content areas.

Honing analytical capacities. I suggest that transformational coaches use a set of analytical tools (the Coach's Optical Refractor presented in Chapter Four). Engaging with the sets of assumptions and questions offered with each lens is a way to expand understanding of core coaching knowledge. Given that there are no formal pathways to coaching roles, many of us who become coaches have not had an opportunity to study adult learning theory. The recommended resources in Appendix E offers suggestions for readings on the theories behind the lenses. A coaching practice can be strengthened by deepening our knowledge of the theoretical basis for coaching.

Rubric Domain 2: Relationships

Domain 2 outlines the relationship building skills that a coach needs. These include enrolling a client in coaching and developing trust (covered in Chapter Five).

Although these elements must be named as practices that a coach should be skilled at, and coaches should be held to these standards, it is also true that they are very hard to measure or evaluate. This domain is included to provoke reflection and conversation.

Cultural competence. In order to develop a relationship with a client in which transformational change is possible, a coach must be able to work across race, ethnicity, gender, class, sexual orientation, age, and language backgrounds; essentially, across any and all real or perceived differences. This ability is sometimes called "cultural competence." Most of us, if not all of us, need to intentionally develop these abilities and not assume that we possess them. We all have our blind spots, prejudices, and fears that may be enforced by our families of origin, home communities, or the media.

First, coaches must actively work to become aware of what those prejudices are. Most of us probably have strong hunches of which kinds of people make us feel uncomfortable or judgmental. We need to explore where these beliefs come from (see the Ladder of Inference in Chapter Two). Then we need to expand our knowledge and understanding about those groups of people who are "other" to us, although not necessarily from our clients directly—their role is not to teach us about being black, or gay, or an immigrant. We can learn by reading books—fiction and nonfiction, attending seminars or lectures, and developing personal and professional relationships with people from cultural groups different from our own.

We also need to cultivate an internal awareness of how our limited viewpoints affect our work. Coaches need to recognize when we're being blocked by our own perceptions, thoughts, feelings, or judgments about someone else because of his or her background, culture, or way of life. This may manifest in our willingness to work with members of certain groups, in the impact we have with them (perhaps always being more effective when coaching someone of the same age range, gender, race, and so forth), or in our commitment to different kinds of clients. A culturally competent coach is effective across differences, cares about and is committed to a client regardless of her background, and isn't limited by what kind of person she works with.

Empathy and compassion. How can a coach develop these capacities? The first step is to notice when our compassion is dwindling, which is a practice we can develop. I often imagine there's a little coach perched on my shoulder who pays attention to how I listen. This coach observes my emotions and thoughts and taps on my shoulder when I become judgmental. I am now much quicker to notice when I descend into judgment and to make a fast return to an open heart. I have a set of statements I say to myself that help me remember what I truly value and believe, that realign me to my coaching vision: What are some other ways to see this person's actions or beliefs? What else might I want to know so I can better understand where this person is coming from? And finally I ask myself, who am I to judge this person? Mentally reciting these questions usually gets me into a more humble and compassionate place.

As you begin to explore compassion consider how you recognize this quality in others. What does it look like when others are compassionate toward you? What do you notice when you feel a lack of empathy from another? To some extent, these expressions are cultural constructs so once we have a definition for ourselves, we may need to engage our clients in a conversation about how they recognize compassion. First, we start with ourselves.

There are many world traditions which emphasize compassion and suggest a range of practices that can help people demonstrate it. A secular practice from the Buddhist tradition is "metta meditation," or lovingkindness meditation, which offers simple ways to cultivate empathy and compassion for others. When I have worked with difficult teachers and principals, I found these practices very helpful. The Recommended Resources in Appendix E offer recommendations for books on lovingkindness practices.

Rubric Domain 3: Strategic Design

The work plan. Improving our strategic design of coaching begins with creating a work plan. Many of the elements named on the rubric are either actions we are taking or not taking. If you've never created a work plan for your coachees, clearly, this is the first step. (See Chapter Seven.)

Moving into the "developing" and "refining" stages of using a work plan in a coaching practice is about the role that the plans play in our work. When I first started using work plans, I'd create them and then forget all about them until I had to write up midyear reports. As I developed my practice, I recognized how I could use work plans to guide every step of the way and to narrow and refine my conversations so that my client reached his goals much faster. Our coaching work plans are the equivalent to the long-term unit plans that intentional teachers create. The careful, methodical planning pays off.

Planning conversations. The more we practice and prepare for conversations, the more effective they will be. This is perhaps a technical side of our art: just as no actor would dream of performing without hours and hours of practice, we can learn how to walk onto our stage well-rehearsed, but also not appearing to read a script. Chapter Four includes a sample debrief plan that illustrates how a coach can prepare for a conversation.

Planning for conversations is especially useful if we engage in a process of analyzing a transcript of a conversation, as is described in the following section. Especially for novice coaches, as we intentionally plan how we'll ask questions, we internalize the language frames and coaching stems that make coaching transformational.

Rubric Domain 4: Coaching Conversations

The wise coach knows when to be silent; when to challenge; when to observe as the client moves into space and behavior that might derail; and when to intervene with humor, a story, a poem, or a practice.

SHOWS AND SCRIBER (2008, P. 16)

Although coaches plan conversations, sometimes we need to change course midway in response to what a client says and does. For me, in order to make these decisions, I must be calm, grounded, and present for my client, and I must listen without attachment to outcome. I also need to constantly refine my listening and questioning skills.

Listen to your own listening. One practice that I regularly engage in and that is perhaps one of the most useful is to listen to my own listening. We're usually not aware that when we're listening our mind is busy. This exercise invites you to open a window into your mind and see what it's doing. You might be surprised to learn that while engaged in a dialogue, you're listening to find something you can connect with and interject your own story. Or perhaps your mind is searching for points it disagrees with so that you can debate the speaker. The purpose for this exercise is to develop awareness of what's going on when we're listening. Just by honing our awareness, the mind quiets a little and we can make decisions about where our thoughts wander.

You can listen to your own listening when talking with friends and colleagues. As you engage in conversation, set an intention to notice how you listen and then keep a notepad close by and jot down your observations as they arise. You might be listening to a friend's story intently and then notice a few minutes later that your awareness has shifted to your hunger or to annoyance that your friend is telling the same story again. Note your impatience and go back to listening. Listening to your own listening is an awareness to cultivate.

Using audio and video to analyze coaching conversations. One of the most powerful ways to reflect on coaching conversations is to record them. I regularly do this with the recording software on my phone. I promise my client that only I will listen so that I can improve my coaching. I place the device out of sight and usually we both forget that it's on.

I often transcribe my statements; transcribing what the client says is very useful but takes much more time. (Software such as Dragon Dictation is worth exploring for this purpose.) Then I consider the following:

1. How much did I talk? I always aim to talk less than roughly one-quarter of the total time.

2. Did I provide wait time when I asked a question? Did I allow for silence? How did the client respond to silence?

3. What kinds of questions did I ask: clarifying or probing, or facilitative or directive?

4. Which stances did I take: confrontational, cathartic, catalytic, supportive, informative, prescriptive?

5. Which questions emerge after applying the coaching lenses?

Then I consider the client's response. Did his thinking deepen? Did he gain clarity, awareness, or insight? In many coaching conversations there can be a turning point, a moment when the client's understanding of the situation he's in changes; he may laugh, sigh, or say something like, "That's a really good question," or "I hadn't thought about it that way." When this happens I try to identify what I said that made it happen.

When conversations don't result in the client moving toward his goals, then I try to anticipate the client's response had I asked the question another way. I always look for clues in the conversation to help me figure out what I might try next time.

When I first began analyzing my conversations, I noticed my tendency to fall into comfortable questioning routines with clients, finding that I often relied on a single stance or approach. I found that if the client had some insights I was happy and didn't dig deeper. Once I became aware that both my clients and I were usually operating only within our comfort zones, I realized I needed to push both of us.

Videotaping yourself in a coaching conversation is also revealing. It is powerful to watch the video without sound so that you can completely focus on your nonverbal communication—often we notice things that our client may subconsciously register.

Make your ego porous.

RAINER MARIA RILKE (SAFRANSKY, 2012, P. 51)

Finally, when a coach asks a client for permission to record a conversation, explaining that "it's because I'm committed to improving my coaching practice," she's modeling the reflective processes that we encourage clients to engage in. We strive to create an environment where constant learning, reflection, and risk taking is the norm.

Listening without attachment. What does it mean to "listen without attachment?" And why is this important?

Inherent within all coaching relationships is a power dynamic because the coach is in a position to exert influence over the client. Furthermore, coaches working in schools are expected to have a knowledge and experience base that usually surpasses those of our clients—at least in some areas. Although we are not experts on everything, our clients also need to know that we have some basis for credibility. These are tricky lines to negotiate and coaches must be extremely mindful of these power dynamics. It is our responsibility to support teachers and leaders to be autonomous, self-sufficient, empowered decision makers; this is what it means to coach adult learners. If we are not working toward this end, we run the risk that clients will shut down to coaching or become dependent on coaches.

Sometimes when I'm listening to a client I notice that I start having opinions about actions that he should take; my questions become subtly suggestive and leading. And then I notice that I'm feeling attached to what he decides—my ego has surged and I am listening with attachment to the outcome.

In order to listen *without* attachment, a coach needs to first become aware of when she is hoping that a client will do this or that, or hoping for a certain result. When we notice those tendencies, we need to consider how this shows up in our coaching, perhaps in the questions we ask or the actions we engage clients in. Being open to outcome is really a philosophical stance and can be strengthened by reconnecting with our coaching vision, beliefs, and core values (see Chapter Three). However, as transformational coaches working for educational equity, we're stuck in a contradiction: we are very attached to an outcome which improves the learning and experience for all children in schools. We must learn to hold two truths: we can only coach if we are not attached to outcome and we must stay attached to the outcome of equity.

Presence. A transformational coach has a calm, grounded presence; we create an expansive spaciousness for our client to explore his deepest beliefs and feelings, to examine his actions, and to dream and envision. We can't create this kind of space if we're filling it without ourselves or if we arrive at a coaching meeting frazzled and distracted.

There is a range of contemplative and centering practices that can help us get grounded. Mindfulness practices based in Buddhist traditions invite us to slow down, or stop, and take careful notice of the present moment. This can be done through sitting meditation—by focusing on the breath for a period of time—or in walking meditation, or in a number of other ways such as eating silently and focusing on our meal, listening to a piece of music, or gazing at a candle. The basic premise is that we focus our attention. Meanwhile, the incessant chatter in our minds quiets. These are exercises that require practice over time.

For some, connecting to the sacred can also deepen and calm the presence with which we show up in coaching. Expressing gratitude, reading inspirational writing or poetry, singing, being in nature, practicing various forms of visualization, and so on can help us feel more grounded. When we have daily practices we can go deeper and deeper into a quiet place from which we can

> *People who engage in reflective practice tend to have a quiet, steady, very calming presence. Their thoughts seem to come from a deeper, more analytical place, and they are often able to slow conversations down to a pace where everyone is thinking more deeply and reflectively.*
>
> O'NEILL AND CONZEMIUS
> (2006, P. 159)

access wisdom and presence. Whenever I meditate, take a long walk, or read poetry I tell myself, "This is work." I am a much more effective coach when I prioritize these activities.

If this is an area you want to work on, identify a practice or two that you'd like to try. Start with a realistic goal: commit to doing the practice for a week or a month and examining the effect it has on your coaching. Make time for it and see what happens.

Rubric Domain 5: Strategic Actions

Just as we reflect on conversations, we also want to reflect on the activities we engage clients in. Document the activities you do together and consider their impact on the client's practice. Then consider different activities in which to engage the client. Similar to what happens in conversations, a coach and client can find their comfort zone and settle into it. Particularly after trust is established, the coach can take the lead on suggesting different activities which can push the client's growth.

One of the harder coaching actions to fully integrate is the skill of working within a client's ZPD and gradually releasing responsibility. In order to do this, we have to develop an acute understanding of the client's ZPD, which is sometimes only identifiable through trial and error. Then we need to anticipate the next steps for the client to take in order to master the desired skill. For many coaches the next stage in developing their practice lies in the domain of planning, particularly in strategizing around the gradual release of responsibility.

The coach's documentation and reflection log in Exhibit 15.3 is a simple tool that coaches can use to reflect on coaching sessions and plan subsequent ones. When reflecting on patterns in her own coaching, a coach can make intentional moves to push her client deeper into her learning, but often we can't identify those next steps without clearly seeing what's already happened. A blank log is available on my website www.elenaaguilar.com.

Rubric Domain 6: Coach as Learner

Several of the elements in the coach as learner domain are clearly actionable— soliciting feedback from clients, gathering a variety of data on our own practice, attending training which can build coaching capacity, or seeking out colleagues to learn with.

Exhibit 15.3. Coach's Documentation and Reflection Log

Coach: E. Aguilar   **Client: Marco Birch**

Date and Time	March 21, 2010, 10 a.m.–12:00
Reflection on my **Presence**	*I began feeling really grounded and centered. I noticed that I listened attentively. I got triggered at one point when Marco made comments about some students that really bothered me. I noticed that my shoulders and jaw tensed and I tried to change the subject. Then worked on letting go of my attachment that he recognize what he was saying and I returned to this topic to explore it with him. I also noticed that at one point when Marco was feeling really overwhelmed I used humor to lighten the space and he responded really well. I think he was surprised that I could be funny and he said he appreciated it. I noticed that at the end of our meeting I didn't feel as tired as I sometimes feel from coaching.*
Coaching **Stances** Taken and Impact	*I recorded this conversation and charted the stances I took. I found that about 80 percent of the time I was facilitative. I noticed that when I was directive, Marco didn't respond as well. His answers to my questions were less thoughtful and a few were evasive.* *I noticed that when I used a catalytic approach Marco was most responsive. Each question I asked from this stance elicited, "That's a good question!" from him. From another I got, "Wow, I'd never thought of that."*
Coaching **Lenses** Applied and Impact	*The lens that kept coming up for me today was the lens of inquiry. This was intentional—I'd planned for this conversation to incorporate many of these questions, but I'd also planned for other lenses. I kept finding myself needing to raise questions from the Lens of Inquiry to push Marco's thinking about the dilemmas he's facing. The lens of inquiry allowed me to help Marco reframe his situation and this was most useful for him—he discovered a number of actions he can take through this line of questioning.*

(continued)

Exhibit 15.3. (*Continued*)

Coaching **Activities** Used and Impact	*There were two activities that worked well today. We role-played a conversation that Marco needs to have with a parent. We actually did this three times—first he played himself and I played the parent, then we reversed roles, and then he played himself again. He requested this and by the end he was feeling really confident and prepared. I was apprehensive about modeling his role—I worried about the impact of this and didn't want him to think my way was the right way—but it actually was OK. He needed to see me demonstrate some ways of communicating that were direct but not confrontational and afterwards he said he really appreciated this.*
	We also did a quick reading together. Last time we met Marco had asked me to bring an article on facilitating team meetings, so we read it and discussed it. He is going to use this information to plan an upcoming meeting. Next week we'll go over his agenda.
Other Reflections	*I noticed that when I allowed for silence after Marco said something, he returned to the topic after a few moments and continued to expand on his thoughts. I'm uncomfortable with silence but I saw how useful it was today.*
Progress toward **Goals**	*Today we were really working on Marco's first goal about how he communicates with all stakeholders. I noticed a number of pieces of evidence (the language frames he used in the role-play, the way he relayed a conversation he'd had last week) that indicate that he's well on track to meet his goals by June. He echoed this—he's feeling really good about the coaching work and feels like he's close to meeting his goals.*
Plans for Next Session	*Debrief the hard conversation with the parent that we role-played. Review agenda for upcoming meeting.*
	I might need to continue modeling some of the communication strategies that Marco is trying to develop. I need to help him recognize the nonverbal cues I give as well as the words I use.

DEVELOPING REFLECTIVE PRACTICES

Coaches are always modeling a way of being—both with our clients and with all others with whom we interact. Emotions are contagious and the way we show up with clients affects them. If teachers see us as frustrated when we interact with a principal, it could reduce their trust in us or activate their own negative feelings. The implications of this can be daunting for a coach: we are always "on" and always need to be mindful of how we're being received. However, this can also be empowering. On many occasions I have seen that when a coach is a quiet, calming presence it sets the tone for a team. Many educators take cues from a coach. We can instantaneously shift the energy in a room just by showing up in a particular way—either positive or negative. Once I got over the pressure of feeling like I was always being watched, and once I developed some strategies to manage my emotions and be calm and grounded, I recognized the invaluable influence I could have. Because of the impact we can have, coaches need time and structures for reflection in order to examine how we show up in our work and how we are received.

The self-aware coaches do the internal work to understand their boundaries, triggers, gifts, and limitations. In this way, the coaches are able to enter the coaching space authentically and confidently.

SHOWS AND SCRIBER (2008, P. 15)

Written journals. Although we may constantly reflect on our work in our minds when we commit our thoughts to paper they get clearer, more concrete, and we can sort through them. We notice patterns and trends in our experiences, thoughts and feelings, and see our own growth over time. For a coach, spending a minimum of ten minutes per day journaling about the day's work can be tremendously effective. Try it for a few weeks and see how your practice changes. Exhibit 15.4 offers a list of reflective questions that could help guide your ruminations. There are prompts for daily or weekly consideration as well as prompts that you might respond to occasionally.

Who you are speaks so loud that I cannot hear what you are saying.

RALPH WALDO EMERSON
(BONAR, 2007, P. 151)

Exhibit 15.4. Reflective Prompts for a Coach

Prompts for Daily or Weekly Reflection

- What happened in today's coaching session?
- What did you notice about your client?
- What did you notice about your own coaching? About your thoughts and feelings today?
- What kind of impact did your coaching have on your client today? How do you know?
- When did your coaching feel effective today? What made it feel that way?
- Was it possible that your client had any "aha" moments today? What led to that moment?
- What was challenging for you in today's session?
- What did you notice about your own listening? About your inner dialogue?
- What do you appreciate about your own coaching today?
- What would your client say about your coaching today?
- What do you think was "not said" by your client today?
- Was your client sharing any stories today? Were these new stories or ones she's told in the past?
- What indicators were there today that your client made progress toward her goals?
- Where do you think your client is ready to go next?
- What are you curious about or do you want to learn more about?
- What is your next coaching move?
- What would help your client move forward?
- What do you want to do or say in your next meeting?

Prompts for Occasional Reflection

- What do you enjoy about coaching? What draws you to this practice?
- When have you felt particularly effective as a coach? What happened?
- How does coaching align to your core values?
- What do you see as the possible effect or potential of coaching?
- What's challenging about coaching? When do you feel frustrated or ineffective?
- What kind of client (gender, age, race, background, experience, and so on) seems the "easiest" for you to coach? What makes coaching him or her easy?
- What kind of client feels the "hardest" to coach? What makes coaching him or her hard?

- What personality types feel easy and challenging to coach? What comes up for you when you need to coach someone whose personality is very different from your own?
- What kinds of thoughts go through your mind when you are introduced to someone who comes from a very different background than you? Who seems very different than you?
- Think of a client with whom you struggled. What might he or she have said or thought about you? What would his or her "side" of the story be?
- Consider your initial beliefs about a client's capacity to grow with what actually happened as you coached him or her. What happened? What did you learn that you might apply when working with future clients?
- What metaphor could represent what coaching is to you?
- What are you learning about yourself through coaching?
- What would you like to pay more attention to?
- What do you want to stay curious about?

Audio journals. Another strategy for capturing our reflections is to use audio recordings. For those of us who spend time in the car each day, using a recording device on a phone, for example, can be a strategic way to gather our thoughts. Even if we never listen to them again, the process of speaking them aloud shifts our thoughts. This is what we do often with clients—give them space and time to speak aloud—and just this act can be helpful.

Personal transformation. This will mean something different for each coach and no one should be evaluated on his or her personal transformation. However, to include it on a rubric is to value it as an area deserving time and attention.

Reflecting on the meaning of personal transformation could be energizing for coaches. Personal transformation might suggest a work-life balance or practicing self-care; this is something many educators strive to attain. Coaches can be very compassionate people toward everyone but themselves so for some practicing radical self-acceptance may be personally transformative. Learning to accept ourselves where we're at can be a major growth area.

Personal transformation could also mean cultivating patience and equanimity or finding ways to bring joy and play into our work. It might mean healing past pain and trauma so that they don't affect work relationships. As each identifies what personal transformation means, he can search out practices that could support this growth.

Masterful coaches not only stand in a place that a difference can be made, they speak, listen, and act from that place, never indulging in cynicism or allowing others to do so. When others give up on an individual or start to gossip, they say, "Transformation is possible."

HARGROVE (2003, P. 51)

In our contemporary society, there are an abundance of practices and practitioners to help us address our inner lives, be reflective, increase our compassion, connect with others, expand our creativity, and so on—yoga, meditation, classes and workshops, therapy, and, of course, personal coaching are just a few resources. Those engaged in coaching for transformation must attend to ourselves, so that we can coach for transformation.

CONCLUSION

Professional development for coaches can be greatly expanded. The first step is to recognize the critical need for PD and then explore the highest leverage structures in which to engage coaches in their own learning. The impact on teacher practice will be far greater when coaches are engaged in rigorous, high-quality professional development. As a result, there could be a much greater likelihood that the experience and outcomes for students will improve. When we tend to the learning needs of all adults in a learning organization, children will benefit.

CONCLUSION

A FINAL STORY

"Do you want to read what I said at the news conference?" the principal said proudly at the end of the 2011–12 school year. Her middle school had been lauded in a report on reducing the suspension rates of African American boys: in one year, by implementing alternative practices, her school cut this number by 72 percent. This is a significant issue in our district, where the suspension rates for African American boys are astronomical and disproportionate to their white counterparts.

"Of course," I said. She handed me her notes. The initiative stemmed, she'd written, from engaging her staff and families in a conversation around the school's vision and mission. Their collaborative reflection led to new systems and structures for addressing student behavior; her staff became committed to ensuring that African American boys attended school every day so that they could learn.

I was stunned by her account of this transformation, because vision and mission were the primary areas on which I'd coached her and her leadership team in our first year working together. And I said so: "This is what we worked on all last year! Vision, mission, what it means to make decisions that stem from a mission, to operate from a living vision."

"Yeah," she said. "Without coaching and all those hours when I could talk through ideas and figure out my next steps I don't know if we would have gotten to the same place."

"This is huge!" I exclaimed. It's not very often that coaches can trace such a direct line between our efforts and large-scale positive impact on kids, particularly for our most vulnerable students. I continued: "I know that there were many factors that led to the reduction of suspensions, but I have to admit, it feels really good to know that I played a little role."

"Definitely," she said.

"But let me clarify," I added. "It wasn't *me;* it was the role I played and the space I held—it was the coaching. And that's what's important in the telling of this story. When administrators look at what you accomplished, and they attempt to replicate it, they need to understand that your accomplishment emerged from deep conversations with stakeholders—it wasn't just the application of a set of strategies or policies that can be plunked down on any site. And what enabled you to hold those conversations and lead this work around vision and mission was coaching—which is a supported space for you to reflect, process, plan, and access your own power and potential."

"Yes," she said nodding. "Of course."

THE ROAD AHEAD

There is much more to say about coaching—about the roles it can play, how we can refine our strategies, how we can make our work public and document its impact. There are distinctions to expand on—for example, there is much more to say about coaching principals, and the art of coaching teams deserves its own volume.

The path toward equitable schools often feels excruciatingly long. As we work to ensure that every child gets what she needs every day in our schools, I am fairly sure of a few things. I know we're going to have to slow down, listen deeply, think before we speak, be mindful and intentional about our actions, and notice and celebrate every victory. Many of our schools need to change immediately; however, operating from urgency is dangerous. We can harness the energy and anger behind our urgency and remember that what we do today creates something for tomorrow. Transformation will be possible if we act with compassion today.

Along this journey, we'll need to attend to adults at all levels of our institutions—from teachers to principals to the cafeteria workers and the custodial staff to central office administrators and superintendents. We'll need to create space and time to heal our wounds, listen to each other, build relationships, and learn new behaviors, beliefs, and ways of being.

Transformational coaching can facilitate this process. It can help build emotional resilience in educators, bring teams together in healthy ways, and change systems. Transformational coaching is an approach to social change that can "minimize the pain" that people experience *and* transform the system—a challenge put forth by Immanuel Wallerstein (2010), an American sociologist. As Wallerstein suggested to a group of activists in summer 2010, we need to find strategies that can do both.

Most of the coaching sessions I engage in these days conclude with my client saying something like, "Thanks, I feel much better now." I know I'm alleviating pain. I also see professional learning and growth that continues after our coaching contract ends. And as illustrated in the example that opened this chapter, I see mounting evidence of systems change as a result of coaching. Most important in my daily visits to schools where I've worked for years, I can see that the outcomes and experiences for children are improving, particularly for our most vulnerable youth.

As I reached the end of writing this book, I took on a new role in the Oakland Unified School District, where I've worked for seventeen years. In the 2012–13 school year, I am leading a team of transformational instructional and leadership coaches who are serving our schools that struggle the most. Although the conditions in our schools are daunting and the task ahead of us is tremendous, I am thrilled to see the art of transformational coaching implemented and to provide the support and professional development required for my fantastic coaches

> *When I dare to be powerful, to use my strength in the service of my vision, then it becomes less and less important whether I am afraid.*
>
> AUDRE LORDE (1997, P. 13)

to do their best work. I am confident that our students will benefit. The fact that our district supports a systemic professional development initiative of this kind increases my conviction that we can and will transform our schools.

FEARLESSNESS AND FAITH

In order for me to engage in this process of transformation, I have accepted that I need to be fearless. For some time, I skirted the shores of despair. I saw former students drop out of school, join gangs, and have babies in their teens. National education policy seems headed in a direction that runs contrary to my core values. Every year the state of California (where I live) cuts funds for schools and increases spending on prisons. I have a young son—an African American boy. There are many reasons to be very afraid.

In her beautiful book *Perseverance*, Margaret Wheatley writes that we all have "a lineage of fearlessness" (2010, p. 33). I've engaged clients in identifying their own fearless ancestors who persevered through adversity and to find inspiration in the struggles of others. I give them permission to adopt local, national, and international figures into their lineage; we need all the fearless ancestors we can get. Wheatley also suggests the term *spiritual warriors* for those fearless people who "wish to be of service to this troubled time." These warriors, she writes, "never use aggression or violence ... The skills that give them power are compassion and insight" (2010, p. 23). The softness and strength of this term appeals to me.

I have a little secret about coaching. Every day when I meet with clients, hear their stories, and witness their learning, commitment, and growth, my fearlessness expands. Every day I am inspired by the movements toward transformation that I see; many of my clients are spiritual warriors in our schools. I am deeply grateful for this experience.

What I witness fuels my faith and inspires me to work in our underfunded urban schools year after year. Every day I make a choice to have faith in the abstract process of transformation. This is often hard in the face of the reality I encounter—too many kids are wasting away in schools, their emotional, social, and intellectual needs ignored, their potential squandered; too many teens are dropping out or being pushed out of school; too many boys are killed on the streets in Oakland. But perseverance is a choice. It's what I chose.

Dr. Martin Luther King Jr. is a central figure in my pantheon of adopted, fearless ancestors and a radiant spiritual warrior. In 1967, he delivered a speech titled, "Where Do We Go from Here?" Decades later these words still uniquely capture the poetry, beauty, and magnitude of what we face as we work to transform our schools and world. The entire speech is worth reading, but the following passage graced the walls of many of the spaces in which I've worked and is appropriate to close this book:

> Difficult and painful as it is, we must walk on in the days ahead with an audacious faith in the future ... Let us realize the arc of the moral universe is long but it bends toward justice. (King, 1967)

The Coach's Optical Refractor (the Coaching Lenses)

	Assumptions	Questions
Inquiry	The way we pose the question determines the nature of the answer. The way we define the problem dictates how we define the solution.	Who is defining the problem? Whose question is this? What data do we have on this problem? What problems do that data say we should address?
	The questions we ask are as important as the answers we find.	Is this a question I really care about? Who does care about this question?
	People can create their own knowledge and solutions.	From what perspective am I seeing this? What other perspectives would help me understand this?
	Seemingly intractable problems can be addressed.	How is this connected to other things?
	It is easier to engage and enroll people to address inequities when we affirm that we don't yet know everything we need to know to create transformed systems, but we have a responsibility to do so, so we must ask questions together and move forward.	
	If you own the question, you will take responsibility for the answer.	
	Evidence and data are critical to making informed decisions and judgments.	
	Multiple forms of data, including authentic and qualitative measures produced by multiple constituencies, are necessary for effective decision making.	
	Knowledge is socially constructed.	
	We never know everything we need to know, but we need to act anyway.	

	Assumptions	Questions
Change Management	Beneficial change is possible.Conditions and strategies can be manipulated to get the system to produce different outcomes. Change can be studied, understood, and influenced. Analysis of conditions for change is necessary for effective implementation. Certain elements need to be present for successful change to occur: leadership, vision, skills, incentives, resources, and a clear plan of action. People need to have the will, skill, knowledge, and capacity to change.	What are the conditions for change here? What are the strengths that can be built on? What is working? Where are the opportunities for leveraging change? What threats to change are present? What is the vision that people are working toward here? What skills are required of people to achieve the vision? What knowledge is necessary? Do people have the skills and knowledge necessary to implement change? Does the will for change exist here? Where? Who are the likely "early adopters" of a change initiative? What incentives are in place for people to change? To improve their practice? What resources are available to support change?
Systems Thinking	What we observe, whatever is happening in this moment, is exactly what is supposed to happen in the system as it is. Everything we observe is the result of a complex set of interactions. We must seek to understand these interactions in order to intervene effectively to change them. Process and product are part of the same whole. Conflict and tension are necessary and natural. Complexity and diversity are good, healthy things. All energy moves in cycles.	How is the current system designed to produce these results? Why did that happen? What happens when this happens? What happens when that happens? What are the relationships between things here? Where is the energy here? Where are the stuck points? If I did this here, what would happen over here?
Adult Learning	Problems of change are problems of learning. People can only be where they are. Every human being is "on a path" from somewhere to somewhere, and it is important to find out both where people have been and where they're going. Each of us enters the work of equity and justice from a very different starting point. If you don't acknowledge progress, you lose people's trust. Adults have had a lot of life experiences that affect how they continue to learn.	What is the goal or objective? What came before? What is the gap between the goal and what is? What progress has been made? Is there evidence of prior learning? Does the will for learning exist?

	Assumptions	Questions
	Adults must feel safe to learn.	
	Adults want to be the origin of their own learning; they want to control certain aspects of it.	
	Adults want and need feedback.	
Systemic Oppression	Oppression and injustice are human creations and can therefore be undone. Systemic oppression exists and negatively affects relationships and the educational process in multiple ways.	Who is at the table? Who isn't? Who has power here? What is that power based on here?
		How are power relations affecting the truth that is told and constructed at any given moment?
	Oppression and systematic mistreatment (such as racism, classism, sexism, and homophobia) are more than just the sum of individual prejudices.	Where and how does each person locate himself or herself in a conversation?
	Systemic oppression has historical antecedents; it is an intentional disempowerment of groups of people based on their identity in order to maintain an unequal power structure that subjugates one group over another.	How are oppression, internalized oppression, and transferred oppression playing out right here, right now (in this school, group, organization, or district)?
		How safe is it here for different people to share their truth?
	Systemic oppression manifests in economic, political, social, and cultural systems.	Does the truth telling connect to shared purposes and commitments for action?
	Systemic oppression and its effects can be undone through recognition of inequitable patterns and intentional action to interrupt inequity and create more democratic processes and systems supported by multicultural, multilingual alliances and partnerships.	How can I build the alliances needed to move forward here?
		How is leadership constructed here? What forms does it take? Who is missing?
		What can we do to make room for different cultural constructions of leadership?
	Discussing and addressing oppression and bias will usually inspire strong emotional responses.	How do I understand my practice as an antiracist, antibias educator, given my differences from and similarities to my colleagues? What about the differences from and similarities to the people I am serving?
		How can I build my practice as a leader for equity, starting with who I am and what I bring because of who I am?

Assumptions	Questions
We are all born with a certain level of emotional intelligence, and we can further develop these skills and capacities.The emotional intelligence of a leader is a primary act of leadership.	**Self-Awareness**
	When does he recognize that his feelings are affecting him at work? How does he speak about his feelings?
There are four areas of emotional intelligence: self-awareness, self-management, social awareness, and relationship management.	When does he recognize his limits and strengths?
	How does he invite or welcome feedback?
	Is he aware of the times when he needs help?
An effective leader can speak about her emotions, welcomes feedback, and knows when she needs help.	**Self-Management**
	How does she respond to disturbing emotions?
An effective leader manages her emotions by demonstrating self-control and by being candid about her beliefs and actions.	How does she manage high stress?
	Is she candid about her feelings, beliefs, and actions? Can she admit mistakes or faults?
Adaptability and flexibility are indicators of high emotional intelligence.	How does she adapt to new challenges?
A high degree of emotional resiliency is an indicator of emotional intelligence—an effective leader sees adversity as opportunity.	Does she welcome and create new opportunities? Or does she wait for them?
	How does she deal with changes and setbacks?
Demonstrating empathy is an expression of social awareness.	**Social Awareness**
	Can he sense the unspoken emotions in a person or group?
Organizational awareness and understanding of power relationships are indicators of emotional intelligence.	Can he detect social networks and key power relationships? How does he recognize political forces in an organization?
Managing relationships between people is a primary skill of an emotionally intelligent leader.	How does he cultivate an emotional climate that ensures that people are getting what they need? How does he monitor the satisfaction of those he serves?
	Relationship Management
	How does she create resonance and move people with a compelling vision or shared mission?
	How does she model what she wants from others?
	How does she try to appeal to different stakeholders? How does she try to enroll key people?
	When does she seem to be genuinely interested in developing her people? How does she learn about their goals, strengths, and areas for growth? Does she give feedback that is useful and well received? If so, when?

(Emotional Intelligence)

Assumptions	Questions
	When does she recognize the need for a change and aim for transformation? When does she strongly advocate for change, even in the face of opposition? How does she find practical ways to overcome barriers to change?
	When there's a conflict, how does she understand different perspectives? How does she surface the conflicts, acknowledge views from all sides, and then redirect the energy toward a shared ideal?
	In what ways does she model respect, concern, and collaboration? How does she build relationships, identity, and spirit?

APPENDIX B

Coaching Sentence Stems

Active Listening Stems

So . . .

In other words . . .

What I'm hearing, then, . . . Is that correct?

What I hear you saying is . . . Am I missing anything?

I'm hearing many things . . .

As I listen to you, I'm hearing . . . Is there anything else you feel I should know?

Clarifying Stems

Let me see if I understand . . .

I'm interested in hearing more about . . .

It would help me understand if you'd give me an example of . . .

So are you saying (or suggesting) . . . ?

Tell me what you mean when you . . .

Tell me how that idea is similar to (or different from) ...

To what extent is ... ?

I'm curious to know more about ...

I'm intrigued by ...

I'm interested in ...

I wonder ...

Nonjudgmental Responses

I noticed how when you ..., the students really ... (to identify something that worked and why it worked)

What did you do to make the lesson so successful?

I'm interested in learning (or hearing) more about ...

Probing Stems

What's another way you might ... ?

What would it look like if ... ?

What do you think would happen if ... ?

How was ... different from (or similar to) ... ?

What's another way you might ... ?

What sort of an effect do you think ... ?

What criteria do you use to ... ?

When have you done something like ... before?

What do you think ... ?

How did you decide ... (or come to that conclusion)?

FACILITATIVE COACHING

Cathartic Stems

I'm noticing that you're experiencing some feelings. Would it be OK to explore those for a few minutes?

What's coming up for you right now? Would you like to talk about your feelings?

Wow. I imagine I'd have some emotions if that happened to me. Are you experiencing strong feelings?

Catalytic Stems

Tell me about a previous time when you ... How did you deal with that?

I hear you're really struggling with ... How do you intend to start?

It sounds like you're unsatisfied with ... What would you do differently next time?

You've just talked about five different things you want to work on this week. The last thing you mentioned is ... How important is this to you?

Supportive Stems

I noticed how when you ... the students really ... (to identify something that worked and why it worked)

It sounds like you have a number of ideas to try out! It'll be exciting to see which works best for you!

What did you do to make the lesson so successful?

I'm interested in learning (or hearing) more about ...

Your commitment is really inspiring to me.

It sounds like you handled that in a very confident way.

You did a great job when you ...

I'm confident that you'll be successful.

DIRECTIVE COACHING

Confrontational Stems

Would you be willing to explore your reasoning about this?

Would you be open to examining the assumptions behind your reasoning?

I'd like to ask you about ... Is that OK?

What's another way you might ... ?

What would it look like if ... ?

What do you think would happen if ... ?

How was ... different from (or similar to) ... ?

What sort of an effect do you think ... would have?

I'm noticing (some aspect of your behavior) ... What do you think is going on there?

What criteria do you use to ... ?

Informative Stems

There's a useful book on that topic by ...

An effective strategy to teaching ... is ...

You can contact ... in ... department for that resource ...

Your principal will be in touch with you about that.

Prescriptive Stems

I would like you to discuss this issue with your supervisor.

You need to know that the school's policy is ...

Have you talked to ... about that yet? Last week you said you planned on doing so.

Would it be OK if I shared some advice that I think might help you? You're welcome to take it or leave it, of course.

I'd like to suggest ...

APPENDIX C

Transformational Coaching Rubric

Beginning	The coach is talking about the strategies, demonstrating awareness of them, and may occasionally try them out.
Emerging	The coach has begun to use these strategies, but is inconsistent in usage and effectiveness.
Developing	The coach consistently uses these strategies and approaches; employing these practices leads to meeting some coaching goals.
Refining	The coach's usage of the strategies and approaches is deeply embedded in the coaching practice and directly results in meeting goals.
Modeling	The coach's practice is recognized as exemplary and is shared with other coaches; the coach shares and creates new knowledge and practice.

1. Knowledge Base Coach understands and applies a set of core coaching knowledge components. Element	Beginning	Emerging	Developing	Refining	Modeling	Evidence
a. Coach has knowledge of the discipline around which he or she coaches (literacy, math, leadership, classroom management, school transformation, or other).	○	○	○	○	○	
b. Coach has knowledge of a range of coaching approaches, including directive, facilitative, cognitive, and ontological, and can apply them as needed.	○	○	○	○	○	

(continued)

(Continued)

	Beginning	Emerging	Developing	Refining	Modeling	Evidence
c. Coach demonstrates understanding of adult learning theory and applies it in analyzing coaching situations and working with clients.	O	O	O	O	O	
d. Coach demonstrates understanding of systemic oppression and applies it in analyzing coaching situations and working with clients.	O	O	O	O	O	
e. Coach demonstrates understanding of systems thinking and applies it in analyzing coaching situations and working with clients.	O	O	O	O	O	
f. Coach demonstrates understanding of an inquiry lens and applies it in analyzing coaching situations and working with clients.	O	O	O	O	O	
g. Coach demonstrates understanding of emotional intelligence theory and applies it in analyzing coaching situations and working with clients.	O	O	O	O	O	
h. Coach demonstrates understanding of change management theory and applies it in analyzing coaching situations and working with clients.	O	O	O	O	O	
2. Relationships Coach develops and maintains relationships based on trust and respect and demonstrates cultural competency in order to advance the work. **Element**	Beginning	Emerging	Developing	Refining	Modeling	Evidence
a. Coach enrolls the client in a coaching relationship and monitors enrollment throughout the work.	O	O	O	O	O	
b. Coach builds trust with client and sustains it over time; coach maintains confidentiality at all times.	O	O	O	O	O	
c. Coach demonstrates cultural competence and the ability to effectively coach across race, ethnicity, gender, class, sexual orientation, age, and language background.	O	O	O	O	O	
d. Coach demonstrates empathy and compassion.	O	O	O	O	O	

3. **Strategic Design** Coach develops strategic work plans based on data and a variety of assessments. Coach is continually guided by the work plan, makes adjustments as necessary, and monitors progress along the way. Element	Beginning	Emerging	Developing	Refining	Modeling	Evidence
a. Coach gathers a variety of data and engages client in assessing data in order to coconstruct work plan.	O	O	O	O	O	
b. Work plan aligns to school or district vision and larger context.	O	O	O	O	O	
c. SMARTE goals drive the work with client; coach regularly gathers data to demonstrate progress toward goals and engages client in this reflection.	O	O	O	O	O	
d. Coach develops a theory of action for coaching each client and applies theory in conversations and actions.	O	O	O	O	O	
e. Coach breaks down the learning into chunks and identifies high-leverage coaching strategies; a plan for gradual release of responsibility is articulated.	O	O	O	O	O	
4. **Coaching Conversation** Coach demonstrates a wide range of listening and questioning skills. Coach is able to effectively move conversations toward meeting the client's goals. Element	Beginning	Emerging	Developing	Refining	Modeling	Evidence
a. Coach plans for and structures coaching conversations to ensure that they align with client's goals and that they are moving the client toward meeting the goals.	O	O	O	O	O	
b. Coach uses a variety of questioning strategies with clients.	O	O	O	O	O	
c. Coach listens for high-leverage entry points that could deepen the conversation and uses them.	O	O	O	O	O	
d. Coach effectively uses a range of conversational coaching approaches in order to push client to find new possibilities for action to meet goals.	O	O	O	O	O	

(continued)

Element	Beginning	Emerging	Developing	Refining	Modeling	Evidence
e. Coach listens with empathy and uses nonjudgmental language in coaching conversations.	O	O	O	O	O	
f. Coach listens without attachment to outcome.	O	O	O	O	O	
g. Coach shows up as a calm, grounded presence.	O	O	O	O	O	
5. Strategic Actions Coach implements high-leverage strategic actions that support client in reaching goals and uses a gradual release of responsibility model to develop a client's autonomy.						
a. Coach observes client in various contexts, gathers data, and offers feedback based on what the client has asked for.	O	O	O	O	O	
b. Coach guides client to develop reflective capacities when receiving feedback.	O	O	O	O	O	
c. Coach engages client in analyzing data (student work, survey data, test scores, and so on) and responding to data.	O	O	O	O	O	
d. Coach models best practices (delivering a lesson, facilitating a meeting, providing professional development, giving difficult feedback, and so on) and engages client in reflecting on the demonstration.	O	O	O	O	O	
e. Coach engages client in other coaching activities (role-playing, visualizing, gathering surveys, using video, and so on) that move the client toward goals.	O	O	O	O	O	
f. Coach works within a client's ZPD and gradually releases responsibility to enable the client to meet his or her goals.	O	O	O	O	O	
g. Coach supports client to identify needs, access resources, and build relationships that can help meet those needs.	O	O	O	O	O	

6. Coach as Learner Coach consistently reflects on his or her own learning and development as a coach and actively seeks out ways to develop his or her skill, knowledge, and capacity. Element	Beginning	Emerging	Developing	Refining	Modeling	Evidence
a. Coach solicits feedback from clients and takes action based on feedback.	O	O	O	O	O	
b. Coach gathers a variety of data (notes, audio recordings, video, and so on) and utilizes a variety of strategies to reflect on coaching practice. Reflection leads to development of practice.	O	O	O	O	O	
c. Coach seeks out professional learning opportunities and consultations with other coaches to develop coaching practice; also stays informed of current research on best practices.	O	O	O	O	O	
d. Coach collaborates effectively with colleagues by supporting their professional growth.	O	O	O	O	O	
e. Coach demonstrates awareness of his or her own emotional intelligence and works to develop emotional resiliency.	O	O	O	O	O	
f. Coach models transformational leadership and demonstrates awareness of how he or she is perceived by others.	O	O	O	O	O	
g. Coach attends to his or her own personal transformation.	O	O	O	O	O	

APPENDIX D

Cheat Sheets and Lists

ESSENTIAL FRAMEWORKS FOR TRANSFORMATIONAL COACHING

The Ladder of Inference. To understand how beliefs are constructed and why we do what we do (Chapter Three).

- *Use this* to help a client deconstruct beliefs and find other ways of seeing a situation.

The Coach's Optical Refractor. An analytical tool that uses six lenses to provide insight into a current reality or dilemma (Chapter Four).

- *Use this* to plan for coaching sessions, to understand problems and dilemmas that arise, and in reflection.

Coaching stances. These are different ways of engaging in coaching conversations and activities (Chapters Nine, Ten, Eleven, and Twelve).

- *Use these* to plan coaching conversations, make decisions during the conversation, and guide the next steps we take.

COACHING FOR SYSTEMS CHANGE

1. Look for the fires
2. Identify root causes and reflect on the impact
3. Plan some changes
4. Communicate those plans
5. Implement the plan
6. Gather data and reflect

TIPS FOR USING DIFFERENT APPROACHES

Tips for Using a Cathartic Approach
- Always ask permission to invite feelings in
- Acknowledge the role that emotions play
- Affirm the value in processing and releasing emotions

Tips for Using a Catalytic Approach
- Nudge gently through questions
- Notice metaphor and symbolic language, then explore them

Tips for Using a Supportive Approach
- Be authentic
- Be specific
- Highlight micromovements of growth

Tips for Using a Confrontational Approach
- Listen for rut stories and interrupt them
- Guide clients down the Ladder of Inference
- Identify mental models that are fixed and constricting
- Rebuild models and mind-sets and create river stories

Tips for Using an Informative Approach

- Be sure to coach within the client's zone of proximal development
- Release responsibility gradually, but as soon as possible
- Offer a selection of resources and guide the client to make decisions

Tips for Using a Prescriptive Approach

- Use this approach to direct behavior around legal, safety, or ethical issues
- Use when the client lacks confidence or can't direct her own learning
- Use with caution

Tips for Shifting Mental Models

- Listen for stories
- Interrupt rut stories and ask, "What are the unintended consequences of this story?"
- Step back and observe facts, then ask, "What are other ways to view what happened?"
- Create a river story

THE COACHING CONVERSATION

Planning for a Coaching Conversation

1. Where does my client need to go?
2. Who do I need to be?

The Arc of a Coaching Conversation

1. Check in and chat
2. Create a plan for the conversation—"What's on your mind?"
3. Check in on previous commitments—"How'd that go?"
4. Engage in coaching stances and approaches
5. Determine next steps
6. Reflect on conversation and ask for feedback

FIVE STEPS FOR A MIDYEAR OR END-OF-YEAR REFLECTION

1. Coach: review work plan and coaching notes and evidence
2. Coach: reflect on data
3. Coach: plan conversation
4. Coach and client: determine the when and where for reflection conversation
5. Coach and client: engage in reflection conversation

APPENDIX E

Recommended Resources

This section presents a short list of places to go for more information.

Research on Coaching (Chapter One)

Allen, Joseph P., and others. "An Interaction-Based Approach to Enhancing Secondary School Instruction and Student Achievement." *Science*, Aug. 2011, 1034–1037.

Anastos, J., and Ancowitz, R. "A Teacher-Directed Peer Coaching Project." *Educational Leadership*, 1987, *45*(3), 40–42.

Barr, K., Simmons, B., and Zarrow, J. "School Coaching in Context: A Case Study in Capacity Building." Paper presented at the American Educational Research Association annual meeting, Chicago, Apr. 2003.

Brown, C., Stroh, H., Fouts, J., and Baker, D. *Learning to Change: School Coaching for Systemic Reform*. Seattle: Bill and Melinda Gates Foundation, 2005.

Burkins, J. M. *Coaching for Balance: How to Meet the Challenges of Literacy Coaching*. Newark, Del.: International Reading Association, 2007.

Center for Collaborative Education. *The Role of the Coach at CCE*. Boston: Center for Collaborative Education, n.d. www.ccebos.org/coaching_intro.doc

The Elementary School Journal, 2010, *3*(1). Contains eight articles about the effectiveness of coaching. It includes the article "Assessing the Value-Added Effects of Literacy Collaborative Professional Development on Student Learning," by G. Biancarosa, A. S. Bryk, and E. R. Dexter.

Elish-Piper, L., and L'Allier, S. K. "Examining the Relationship Between Literacy Coaching and Student Reading Gains In Grades K–3." *Elementary School Journal*, 2011, *112*(1), 83–106.

Lockwood, J. R., McCombs, J. S., and Marsh, J. "Linking Reading Coaches and Student Achievement: Evidence from Florida Middle Schools." *Educational Evaluation and Policy Analysis*, 2010, *32*(3), 372–388.

Marsh, J. A., McCombs, J. S., and Martorell, F. "How Instructional Coaches Support Data-Driven Decision-Making: Policy Implementation and Effects in Florida Middle Schools." *Educational Policy*, 2010, *24*(6), 872–907.

McCombs, J. S., and Marsh, J. "Lessons for Boosting the Effectiveness of Reading Coaches." *Phi Delta Kappan*, 2009, *90*(7), 501–507.

Neufeld, B., and Roper, D. *Coaching: A Strategy for Developing Instructional Capacity.* Washington, D.C.: The Aspen Institute Program on Education and the Annenberg Institute for School Reform, 2003.

von Frank, V. "Coaches Root out Deep Bias." *Journal of Staff Development*, 2010, *31*(4), 20–25. Reports on the National Equity Project's coaching model.

Race, Racism, and Systemic Oppression (Chapters One and Four)

Boykin, A. Wade, and Noguera, Pedro. *Creating the Opportunity to Learn: Moving from Research to Practice to Close the Achievement Gap.* Alexandria, Va.: ASCD, 2011.

Delpit, Lisa. *Other People's Children: Cultural Conflict in the Classroom.* New York: The New Press, 1995.

Delpit, Lisa. *The Skin That We Speak: Thoughts on Language and Culture in the Classroom.* New York: The New Press, 2002.

Hooks, Bell. *Teaching to Transgress: Education as the Practice of Freedom.* New York: Routledge, 1994.

Horton, M., Freire, P., Bell, B., Gaenta, J., and Peters, J., eds. *We Make the Road by Walking: Conversations on Education and Social Change.* Philadelphia: Temple University Press, 1990.

The National Equity Project offers powerful and engaging workshops: www.nationalequity project.org

Rios, Victor. *Punished: Policing the Lives of Black and Latino Boys.* New York: NYU Press, 2011. An essential book to read to gain an understanding of the larger systemic oppression that manifests in our criminal justice system.

Steele, Claude. *Whistling Vivaldi and Other Clues to How Stereotypes Affect Us.* New York: Norton, 2010.

Tatum, Beverly D. *"Why Are All the Black Kids Sitting Together in the Cafeteria?" and Other Conversations About Race.* (Rev. ed.) New York: Basic Books, 1999.

Wise, Tim. *White Like Me: Reflections on Race from a Privileged Son.* Berkeley, Calif.: Soft Skull Press, 2008.

Coaching Models (Chapter Two)

Bloom, Gary, Castagna, Claire, Warren, Betsy, and Moir, Ellen. *Blended Coaching.* Thousand Oaks, Calif.: Corwin, 2005. A classic in this field. It's a foundational read for all coaches and extremely useful for leadership coaches.

Costa, Arthur, and Garmston, Robert. *Cognitive Coaching: A Foundation for Renaissance School.* Norwood, Mass.: Christopher-Gordon, 1994. Costa and Garmston are the pioneers of cognitive coaching.

Hargrove, Robert. *Masterful Coaching.* San Francisco: Jossey-Bass, 2003. Those interested in transformational coaching might start by reading this core text.

Killion, Joellen, and Harrison, Cindy. *Taking the Lead: New Roles for Teachers and School-Based Coaches.* Oxford, Ohio: National Staff Development Council, 2006. Very useful for those setting up coaching programs.

Knight, Jim. *Instructional Coaching: A Partnership Approach to Improving Instruction.* Thousand Oaks, Calif.: Corwin, 2007.

Knight, J., ed. *Coaching Approaches and Perspectives.* Thousand Oaks, Calif.: Corwin, 2009.

Psencik, K. *The Coach's Craft: Powerful Practices to Support School Leaders.* Oxford, Ohio: Learning Forward, 2011. A recent contribution to the field of coaching leaders in education.

Reeves, D. B., and Allison, E. *Renewal Coaching: Sustainable Change for Individuals and Organizations.* San Francisco: Jossey-Bass, 2009.

Tschannen-Moran, Bob, and Tschannen-Moran, Megan. *Evocative Coaching.* San Francisco: Jossey-Bass, 2010. An excellent resource for coaches with a few years of experience to help deepen their practice.

Wahl, Christine, Scriber, Clarice, and Bloomfield, B., eds. *On Becoming a Leadership Coach.* New York: Palgrave MacMillan, 2008. A volume of twenty-three brilliant, insightful essays that are not specific to education but are incredibly useful.

Beliefs (Chapter Three)

Coyle, Daniel. *The Talent Code: Greatness Isn't Born, It's Grown. Here's How.* New York: Bantam, 2009.

Dweck, Carol S. *Mindset: The New Psychology of Success.* New York: Ballantine, 2006.

Senge, Peter. *The Fifth Discipline: The Art and Practice of the Learning Organization.* New York: Doubleday, 1990.

Theoretical Foundations for Transformational Coaching (Chapter Four)

Argyris, Chris, Putnam, R., and Smith, D. *Action Science*. San Francisco: Jossey-Bass, 1985.

Argyris, C., and Schön, D. *Theory in Practice: Increasing Professional Effectiveness*. San Francisco: Jossey-Bass, 1975.

Goleman, Daniel, Boyatzis, Richard, and McKee, Annie, *Primal Leadership*. Boston: Harvard University Press, 2002.

Heath, Chip, and Heath, Dan. *Switch: How to Change Things When Change Is Hard*. New York: Broadway Books, 2010.

Senge, Peter. *The Fifth Discipline: The Art and Practice of the Learning Organization*. New York: Doubleday, 1990.

Senge, Peter. *The Fifth Discipline Fieldbook*. New York: Doubleday, 1994.

Vella, J. *Learning to Listen, Learning to Teach: The Power of Dialogue in Educating Adults*. (Rev. ed.) San Francisco: Jossey-Bass, 2002.

Wheatley, Margaret. *Leadership and the New Science: Discovering Order in a Chaotic World*. (3rd ed.) San Francisco: Berrett-Koehler, 2006.

Wheatley, Margaret. *Turning to One Another: Simple Conversations to Restore Hope to the Future*. San Francisco: Berrett-Koehler, 2009.

Wheatley, Margaret. *Perseverance*. San Francisco: Berrett-Koehler, 2010.

Wheatley, Margaret, and Frieze, Deborah. *Walk Out, Walk On: A Learning Journey into Communities Daring to Live the Future Now*. San Francisco: Berrett-Koehler, 2011.

Trust (Chapter Five)

Anthony S. Bryk and Barbara Schneider's work on relational trust is essential to understand the role of trust and system change. I recommend starting with "Trust in Schools: A Core Resource for School Reform." *Educational Leadership*, 2003, *60*, 40–45.

Covey, Stephen M. R *The Speed of Trust*. New York: Free Press, 2008.

Stephenson, Susan. *Leading with Trust*. Bloomington, Ind.: Solution Tree, 2009. Includes a wealth of research about trust and very useful reproducible ideas.

Personality Assessments (Chapter Six)

Dr. Martin Seligman's website: www.authentichappiness.sas.upenn.edu

The National School Reform Faculty website: www.nsrfharmony.org

Goal Setting (Chapter Seven)

O'Neill, Jan, and Conzemius, Anne. *The Power of SMART Goals*. Bloomington, Ind.: Solution Tree, 2006.

Listening (Chapter Eight)

Julian Weissglass's articles, such as "*Constructivist Listening for Empowerment and Change.*" *The Educational Forum*, 1990, *54*, 351–371.

Wheatley, Margaret. *Turning to One Another*. San Francisco: Berrett-Koehler, 2009.

Coaching Conversations (Chapters Nine and Eleven)

Heron, John. *Helping the Client*. (5th ed.) Thousand Oaks, Calif.: Sage, 2001.

Kegan, R., and Lahey, L. *How the Way We Talk Can Change the Way We Work: Seven Languages for Transformation*. San Francisco: Jossey-Bass, 2001.

Patterson, Jerry L., and Kelleher, Paul. *Resilient School Leaders: Strategies for Turning Adversity into Achievement*. Alexandria, Va.: ASCD, 2005.

Robbins, Mike. *Focus on the Good Stuff*. San Francisco: Jossey-Bass, 2007.

Ross, Rick, "The Five Whys." In P. Senge, *The Fifth Discipline Fieldbook*. New York: Doubleday, 1994, pp. 108–112.

Stoltzfus, T. *Coaching Questions: A Coach's Guide to Powerful Asking Skills*. Virginia Beach, Va.: Pegasus Creative Arts, 2008.

Coaching Actions and Activities (Chapters Ten and Twelve)

Alterio, M. "Collaborative Journaling as a Professional Development Tool." *Journal of Further and Higher Education*, 2004, *28*(3), 321–332.

Bambrick-Santoyo, P. *Driven by Data: A Practical Guide to Improve Instruction*. San Francisco: Jossey-Bass, 2010.

Blackstone, P. "The Anatomy of Coaching: Coaching Through Storytelling." *Journal of Language and Literacy Education*, 2007, *3*(1), 48–58.

Dyer, K. "The Power of 360-Degree Feedback." *Educational Leadership*, 2001, *58*(5), 35–38.

Schwarz, Dale, and Davidson, Anne. *Facilitative Coaching*. San Francisco: Pfeiffer, 2008.

Coach Habits of Mind and Heart (Chapters Thirteen and Fifteen)

Foster, Rick, and Hicks, Greg. *How We Choose to Be Happy*. New York: Perigree, 2004.

The International Coach Federation: www.coachfederation.org

International Reading Association. "Standards for Middle and High School Literacy Coaches," 2006. www.reading.org/resources/issues/reports/coaching.html

Intrator, Sam, and Scribner, Megan, eds. *Teaching with Fire: Poetry That Sustains the Courage to Teach*. San Francisco: Jossey-Bass, 2003.

Palmer, Parker. *The Courage to Teach*. San Francisco: Jossey-Bass, 1998.

Salzberg, Sharon. *Lovingkindness: The Revolutionary Art of Happiness*. Boston: Shambhala, 1995.

Salzberg, Sharon. *The Kindness Handbook: A Practical Companion*. Boulder, Colo.: Sounds True, 2008.

Rosenberg, Marshall. *Nonviolent Communication*. Encinitas, Calif.: PuddleDancer Press, 2003.

Wheatley, Margaret. *Perseverance*. San Francisco: Berrett-Koehler, 2010.

APPENDIX F

Glossary

Achievement gap: The disparity between the academic performance of groups of students, especially groups defined by race/ethnicity, gender, and socioeconomic status. However, when structural, economic factors are causing the gap in performance, then the *achievement gap* may actually be an *opportunity gap*.

Active listening: A communication strategy where the listener feeds back what the speaker said by restating or paraphrasing what was heard. The listener seeks confirmation that he understood what the speaker was saying.

Adult learning: A theory holding that there are key differences between the ways adults learn and the ways children learn. Adults want to be the origin of their own learning and want control over the what, who, how, why, and where of their learning. They need to see that what they are learning is applicable to their day-to-day activities and problems. Adults also need direct, concrete experiences to apply what they have learned to their work.

Beliefs: Strongly held opinions; we often think they are truths.

Capacity: A person's potential to learn or retain knowledge; their potential for growth, development, or skill building.

Change management: A lens that suggests an analysis of the conditions for change; reminds us to consider a person's will, skill, knowledge, and capacity to change; and reminds us that beneficial change is always possible.

Coaching: Professional development.

Cognitive coaching: Coaching that addresses ways of thinking in order to change the way we behave.

Compassion: The ability to suspend judgment of ourselves and others, appreciating that each of us makes choices based on the information and skills we have at any given time.

Core values: Deeply held personal codes that reflect our ethics and what is most important to us; they are usually deeper than our beliefs and are a source for resilience.

Deep listening: Nonjudgmental listening for the purpose of the speaker so that he can process thoughts, feelings, experiences.

Directive coaching: Coaching that focuses on changing behaviors. Also called instructive coaching.

Equity: Every child gets what he or she needs in our schools—*every child* regardless of where they come from, what they look like, who their parents are, what their temperament is, or what they show up knowing or not knowing. Every child gets what he or she needs every day in order to have all the skills and tools that he or she needs to pursue whatever he or she wants after leaving our schools, to live a fulfilling life. Equity is about outcomes and experiences—for *every child, every day*.

Emotional intelligence: A set of competencies and dispositions; the capacity to recognize our own feelings and those of others, to motivate ourselves, and to manage emotions well in ourselves and in our relationships.

Enrollment: The process in coaching of inviting a client to buy into coaching and be open to the possibilities that might come as a result.

Facilitative coaching: Coaching that builds on changes in behavior to support someone to develop ways of being, or explores beliefs in order to change behaviors.

Gradual release of responsibility: Also known as "scaffolded" instruction. When a learner is in the zone of proximal development, if he is provided with appropriate assistance and tools—the scaffolding—then he can accomplish the skill. Eventually the scaffolding can be removed, the responsibility can be released, and the learner can complete the task independently.

Heron's coaching stances: An analytical framework to apply in coaching conversations; six approaches (cathartic, catalytic, supportive, confrontational, instructive, and prescriptive) that can be used for different reasons and have different effects. See Chapter Nine.

Inquiry thinking: A stance, or lens, that values asking questions as much as finding answers. It suggests that the way we define the problem dictates how we define the solution; it encourages us to collect multiple forms of data.

Instructive coaching: Coaching that focuses on changing behaviors. Also called *directive coaching*.

Ladder of Inference: An analytical framework used to explore how beliefs are formed and to help a client unpack belief systems.

Mental model or mind-set: Our beliefs, assumptions, and ideas about how things work. Mental models are often hidden, even from ourselves. Made up of our values and beliefs and a series of assumptions about how the world works.

Ontological coaching: Coaching that focuses on our way of being which shows up in our language, emotions, and body. Our way of being contains deep-seated attitudes and is the underlying driver of our behavior and communication.

Optical refractor for coaches: The set of six coaching lenses based on theoretical frameworks introduced in Chapter Four.

Paraphrasing: Rendering the message a speaker shared using similar words and phrases as the one used by the speaker.

Prejudice: A preconceived judgment or opinion, usually based on limited information. We are continually exposed to misinformation about others—which is how we end up with prejudices. Stereotypes, omissions, and distortions all contribute to the development of prejudice.

Racism: A system of advantage based on race; a personal ideology and a system of institutional policies and practices that manifest in the beliefs and actions of individuals. Racism is prejudice plus power—racial prejudice combined with social power (access to resources and decision making) leads to an institutionalization of racist policies and practices. Racism is more than just a set of individual beliefs and attitudes; it is systemic.

Reframing: Helping people change the way they see things to find alternate ways of viewing ideas, events, or situations.

Resilience: The ability to emerge from adversity stronger than before; an emotional quality that can be learned and developed.

River stories: A river story is a commitment to learn and grow; it doesn't limit us.

Rut stories: A story that develops when people use defensive reasoning to protect themselves. A rut story is constricting and usually leaves us feeling somewhat powerless.

Scaffolding: When a learner is in the zone of proximal development, if he is provided with appropriate assistance and tools—the scaffolding—then he can accomplish the skill. Eventually the scaffolding can be removed and the learner can complete the task independently. Scaffolded instruction is also known as a gradual release of responsibility.

SMARTE goal: A goal that is strategic and specific, measurable, attainable, results-based, time-bound, and equitable.

Stories: Interpretations of what happens to us. Coaches help people surface, question, and redefine their stories when the current story is called into question or breaks down.

Systemic (or structural) oppression: The theory that oppression resides in systems and structures (such as our education system and school structures), as well as within individual consciousness.

Systems thinking: A conceptual framework for seeing interrelationships and patterns of change, rather than isolated events. It helps us identify the structures that underlie complex situations and discern high- and low-leverage changes.

Theory of action: A theory for change that directs our actions; often framed as if-then statements.

Transformation: A change so massive, thorough, and comprehensive that the result is almost unrecognizable from its previous form; it is almost unimaginable.

Transparency: An authentic openness to others about one's feelings, beliefs, and actions.

Unattachment to outcome: A stance in which a coach isn't attached to a client's decisions or choices.

Webs of belief: The interconnected threads of beliefs that mutually reinforce one another and guide our actions; together they form a mind-set (Drath and Van Veslor, 2006).

Zone of proximal development (ZPD): The difference between what a learner can do without help and what he can do with help. It is the range of abilities that he can perform with assistance, but cannot yet perform independently. A learner needs "scaffolding" in order to move out of the ZPD.

ACKNOWLEDGMENTS

I have been fortunate to work with and learn from many committed, fantastic educators in the Oakland public schools. The following teachers and administrators have profoundly influenced me: Larissa Adam, Miranda Bergman, Elia Bustamante, Shannon Carey, David Chambliss, Cassandra Chen, Matt Duffy, Michael Hatcher, Cheryl Lana, Viet Nguyen, Angela Parker, Jenny Rienzo, Hattie Saunders, Michael Scott, Eyana Spencer, Keiko Suda, Jessie Thaler, Aaron Townsend, Hae-Sin Kim Thomas, Alexandra Kulka-Wells, Kathryn Williams, and Sarah Wilner. To those I coached, I am most grateful to have been a witness to your learning and transformation. I am sincerely humbled by your trust in me.

I wouldn't be the coach I am today without the generosity and grace of the following coaches, whom I met through BayCES (an organization now known as *the National Equity Project*): Leslie Plettner, Shane Safir, Mark Salinas, Liz Simons, and Ken Yale. Each of you played a key role in helping me navigate the wild waters of our schools and the domain of coaching. Your refined skills, dedication, and integrity inspire me every day. Thank you.

To my former team of transformational leadership coaches, you are deep in my practice: Davina Goldwasser, Mary Hurley, Lisa Jimenez, Jennifer Lutzenberger-Phillips, and Annie Prozan. For your friendships, unwavering support, brilliance, and insight, I am most grateful. Kristina Tank-Crestetto, the master coach and manager extraordinaire of this team: your leadership, courage, and perseverance allowed me to become a transformational coach. My gratitude is immeasurable.

My 2012–13 group of transformational coaches is a dream team of deep thinkers. Thank you Noelle Apostol Colin, David Carter, Rafael Cruz, John Gallagher, Anna Martin, Manny Medina, Han Phung, and Michele Reinhart. What a gift and a joy to continue on this journey with all of you.

ASCEND, a small Oakland school, is my evidence that transformation is possible, that the experience and outcomes for urban youth in public schools can be radically different. My appreciation to all who contributed to this effort is extensive.

John Norton—writer, editor, and educator—was my fairy godmother. This book might not have materialized without his encouragement. In addition, he connected me with my editor at Jossey-Bass and offered invaluable advice along the publishing path. We've never met or even spoken—which makes him feel even more mythical—but through our e-mails, I have developed a profound admiration for him, as well as a volume of gratitude.

At Jossey-Bass, I am grateful for Kate Gagnon's enthusiasm for this project and her editorial guidance along the way. Between Kate's support and that of senior editorial assistant Tracy Gallagher, the process of writing a book was far easier than I'd expected.

I first experienced the transformational power of coaching through my dear friend, Lettecia Kratz, who is a phenomenal coach and teacher in the Denver public schools. Many years ago, her coaching helped move my life in new directions. Most recently, Lettecia read long portions of this manuscript and provided invaluable feedback that made the final version much stronger. My heart is filled with gratitude for her friendship.

My Aunt Jeanne and my father, Gilbert, are farmers who have the patience and attentiveness necessary to cultivate land. I strive to emulate these basic dispositions in my coaching. Even in the most difficult moments, my father has helped me find the bright spots and reframe my perception. My aunt and father also cheer and champion my work without understanding much about the context, details, or substance. I am deeply grateful for their support and presence in my life.

This book is dedicated to my mother, my first coach, who is sadly no longer a living presence in my life. She was deeply and passionately committed to alleviating pain and transforming the world. From her, I learned the extraordinary gifts of listening, unconditional love, and compassion. She also encouraged me to laugh at any predicament and use humor as a vehicle for healing. In my coaching I recognize her dedication, influence, and lightness.

And Stacey—my husband, best friend, and comrade—I can't imagine a better partner for this journey. Thank you for Sundays, for the endless technical support, for suggesting that I blog, insisting that I write, and understanding this creative compulsion that keeps us both enthralled. I've reached the outer limit of language; I just don't have words to express my gratitude.

To my beautiful boy, Orion: thank you for all your encouragement while I wrote. Every time you came up to my office and cheered, "Go mama!" my heart burst with joy and I got the energy I needed to go on. You inspire me to be the best person I can be, to be mindful with my words, to be in the present moment, and to be kind and empathetic. I work for transformation for you, my dear, and for all the other beautiful little people in our schools.

REFERENCES

Annenberg Institute for School Reform. "Instructional Coaching: Professional Development Strategies That Improve Instruction." Providence, RI: Brown University, 2004. annenberginstitute.org/pdf/InstructionalCoaching.pdf

Argyris, C. *Overcoming Organizational Defenses.* New York: Simon and Schuster, 1990.

Ball, F. "Continued Development: Self-Authorship and Self-Mastery." In C. Wahl, C. Scriber, and B. Bloomfield, eds., *On Becoming a Leadership Coach.* New York: Palgrave MacMillan, 2008.

Banks, C., trans. *The Essential Rumi.* San Francisco: HarperCollins, 1995, *35.*

Barth, R. *Learning by Heart.* San Francisco: Jossey-Bass, 2001.

Biancarosa, G., Bryk, A., and Dexter, E. "Assessing the Value-Added Effects of Literacy Collaborative Professional Development on Student Learning." *The Elementary School Journal*, 2010, *3*(1), 7–34.

Block, P. *Flawless Consulting.* (3rd ed.) San Francisco: Jossey-Bass/Pfeiffer, 2011.

Bloom, G., Castagna, C., Warren, B., and Moir, E. *Blended Coaching: Skills and Strategies to Support Principal Development.* Thousand Oaks, Calif.: Corwin, 2005.

Bonar, C. A. *Amen, I Say to You: Sunday Homilies for Cycles A, B, and C and Homilies for Holy Days of Obligation.* Bloomington, IN: Xlibris Corporation, 2007.

CampbellJones, F., Lindsey, R. B., and CampbellJones, B. *The Cultural Proficiency Journey: Moving Beyond Ethical Barriers Toward Profound School Change.* Thousand Oaks, Calif.: Corwin, 2010.

Churchill, W. Retrieved from http://thinkexist.com/quotation/courage_is_what_it_takes_to_ stand_up_and_speak/150104.html, n.d.

Covey, S. R. *Seven Habits of Highly Effective People*. New York: Free Press, 1989.

Covey, S.M.R. *The Speed of Trust*. New York: Free Press, 2008.

Coyle, D. *The Talent Code: Greatness Isn't Born, It's Grown. Here's How*. New York: Bantam, 2009.

Darling-Hammond, L., Wei, R. C., Andree, A., Richardson, N., and Orphanos, S. "State of the Profession: Study Measures Professional Development." *Journal of Staff Development*, 2009, *30*(2) 42–50.

Delpit, L. *Other People's Children: Cultural Conflict in the Classroom*. New York: The New Press, 1995.

Drath, W., and Van Veslor, E. "Constructive-Developmental Coaching." In S. Ting and P. Scisco, eds., *The CCL Handbook of Coaching*. San Francisco: Jossey-Bass, 2006.

Drucker, P. *The Essential Drucker: The Best of Sixty Years of Peter Drucker's Essential Writings on Management* (Collins Business Essentials). New York: HarperCollins, 2008.

Echeverría, R., and Olalla, J. *The Art of Ontological Coaching*. Boulder, CO: Newfield Network. 1993.

Evans, Alice. "Leaning into the Light: An Interview with Barry Lopez." *Poets & Writers*, March/April 1994, *22*(2), 62–79.

Gallwey, T. *The Inner Game of Work*. New York: Random House. 2000.

Gawande, A. "Personal Best." *New Yorker*, Oct. 3, 2011.

Gladwell, M. *Outliers: The Story of Success*. New York: Little, Brown, 2008.

Goleman, D., Boyatzis, R., and McKee, A. *Primal Leadership: Learning to Lead with Emotional Intelligence*. Boston: Harvard University Press, 2002.

Hansen, R. *The Buddha's Brain: The Practical Neuroscience of Happiness, Love, and Wisdom*. New Harbinger, 2009.

Hargrove, R. *Masterful Coaching*. San Francisco: Jossey-Bass, 2003.

Hartman, A. "Words Create Worlds," *Social Work*, 1991, *36*(4), 275.

Jones, D. 2012. "Celebration Quotes." Retrieved from www.celebratewhatsright.com/inspire/ quotes?page=5

Jones, J. E. *360-Degree Feedback: Strategies, Tactics, and Techniques for Developing Leaders*. Minneapolis: Lakewood Publications, 1996.

Joyce, B., and Showers, B. "Transfer of Training: The Contribution of Coaching." *Journal of Education*, 1981, *163*(2), 163–172.

Killion, J., and Harrison, C. *Taking the Lead: New Roles for Teachers and School-Based Coaches*. Oxford, Ohio: National Staff Development Council, 2006.

King, M. L. "Where Do We Go from Here?" Speech to the Southern Christian Leadership Conference. Atlanta, GA, August 16, 1967.

Krishnamurti, J. "You Are the World." First public talk at University of California Berkeley, February 3, 1969. www.jkrishnamurti.org/krishnamurti-teachings/view-text.php?tid=19&chid=68563&w=%22When+you+are+listening+to+somebody%2C+completely%2C%22

Lewicki, R., and Wiethoff, C. *Trust, Trust Development, and Trust Repair: The Handbook of Conflict Resolution — Theory and Practice*. San Francisco: Jossey-Bass, 2000.

Loeb, Paul. *The Impossible Will Take a Little While: A Citizen's Guide to Hope in a Time of Fear*. New York: Basic Books, 2004, 9.

Lorde, A. *The Cancer Journals*. San Francisco: Aunt Lute Books, 1997.

Lorde, A. *Sister Outsider: Essays and Speeches*. Berkeley, CA: Crossing Press, 1984.

Matsumura, L. C., Garnier, H. E., Correnti, R., Junker, B., and Bickel, D. D. "Investigating the Effectiveness of a Comprehensive Literacy Coaching Program in Schools with High Teacher Mobility." *The Elementary School Journal*, 2010, 3(1).

McNeil, P., and Klink, S. "School Coaching." In L. B. Easton, ed., *Powerful Designs for Professional Learning*. Oxford, OH: National Staff Development Council, 2004, pp.185–194.

Menninger, K. *Love Against Hate*. New York: Harcourt Brace, 1942, 275–276.

Naparstek, B. *Staying Well with Guided Imagery*. New York: Warner Books, 1994.

National Equity Project. 2007. *The National Equity Project Coaching Lenses*. Oakland, CA: Author.

Nhat Hanh, T. 2011, www.tnhtour.org/faq.html.

Nhat Hanh, T. 2012, www.katinkahesselink.net/tibet/Thich-Nhat-Hanh-love-q.html.

O'Neill, J., and Conzemius, A., with Commodore, C., and Pulsfus, C. *The Power of SMART Goals*. Bloomington, Ind.: Solution Tree, 2006.

Patterson, J. L., and P. Kelleher. *Resilient School Leaders: Strategies for Turning Adversity into Achievement*. Alexandria, Va.: ASCD, 2005.

Ravitch, D. *The Life and Death of the Great American School System: How Testing and Choice Are Undermining Education*. New York: Basic Books, 2010.

Roy, A. 2003. "Confronting Empire," speech given in Porto Alegre, Brazil, January 27, 2003.

Safransky, S. *Sunbeams, Revised Edition: A Book of Quotations*. Berkeley, CA: North Atlantic Books, 2012.

Sailors, M., and Shanklin, N. L. "Growing Evidence to Support Coaching in Literacy and Mathematics." *The Elementary School Journal*, 2010, 3(1), 1–6.

Schwarz, D., and Davidson, A. *Facilitative Coaching: A Toolkit for Expanding Your Repertoire and Achieving Lasting Results*. San Francisco: Pfeiffer, 2008.

Senge, P. *The Fifth Discipline: The Art and Practice of the Learning Organization*. New York: Doubleday, 1990.

Senge, P. *The Fifth Discipline Fieldbook: Strategies and Tools for Building a Learning Organization*. New York: Doubleday, 1994.

Senge, P., and others. *The Dance of Change: The Challenges to Sustaining Momentum in Learning Organizations*. New York: Doubleday, 1999.

Shows, J. K., and Scriber, C. L. "Sacred Space: Where Possibilities Abound and Change Is Engendered." In C. Wahl, C. Scriber, and B. Bloomfield, eds., *On Becoming a Leadership Coach: A Holistic Approach to Coaching Excellence*. New York: Palgrave MacMillan, 2008.

Stevenson, A. E. Speech. Richmond, VA, September 20, 1952.

Stoltzfus, Tony. *Coaching Questions: A Coach's Guide to Powerful Asking Skills*. Pegasus Creative Arts, 2008.

Wallerstein, I. In Conversation with Grace Lee Boggs and Immanuel Wallerstein (video). U.S. Social Forum, Detroit, Mich., 2010. http://vimeo.com/13407876

Weissglass, J. "Constructivist Listening for Empowerment and Change." *The Educational Forum*, 1990, *54*(4), 351–371.

Wheatley, M. *Turning to One Another: Simple Conversations to Restore Hope to the Future*. San Francisco: Berrett-Koehler, 2009.

Wheatley, M. *Perseverance*. San Francisco: Berrett-Koehler, 2010.

Zohar, D. *Rewiring the Corporate Brain*. San Francisco: Berrett-Koehler. 1997.

INDEX

O

Oakland Unified School District, 14, 289–290

Observation: activities, 212–229; of client, 107–108, 115, 212–227; debriefing, 213–214; in exploration stage, 107–108; feedback from, 215–217, 222–224; focus of, 212, 225; of meetings, 115–116; tools, 214–215, 217–220

Office administrators, 86, 264

Olalla, Julio, 75, 92–93, 172

O'Neill, Jan, 121, 125–126, 140, 279

On-the-spot coaching, 223–224

Ontological coaching, 24–25

Openness, 87–88

Oppression, systematic, 57–59, 63–65, 71, 99–100

Optical refractor: for coaches, 48–65, 271, 274; Delgado using, 51–55, 57, 59, 61–65, 69–70. *See also* Lenses

Outcome, attachment to, 42

P

Paraphrasing, 153

Parenting, 6–7

Passions, uncovering, 103–104, 117

PD. *See* Professional development

Permission, 88–89, 216, 218, 278

Perseverance (Wheatley), 290

Personal transformation, 24, 29, 285–286

Personality self-assessments, 106–107, 116

Phrasing, 217

Planning: conversations, 232, 234–237, 249–252, 276, 282; exploration stage and, 111; lesson, 223; for meetings, 234–237; PD, 269–282; trust and, 79–81; unit, 223. *See also* Work plan

Plettner, Leslie, 33–34

Positive psychology, 106

Positive self-talk, 182–184

The Power of SMARTE Goals (O'Neill and Conzemius), 126

Prejudice, 57–58, 274

Prescriptive approach, 202, 204–205

Presence, 279, 281

Primal Leadership: Learning to Lead with Emotional Intelligence (Goleman, Boyatzis, and McKee), 59

Principals, 205–207, 287–288; confrontational approach and, 202; data on, 114; observation of, 107; supportive role of, 171; surveys and, 108–109, 191–192; videotaping, 180–181; work plans and, 123–125, 128, 134–135, 137. *See also specific principals*

Probing questions, 159–160, 169

Professional development (PD): coaches and, 7–8, 10, 16, 18, 79–81, 98, 140, 176, 232, 267–286; first meeting questions about, 79–81; focus of, 268–269; learning activities for, 270–273; planning, 269–282; reflective practices, 283–286; rubric and, 270, 273–282; for teachers, 7–8, 18, 55, 98, 155, 176

Program enforcement, 19

Progress: end-of-year report, 254; indicators, 122, 133–134, 143; midyear report, 254; monthly report, 84, 249, 250–251

Psychological self-assessments, 106–107, 116

Q

Question stems, 186–187

Questioning: in beginning of relationship, 79–81, 85; challenges and helpful responses, 160–161; clarifying, 85, 151, 158–159, 169; in interviews, 11–14; lenses for, 160–161; listening and, 147–148, 151, 158–160; probing,

ABOUT THE AUTHOR

Elena Aguilar is a teacher, coach, and consultant with more than 20 years of experience working in schools. She has taught Grades 2–10 and has a particular love for middle school students. She has been an instructional coach, a leadership coach, and a central office administrator.

Elena is the founder of Elena Aguilar Consulting (www.elenaaguilar.com). She and her associates facilitate professional development for coaches, teachers, and administrators in public, charter, and private schools across the United States. Elena also consults with districts that are developing a coaching program and with leaders engaging in transformational change. She continues to coach school leaders in the San Francisco Bay Area.

Elena is also the author of The Art of Coaching Teams: Building Resilient Communities that Transform Schools (Jossey-Bass, 2016). She has been a frequent writer for Edutopia since 2008 and writes a blog on EdWeek Teacher for coaches. Elena lives in Oakland, California, with her husband and son.